THE ROUTLEDGE INTRODUCTION TO ITALIAN LINGUISTICS

The Routledge Introduction to Italian Linguistics offers a systematic and comprehensive overview of the linguistic structure of the Italian language, including phonetics and phonology, morphology and morphosyntax, syntax, semantics, and sociolinguistics.

The manual includes a historical sketch of the Italian language, which outlines the central phases of its emergence and process of standardization. Written in clear, concise language and taking a descriptive, theory-neutral approach, this is the ideal companion for advanced students of the Italian language and those studying Italian and Romance linguistics. After sketching the most important phases of the process of standardization of Italian and introducing the main varieties of Italian as classified from a social and geographical perspective, this introductory text addresses the core topics of Italian linguistics as pertaining to the sound system and word and sentence structure.

The text adopts a descriptive approach and requires no previous knowledge of linguistics since technical terms are carefully explained and illustrated by numerous examples. Thus, it can serve as a reference tool for instructors of Italian and anyone interested in advancing their knowledge of the Italian language or familiarizing themselves with Italian linguistics.

Cinzia Russi is Professor of Italian and Romance Linguistics at the University of Texas at Austin, USA.

THE ROUTLEDGE INTRODUCTION TO ITALIAN LINGUISTICS

Cinzia Russi

Routledge
Taylor & Francis Group

LONDON AND NEW YORK

First published 2023
by Routledge
4 Park Square, Milton Park, Abingdon, Oxon OX14 4RN

and by Routledge
605 Third Avenue, New York, NY 10158

Routledge is an imprint of the Taylor & Francis Group, an informa business

British Library Cataloguing-in-Publication Data
A catalogue record for this book is available from the British Library

Library of Congress Cataloging-in-Publication Data
Names: Russi, Cinzia, 1966– author.
Title: The Routledge introduction to Italian linguistics / Cinzia Russi.
Other titles: Italian linguistics
Description: Abingdon, Oxon ; New York, NY : Routledge, 2023. | Includes
    bibliographical references and index.
Identifiers: LCCN 2022041107 (print) | LCCN 2022041108 (ebook) |
    ISBN 9780367523459 (paperback) | ISBN 9780367523435 (hardback) |
    ISBN 9781003057536 (ebook)
Subjects: LCSH: Italian language.
Classification: LCC PC1073 .R83 2023 (print) | LCC PC1073 (ebook) |
    DDC 450—dc23/eng/20221018
LC record available at https://lccn.loc.gov/2022041107
LC ebook record available at https://lccn.loc.gov/2022041108

ISBN: 978-0-367-52343-5 (hbk)
ISBN: 978-0-367-52345-9 (pbk)
ISBN: 978-1-003-05753-6 (ebk)

DOI: 10.4324/9781003057536

Typeset in Bembo
by Apex CoVantage, LLC

To Chiara and Alice, my beacons and my joy.

CONTENTS

TABLES

FIGURES

PREFACE

This textbook offers a systematic and comprehensive introduction to the linguistic structure of the Italian language. After sketching the most important phases of the process of standardization of Italian and introducing the main varieties of Italian as classified from a social and geographical perspective (namely, standard, neo-standard, sub-standard varieties, and the dialects and regional varieties), it addresses the core topics of Italian linguistic as pertaining to the sound system (phonetics and phonology) and word and sentence structure (morphology, morphosyntax, and syntax).

This textbook is intended primarily as a supporting tool in the development of a key component of the curriculum of undergraduate (intermediate and advanced) courses in Italian language and Italian linguistics at US (and other English-speaking countries') universities. It is designed specifically to assist English-speaking students in developing the skills to achieve a proper and comprehensive understanding of the Italian language as a whole, and to help them build the foundations for conducting research in Italian linguistics. It adopts a descriptive approach and requires no previous knowledge of linguistics since technical terms are carefully explained and illustrated by numerous examples. Thus, it can also serve as a reference tool for instructors of Italian, as well as anyone interested in advancing their knowledge of the Italian language or familiarizing themselves with Italian linguistics.

Many people contributed, in different ways and to different extents, to the realization of this work, and I could hardly hope to thank all of them individually here. I am deeply grateful to my dear friend Adria Frizzi for her invaluable advice on some challenging English translations, and to Nicholas Mireles for his superb proofreading. Some of the material included in this textbook were 'tested' on the students who attended my course *Introduction to Italian Linguistics* in fall 2020. I warmly thank them for bearing with me and providing important, constructive feedback. Sincere thanks also go to two anonymous reviewers for offering pertinent and insightful comments and suggestions (which I did my best to address adequately) and the editorial staff at Taylor & Francis for their kind assistance and patience. Any inaccuracies or mistakes remain, of course, my own. Last but definitely not least, I want to thank my family for their unceasing encouragement and inspiration, and for cheering me up every time I felt overwhelmed.

Cinzia Russi

Austin, April 2022

1

THE ITALIAN LANGUAGE

This chapter provides an introductory characterization of the Italian language. It starts with tracing the key junctures in the development of Italian as a unitary standard language. Next, the chapter introduces the core varieties of Italian that shape the current linguistic repertoire of the Italian people. Specifically, it first reviews the basic language varieties that are traditionally distinguished in reference to social parameters: standard, neo-standard, and non-/sub-standard. Then it addresses the varieties that are identifiable along the geographical dimension: the dialects and the regional varieties, *italiani regionali*. For both sets of varieties, the discussion focuses on the key aspects of a general process of restructuring (or 're-standardization'), through which the different varieties of Italian have been converging since the middle of the past century.

1.1 The development of the Italian language

Italian is a Romance language often credited for its close similarity to Latin and is 'considered by many to be the most beautiful of the world's languages' (Katzner & Miller, 2002, p. 62).[1] It is the official language of the Republic of Italy, the Republic of San Marino, and Vatican City, and one of the four official languages of Switzerland (Cantons of Ticino and Grisons). It is also widely spoken in the Unites States, Canada, Argentina, and Brazil. Compared to the other major Romance languages (except Romanian), Italian is distinguished by a long and complex history of linguistic unification which, for a long time, concerned only the written language. This prolonged linguistic fragmentation has had a consequential role in shaping Italy's distinctive linguistic scenario, especially regarding dialectal differentiation.

The roots of the Italian language lie in Vulgar Latin (i.e., the Latin spoken by the people; Latin VULGARIS < VULGUS 'people') – in other words, the spoken Latin of common usage around the end of the Western Roman Empire (476 CE). Around this time, Vulgar Latin fragmented into an array of local vernaculars characterized by flexible geographical (and linguistic) boundaries and different degrees of prestige. The Florentine vernacular would eventually tower all the other vernaculars spoken in the Italian peninsula and become the foundation of modern-day Italian.

DOI: 10.4324/9781003057536-1

1.1.1 The rise of Florentine

The thirteenth century saw the budding of the conditions which enabled Florentine to secure a privileged, central status among the many Italian vernaculars. Among the most pivotal of these conditions was the establishment of a new social class involved in industry, commerce, and banking. This transformed socio-economic setting also brought about radical changes at the juridical, administrative, and cultural level, setting off the exceptional economic growth that Tuscany first, and then Florence, in particular, gained during this period. Clearly, literacy was imperative to the members of this new social class, because the success of their ventures depended on tasks that required being able to read and write, as well as being versed in arithmetic – keeping record of transactions and accounts, corresponding with clients, staying informed on current commercial trends, and also writing *libri di famiglia* 'family books,' miscellanea including a variety of topics (e.g., good household practices, lineage, important family events, astronomical bulletins, proverbs, spells, and charms). These emerging professional groups were either educated by private tutors or in schools run by laymen (*scuole d'abaco* 'abacus schools'), and the language of instruction was the vernacular, not Latin. Even though Latin was (and would continue to be until the eighteenth century) the language of 'higher' education, it was not suited to serve the linguistic needs of this new society.[2] The first Florentine text available to us, *Frammenti d'un libro di conti di banchieri fiorentini* (1211), is indeed the product of this new socio-economic (and cultural) context.

Thanks to its rapidly flourishing economic prominence and prosperity, Florence became one of the most lively and influential cultural centers of the time and also acquired great political power.[3] Particularly significant from a linguistic perspective is the fact that Florence became the foremost center for the distribution of literary texts written in vernaculars other than Florentine, including poetry by the exponents of the highly prestigious *Scuola siciliana* 'Sicilian school.'[4] By the fourteenth century, Florence had also become the birthplace of the most important literary production in Florentine, embodied by the works of Dante Alighieri (1265–1312), Francesco Petrarca (1304–1374), and Giovanni Boccaccio (1313–1375), known as the *Tre Corone* 'three crowns.' Albeit in different ways, all three authors felt the need to find a *volgare illustre* 'illustrious vernacular' which they could use instead of Latin for (some of) their literary works. They found it in Florentine, and even though their linguistic repertoires were rather dissimilar, the language of their masterpieces would become the primary reference point in the search and development of a common, unitary, 'high' (i.e., written literary) language.

The language of Dante's *Commedia* (the adjective *divina* 'divine' is a later addition to the work's title) stands out for its exceptional composite multilingualism. In addition to Florentine, the *Commedia* features a rich and diverse array of languages/vernaculars, including Latin. Such remarkable multilingualism is accompanied by an equally outstanding use of a full range of registers and styles, from the most refined to the lowest or even scurrilous. Moreover, the incomparable originality of the *Commedia*'s linguistic repertoire is enhanced by the fact that each language variety, register, and style are craftly selected to meet the work's thematic richness and complexity. Dante expressed his views about the need to find a vernacular that could replace Latin as 'elevated' language of culture in *De vulgari eloquentia* 'On vernacular eloquence,' an unfinished essay written in Latin around 1302–1305. Here, he reviewed and appraised the main Italian vernaculars to establish if any of them could suit such purpose. However, he found that none could, and concluded that a distinguished vernacular to be used as common language of culture must be devised drawing from the language practices of prominent literary figures of the time, himself included. *De vulgari eloquentia* displays perceptive, 'modern' linguistic intuitions, but unfortunately, it remained unknown until the sixteenth century.

Francesco Petrarca restricted the use of Florentine to his verse production, the *Canzoniere*, while keeping to Latin for his prose. Petrarca's Florentine differs notably from Dante's since he aimed to achieve a 'high,' polished, cultivated (hence, elite) lyric language. Petrarca, then, purged Florentine from any trait perceived as 'low,' and this is why he is considered the initiator of the most learned, most refined Italian poetic tradition.

The Florentine model pursued by Giovanni Boccaccio in his prose masterpiece, the *Decameron*, is also quite different from those of Dante's and Petrarca's. Since the *Decameron* includes characters and themes from the whole range of social classes and from different geographical areas, Boccaccio needed a linguistic repertoire that could reflect such a multifaceted array of social and ethnic variety. Thus, the most distinctive qualities of the Florentine employed by Boccaccio are its wide diversity and versatility, which made it suitable for practically any style and register.

The linguistic practices of the *Tre Corone* were undoubtedly consequential for Florentine to become the model for a common, non-local, written literary language. However, Florentine and the Tuscan vernaculars in general were also more linguistically 'conservative' compared to the other vernaculars; their phonological and morphological systems had remained closer to Classical Latin phonetic, which would make them *a priori* more suitable to become a unitary variety.

By the fourteenth century, Florentine was able to attain the status of a true language of culture, though not that of a national language, due to the political fragmentation that would continue to characterize the Italian peninsula until it became a unified country, the Kingdom of Italy, in 1861. The fortune of Florentine, then, is not to be linked to the pressure of a political authority but to the influence of a newly established, highly prestigious cultural and literary tradition.

The prestige of Florentine grew in the second half of the fourteenth century, thanks to the swift and vast success of the *Tre Corone*'s works, but would decline in the next century. The Renaissance humanism of the fifteenth century restored Latin as the privileged medium of knowledge and culture, while deeming the vernacular acceptable only for practical purposes. Two notable opponents of this pervasive pro-Latin stance were Leonardo Bruni (1370–1444) and Leon Battista Alberti (1404–1472). Bruni, who is considered one of the most important humanists of the early Renaissance, was a renowned historian and statesman and a great admirer of Dante. He was not against the use of vernacular as language of culture, because he believed a writer's language to be secondary to the quality of their work. Alberti was a prominent, highly versatile intellectual and the author of *Grammatica della lingua toscana* 'Grammar of the Tuscan language' (1438–1441, best-known as *Grammatichetta vaticana*), the first descriptive grammar of an Italian vernacular. An exceptionally 'modern' work aimed at drawing attention to the live Tuscan of the time (*'in quale io raccolsi l'uso della lingua nostra in brevissime annotazioni'* 'where, in very brief notes, I recorded the use of our language'), the *Grammatichetta* was unfortunately discovered only in the nineteenth century. Alberti then believed that the Tuscan vernacular could become the common language of culture if promoted and furthered by the learned classes.

The sixteenth century witnessed a decisive turn in the rise of Florentine to the status of common language. A key event in this respect was the invention of the printing press, which spurred the need of establishing orthographic (and linguistic in general) norms. It is at this time that the so-called *questione della lingua* 'the language question' began, the debate on what kind Florentine should be elevated to 'national' language, which would last until the nineteenth century. The first three decades of the century saw the most animated stages of the dispute, and three main positions developed proposing three different models.

The first was the one expounded by Pietro Bembo (1470–1547) in his *Prose della vulgar lingua* 'The prose of the vernacular tongue' (1525), a work that reveals a keen awareness of the need of a unified literary language even though Italy was not a unified country yet. Bembo championed the 'natural' superiority of fourteenth-century Florentine, which he considered an inherently better language variety, and launched the principles of linguistic purism. The *volgare* he proposed as suitable replacement for Latin as written language of culture was modeled on Petrarca's language for poetry and Boccaccio's for prose. Dante, on the other hand, was discounted because according to Bembo, the language of the *Commedia* was tainted by varieties and features that he reputed too unbecoming. The second position, whose leading advocates included Vincenzo Colli (known as Calmeta, ca. 1460–1508), Baldassare Castiglione (1478–1529), and Gian Giorgio Trissino (1478–1550), endorsed the *lingua cortigiana* 'language of the courts,' a variety in which Florentine (or Tuscan) was still prevalent but which also accepted regional forms that had become established. Clearly, both these views strived for a language that was meant for a restricted intellectual elite rather that for the general public. The third position, on the other hand, supported contemporary spoken Florentine. One of its main promoters was Niccolò Machiavelli (1469–1527), who, in his *Discorso intorno alla nostra lingua* 'A discourse about our language' (1524), presented contemporary, 'live' Florentine as a direct continuation of fourteenth-century Florentine as the only variety that could become a common literary language.

Bembo's position prevailed, leading to the emergence of a written language for aristocratic intellectuals as opposed to the spoken language of the (uneducated) people. As already mentioned, however, Latin would remain the official language of high education – as well as of the liturgy (the use of vernaculars is banished by the Council of Trento, 1545–1563) – acquiring, in fact, the status of international language of science and academia all over Europe.[5]

In 1538, the *Accademia della Crusca* 'Academy of the bran' was founded in Florence (https://accademiadellacrusca.it/). Its members were strong supporters of Bembo's linguistics views, and their primary goal was to sieve *il fior di farina* 'the finest of flour' (i.e., the 'good' language) from *la crusca* 'the bran' (i.e., the language 'impurities'). To achieve this purpose, the *Accademia* embarked on the compilation of a dictionary based on a corpus of distinguished fourteenth-century Florentine literary works. The first edition of *Vocabolario degli Accademici della Crusca* was published in Venice in 1612 and would contribute significantly to the standardization of orthography.

The scientific progress that characterized the seventeenth century had crucial consequences for the advancement of a common Italian, particularly at the level of the lexicon which needed to be renewed in order to express new discoveries and notions. Galileo Galilei (1564–1642) was a foremost figure in this respect. Since he believed that for science to be accessible to the largest possible audience, the language of science should be close to the audience's actual language, Galilei systematically used Italian in his writings, making a vital contribution to the development of the modern scientific language, above all the language of physics. Galilei relied heavily on clarity of exposition; he favored a precise lexicon and often used ordinary words accompanied by comments to clarify their technical, specialized meaning, as well as metaphors and neologisms. Some examples include *stropicciamento de' corpi solidi* 'rubbing of solid bodies' instead of *attrito* 'friction,' *occhialetto per vedere le cose da vicino* 'small spectacles to see things close' for *microscopio* 'microscope,' *istrumento per misurare il caldo e il freddo* 'instrument to measure heat and cold' rather than *termometro* 'thermometer,' *cannocchiale* (from *cannone* 'cannon' + *occhiale* 'spectacles') to replace *telescopio* 'telescope.'

1.1.2 Toward a linguistic unification

An increasing awareness of the complexity and dynamicity of language permeated the eighteenth century, drawing attention to the need to renew and modernize it in order to narrow the gap between literary (written) language and everyday (spoken) language. Two events were consequential in this respect. First, in the second half of the century, particularly in the north, the school system underwent a significant process of restructuring and improvement. Italian became the language of instruction and began to be taught in schools, which led to the publication of grammars and textbooks; most importantly, though, more and more young people became exposed to it. Secondly, there was a considerable surge in the publication of periodicals (especially newspapers and gazettes), thanks to which Italian could reach a wider adult readership also outside the privileged intellectual niches. Moreover, a debate arose, stimulated by the Enlightenment, about French (and English) as viable linguistic models for Italian. On the one hand, these two languages were praised for their concreteness, precision, and clarity, qualities which Italian (allegedly) lacked. For instance, in his essay *Difetti della letteratura* 'The defects of literature,' author Alessandro Verri (1741–1816) commented that the English intellectuals wrote without paying excessive care to order and the French used short energic sentences, producing a prose that follows the flow of their thoughts, whereas the Italians' prose felt tight, convoluted, shy, and overflowing (in Francioni & Romagnoli, 1998, p. 539). Others, however, took the opposite stand. For instance, Venetian playwright Carlo Gozzi (1720–1802), a follower of the most conservative, patriotic views on language and politics, fiercely opposed the influence of French and supported the Florentine/Tuscan linguistic model (hence, endorsing an aristocratic, privileged model of culture). Carlo Goldoni (1707–1793), another playwright from Venice, embraced yet a different position. He believed that comedy must reflect authentic people's speech, not writing; therefore, in his works he used a wide-ranging linguistic repertoire, drawing from different dialects (and foreign languages) and different registers. The language of Goldoni's comedies has been reputed the first concrete manifestation of the integration of an array of language varieties, a language able to meet a full range of expressive and communicative needs and to reach a national, rather than regional, audience.

In 1861, Italy achieved its political unification, and the Kingdom of Italy was born. Yet Italy's linguistic unification was still far. Most Italians only spoke their local dialect, and the rate of illiteracy was exceedingly high. Only a very restricted group of literates knew (and used) the 'Italian' that had been shaping and spreading since the sixteenth century.[6] In 1868, Minister of Education Emilio Broglio appointed a committee, chaired by the renowned author and prominent political figure Alessandro Manzoni (1785–1873), to devise a plan for the establishment, implementation, and spread of a national language, that is, to identify strategies and instruments to achieve Italy's linguistic unification. Manzoni played a central role in the *questione della lingua*, turning it from a debate about the written literary language to one focused on creating a language that the Italian people at large could use to communicate effectively both at the spoken and written level. Manzoni viewed language as a common social tool, and his main objective was to narrow the gap between written and spoken language. Therefore, he took language usage as main point of reference and proposed contemporary spoken (but educated) Florentine – the same language variety he had taken as model for the final version of his novel *I promessi sposi* 'The betrothed' (1840) – as the foundation of a national standard Italian. The instruments and tactics he recommended for achieving Italy's linguistic unification included (a) the compilation of a vocabulary of 'live' Florentine to be used in schools, as well as of vocabularies of the dialects to facilitate the acquisition of Italian among speakers who only spoke dialect, (b) preferably appointing elementary teachers from Tuscany, or teachers who had studied in Tuscany, and sending non-Tuscan teachers to Florence to learn the language. Manzoni's attempts would not be very successful, because Italy was still too fragmented, not only linguistically (and culturally, in general), but also socially, economically, and politically. Italian would continue to be a heritage language of an overall too small social group, and the gap between those who knew and used Italian and those who did not remained large, especially in the south of the country, where the school system was in dreadful conditions and the illiteracy rates were the highest.[7]

Manzoni's plan for linguistic unification was cogently criticized by leading linguist and dialectologist Graziadio Isaia Ascoli (1829–1907), who was against imposing any kind of rigid linguistic model. Ascoli firmly believed that language change proceeds jointly with historical evolution and social renovation. Thus, he argued that Italy's linguistic unification could only be reached by transforming society first. In his *Proemio* to *Archivio Glottologico Italiano* (a still-active journal he founded in 1873), he commented that throughout its history, Italy had lacked continuity of thought and ideals. Italy had never developed a cultural tradition of vast circulation or hegemonic cities (comparable, for instance, to Paris), and it still lacked intellectual and civic unity, as, for example, Germany, a country he considered a model for linguistic unification. According to Ascoli, a unitary language could only result from natural evolution; Italian must be spread, but not to the detriment of the dialects, because the dialects constituted the very basis of the Italian people's social and cultural identity. For Ascoli, then, increasing and widening the distribution of culture across lower social classes was instrumental and imperative for the achievement of linguistic unification.

Since its unification through the first decades of the nineteenth century, Italy experienced a series of momentous social and economic transformations which contributed to the progress toward its linguistic unification. A unified administrative system was created which required a unified language. Although it was highly specialized and formal, the language of bureaucracy became the only model of Italian available to the 'common' people, the only viable alternative to their dialect they had to communicate with speakers of other dialects. Moreover, the administrative body employed individuals who came from all over the country but needed to use a common language, Italian, to communicate effectively among each other in the workplace.

Mandatory conscription (which was instituted in 1861, to last until 2005) contributed to the spreading of Italian as well by bringing together young men who didn't know (or barely knew) Italian but had to use it to communicate among each other and with their superiors. Thus, the slang of the barracks started to develop, an Italian infused with dialectal features some of which would be absorbed into Italian.

A massive external migration set off between 1871 and 1915. It's estimated that during this period, about seven million Italians left Italy in search of better life opportunities. Most of them came from southern Italy, where poverty was most severe and illiteracy most pervasive. Abroad, the immigrants needed to use Italian to fit in the local multi-dialectal Italian communities, and they also needed to know it to write to their families at home. External migration, then, had a significant impact on both the diffusion of Italian and the rise of literacy rates, which registered an estimated drop of 22.2% during the first decades of the twentieth century.

During the first decades of the twentieth century, a considerable internal migration started as well. Due to the combined effects of urbanization and industrialization, many Italians moved from the poorer rural areas (again, predominantly from the south) to the large urban areas in the north, where industries were developing. The phenomenon of internal migration would continue throughout the century (peaking between the 1950s and 1960s) and was as influential at the linguistic level as external migration.

The school system also underwent major developments. In 1860, education became public, and a 12-year national program was implemented, the first two years of which were compulsory and free. More progress followed in 1877; the elementary school curriculum was extended from four to five years and made compulsory for the first three, and a fine was instituted to enforce mandatory attendance. Furthermore, the core national curriculum was expanded to include more subjects and new materials (e.g., Dante's *Commedia* and Manzoni's *I promessi sposi*, both still part of today's curriculum).[8] In the twentieth century, the economic growth Italy experienced after WWII (the *boom economico* 'economic miracle' that peaked in the early 1960s) and the extension of compulsory education to lower secondary school (i.e., from age 11 to age 14) significantly contributed to boost the nation's literacy rates.

Last but not least, we must mention the development of the mass media. At the end of the nineteenth century, leading national newspapers started to be published – *La Stampa* (1867), *Corriere della Sera* (1876), and *Messaggero* (1878) – spurring an increase in the readership. Then, radio, cinema, and television would speed up the diffusion of standard Italian exponentially.

To conclude, on the one hand, we could say Italy's linguistic unification was overall completed by the twentieth century. On the other hand, however, it could be said that it has not really stopped, because the increased distribution of standard Italian among larger and larger population groups as well as a general waning of linguistic prescriptivism and a changed attitude toward the dialects have involved a transformation of the language which is still ongoing. Since the second half of the last century, Italy's society, culture, and economy have been transforming drastically (and fast). As a result, standard Italian has been undergoing a (relatively) rapid process of general 'restructuring,' or **re-standardization**. The boundaries of (prescriptive) standard Italian have gradually been loosening to let in forms and structures from non-standard varieties, some of which had been attested for centuries but shunned as unbecoming to the 'proper' language. In other words, the different varieties of Italian are coming together to form one 'single' Italian. The next sections review the most important aspects of this process of language restructuring.

1.2 Varieties of Italian

Natural languages are not abstract, static entities; rather, they live, change, and die, through the usage speakers make of them.[9] As such, all natural languages comprise multiple interdependent varieties which are shaped and governed by their users' traits and experiences, both individual and collective. Thus, the notion of language as a perfectly homogenous, invariable entity is just a myth, an illusion cherished and perpetrated by linguistic prescriptivism.

Language variation is measured with respect to five main dimensions (or **variables**, in sociolinguistic terminology), as summarized in (1).

(1) a. **Space** (i.e., geographical areas)
   b. **Society** (i.e., speakers' socio-economic status, level of education, occupation, gender, age)
   c. **Communicative situation** (i.e., registers or styles, as measured in terms of degree of formality of both the situation itself and the interlocutors' relationship with one another)
   d. **Communicative channel** (i.e., spoken, written, transmitted)
   e. **Time** (i.e., diachronic stages)

These variables are neither absolute nor self-contained. They represent **interconnected series** (or **continua**) of related 'sub'-variables which are delimited by two 'opposite,' somewhat-discrete varieties. To give an example, the boundaries of communicative situation can be identified as 'maximally formal' (e.g., academic conference) and 'minimally informal' (e.g., casual conversation among close friends or family members). Within these two edges lies a continuum of varieties with shared features, and the closer the varieties are to each other, the larger is the number of features they have in common. But communicative situation crosses with communicative channel (e.g., scientific paper vs. text message), as well as with space (absence of regional features vs. abundance of dialectal features) and society (e.g., the linguistic repertoire of an old male vs. that of a young female). These interconnections bring about many other, more specific language (sub-)varieties, such as, for instance, the language of specific academic/scientific disciplines (e.g., the language of linguistics, medicine, mathematics) or media (the language of newspapers, television, internet) or of specific groups of people (e.g., the language of the youth, the language of women/men). The sentence variants in (2) illustrate the interconnected network of varieties showing the range of 'marked' renderings of the notion 'I don't know at all what they told her.' (The labels are approximative, and the sample sentences are adapted from Berruto, 1987, p. 30).

(2) a. Highly formal written standard: *Non sono affatto a conoscenza di che cosa le sia stato detto.*
   b. Formal (written) standard: *Non sono affatto a conoscenza di che cosa le abbiano detto.*
   c. Standard: *Non so affatto che cosa le abbiano detto.*
   d. (Spoken) neo-standard: *Non so affatto che cosa gli abbiano detto.*
   e. (Spoken informal) neo-standard: *Non so mica che gli hanno detto.*
   f. Informal spoken neo-standard: *Mica lo so che gli hanno detto.*
   g. Informal/colloquial: *Mica lo so che cazzo gli hanno detto.*
   h. Regional informal/colloquial: *Mica lo so che ci hanno detto.*
   i. Dialect: /mikə lə satʃːə   k   jə   anomədittə/[10]
            'not   it   I.know   what   to.her   they said'

The forms and constructions which serve as referent point to measure variation are illustrated in (3).

(3) a. Negation: discontinuous **periphrastic** form *non . . . affatto* 'not at all' vs. **simple** *mica*.
   b. Rendering of 'to know': **lexical periphrasis** *essere a conoscenza* 'to be in the knowledge' vs. **simple verb** *sapere* 'to know.'
   c. Verb diathesis: **passive** form *sia stato detto* 'has been said' (2a) vs. **active** form *abbiano detto* 'have said' (2b–d) and *hanno detto* (2e–i).
   d. Verb mood: **subjunctive** *sia stato detto* (2a) and *abbiano detto* (2b–d) vs. **indicative** *hanno detto* (2e–i).
   e. Third-person singular indirect object pronoun: **feminine** *le* 'to her' (2a–c) vs. **masculine** form *gli* 'to him' (2d–g) vs. **non-standard/regional** *ci* (2h).
   f. Interrogative 'what': **periphrastic** form *che cosa* (2a–d) vs. **simple** form (geographically marked) *che* (2e–i).
   g. Presence vs. absence of the unstressed pronoun *lo* 'it' (2f–i).
   h. Use of the expletive (**dysphemism**) *cazzo* (literally 'penis') (2g).

On the whole, the sentence variants in (2) point to a tendency toward '**simplification**,' a movement toward a 'more concise' and 'more uniform' language (Berruto, 1987, p. 83), where periphrastic expressions give way to simple ones, and the pronominal paradigm is leveled (i.e., the masculine form the third-person singular indirect object pronoun *gli* replaces the feminine form *le*). This tendency is examined in more detail in the following section. Note, however, that the term 'simplification' does not imply 'shift toward a **simpler** language' (i.e., to a language variety that is 'less complex' in the sense of 'less adequate'), because the notion of a 'simple language' is meaningless.

Summarizing, present-day Italian comprises three primary components: (a) the core grammar (i.e., a set of sounds, words, constructions) of standard Italian; (b) an array of different varieties (geographical, social, stylistic, specialistic/technical); and (c) the dialects. Due to scope (and space) constraints, we will only address language variation along the social and geographical dimensions, reviewing only the main varieties, namely, standard, neo-standard, and non-/sub-standard Italian (or *italiano popolare*) for the former, and dialects and regional varieties for the latter.[11]

1.2.1 Standard, neo-standard, non-standard

Standard language denotes

> [a] particular variety of a language, usually both spoken and written, which is accepted as the norm for educated usage. The standard variety is taught in schools and used for almost all publication; educated speakers speak it in all circumstances, except possibly in speaking to relatives and close friends from the same background. Not every language has such a standard form.
>
> *(Trask, 2014, p. 207)*

For Italian, Berruto (1993, pp. 84–85) proposes three possible interpretations of 'standard': (a) 'neutral' (i.e., unmarked for all the parameters in (1)); (b) 'prescriptive' (i.e., codified by grammars and instruction and collectively accepted as 'good/proper,' as in Trask's definition); and (c) 'normal' (i.e., statistically most widespread among the educated speakers). The first interpretation is rather unrealistic/highly abstract because it entails a language variety completely divorced from language use, but even a prescriptive standard is marked at some level by the grammarians' rules.

As outlined in the preceding section, from a diachronic perspective, standard Italian is the landing point of a language that originated in the written Florentine of the fourteenth century, based primarily on Dante's, Petrarca's, and Boccaccio's masterpieces. Then, starting in the sixteenth century, it went through a process of codification which basically ended in the nineteenth century for written Italian but continued until the late twentieth century for spoken Italian (and, to some extent, is still ongoing). This process of codification cleansed Florentine of a number of features (phonetics, morphological, syntactic, and lexical) which were deemed too 'vernacular.' Thus, the somewhat-common beliefs that Italian has not changed as much since medieval times and that the average educated Italian can understand 'Old Italian' (i.e., fourteenth-century Florentine) relatively well are only true to a certain point.

Strictly speaking, however, standard Italian is not the native language for the majority of Italians (especially as spoken language) because it is not the variety they acquire spontaneously as children but the language they learn formally in school. Overall, then, standard Italian is a virtual entity or, at best, a variety characterized by a rather-restricted usage. In other words, it is the variety used essentially (perhaps exclusively) in written (formal) contexts. As a written variety, standard Italian is a unitary language at the level of spelling, generally unitary at the level of morphology/morphosyntax and syntax and less unitary at the level of vocabulary. Differently put, Italian appears to be on the way to becoming a 'partially standardized' variety, that is, a variety displaying higher degree of standardization in morphology/morphosyntax and syntax but a lesser degree in the vocabulary. As a spoken variety, on the other hand, standard Italian remains a virtual variety because pronunciation is always considerably marked by regional features (Palermo, 2020, p. 215). The standard pronunciation (or *pronuncia fiorentina emendata* 'edited Florentine pronunciation,' i.e., a pronunciation edited to remove Florentine features considered dialectal) is a reality only for a very restricted group of people (e.g., actors, dubbers, teachers, linguists, language purists) and, as a matter of fact, is fading away also within these groups. Among the 'common' people, it has never actually existed. Pronunciation, then, remains the domain where the speakers' geographical origins strongly prevail.

As noted earlier, standard Italian has been undergoing a process of 're-standardization' which started to draw the attention of (Italian) linguists around the 1970s, and the first formal accounts appeared in the mid-1980s. The two best-known views on and characterization of this 'new' standard are summarized in (4). Although they overall refer to the same linguistic entity, Berruto's label (4b) is the one that gained more success and is the most commonly used.

(4) a. *Italiano **dell'uso medio*** 'Italian of average usage' (Sabatini, 1985): the Italian used daily both in spoken and written settings, as well as in formal and informal ones.
   b. *Italiano **neo-standard*** (Berruto, 1987): a variety that has accepted forms and constructions from other (lower) varieties (i.e., non-/sub-standard varieties), some of which were still frowned upon by prescriptivist/purists.

Neo-standard Italian, then, denotes the language variety regularly used by Italian speakers from the upper and middle classes in most communicative situations and which has replaced

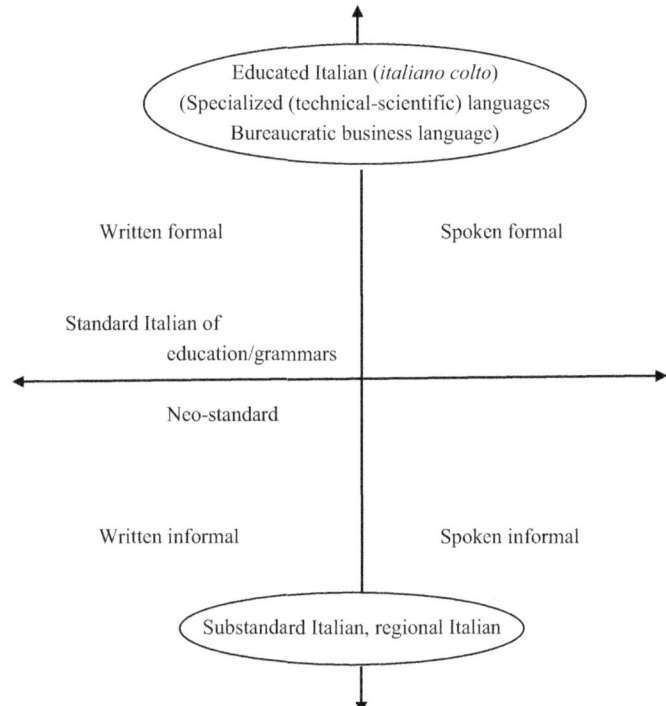

FIGURE 1.1 The structure of contemporary Italian. Horizontal axis = communicative channel; vertical axis = communicative situation.

standard Italian at the spoken level. Berruto (1987, p. 21) proposed a very successful pictorial representation (an 'architecture') of contemporary Italian. A modified version (drawing from Palermo, 2020, p. 219) is given in Figure 1.1.

Before reviewing the most representative features of neo-standard Italian, we will review the notion of non-/sub-standard variety and introduce its most distinctive features since, as just mentioned, some of them have been 'breaking into' the neo-standard.

A **non-standard** language variety is distinguished by forms and constructions that 'officially' do not belong to the standard variety, even though some communities of speakers commonly use them. A **sub-standard** variety also includes forms and constructions that are not part of the standard variety (i.e., non-standard features), yet there is an important difference between the two: non-standard varieties are not inherently characterized by a negative connotation, whereas sub-standard varieties are by the prefix 'sub' (from the Latin preposition *sub* 'under'), which means 'below' in this context. This is clear in the *Oxford English Dictionary*'s definition of the adjective 'sub-standard': '1. Of less than the required or normal quality or size; of a lower standard than required, inferior. 2. Of speech: not conforming to standard usage, nonstandard; *spec.* employing forms which are widely used but are considered incorrect' (https://www-oed-com.ezproxy.lib.utexas.edu/view/Entry/193046?redirectedFrom=sub-standard#eid).

At beginning of the 1970s, Italian linguists stared to call attention to a non-standard variety that had emerged and had been spreading after Italy's political unification, when the newly established standard Italian was instituted. The term *italiano popolare* was first introduced by internationally renowned linguist (and Minister of Education) Tullio De Mauro, who described it as the language variety uneducated Italians resorted to when they needed to communicate in the national language 'optimistically called "Italian,"' a language they never or only marginally learned in a formal setting (i.e., in school) (De Mauro, 1970, p. 49). In the Italian sociolinguistic literature, De Mauro's definition of *italiano popolare* is commonly compared to the definition provided by another highly influential sociolinguist, Manlio Cortelazzo, who characterized *italiano popolare* as the 'type of Italian imperfectly acquired by individuals whose native language is a dialect' (Cortelazzo, 1972, p. 11). De Mauro's and Cortelazzo's characterizations are similar in that they both take low social class and low level of education as main defining parameters, but they also differ. De Mauro's definition underscores that these varieties pertain primarily to the level of individual linguistic competency (i.e., it focuses on the speakers' degree of Italian competency); therefore, *italiano popolare* is viewed as an individual phenomenon. In contrast, Cortelazzo's definition focuses on the speakers' native language; hence, *italiano popolare* is viewed as a collective (supra-individual) phenomenon.

Is *italiano popolare* a non-standard or a sub-standard variety of Italian? Strictly speaking, it is a non-standard variety, because it includes forms and constructions that standard Italian rejects. But it may be (indeed, has been) deemed sub-standard because of the social stigma associated with its users, low-class, low-educated/uneducated Italians.

Clearly, *italiano popolare* is primarily a spoken variety, even though it has been studied essentially through written corpora (correspondence, diaries, other autobiographic materials).[12]

Finally, it should be noted that *italiano popolare* must not be equated with dialect; although it is indeed very much influenced by the dialects (because the dialects are the native languages of speakers of *italiano popolare*), it is independent of them. In other words, *italiano popolare* always displays local regional traits, but the dialects do not exhibit features of *italiano popolare*.

The notion of *italiano popolare* has always been quite controversial. For instance, Berruto (1993, p. 58) characterizes it as thus:

> [T]he social variety par excellence; that is, the set of language practices which frequently recur in the speech (but also the writing) of uneducated people who in everyday life normally use only their dialect, and which characterized by numerous deviations from normative standard Italian.

But he regards the label *popolare* questionable and the notion itself debatable. As noted earlier, Italy's linguistic scenario has been changing rapidly for the past 70 years or so, and *italiano popolare* no longer seems a plausible reality because, presently, no/barely any Italians would fit the profile of a speaker of such a variety. The number of semi-/illiterate dialect monolingual Italians is, at best, marginal, and this category is destined to disappear completely before long. In any case, these individuals have had an extensive active exposure to standard Italian, both in public settings (e.g., administrative and health services, stores, public transportations) and private ones (e.g., interaction with family members and friends who use only or primarily Italian) and, of course, through the media (internet included). In fact, Berruto (2005, p. 334) claims that *italiano popolare* 'no longer exists in the linguistic landscape of Italy, neither as an actual entity nor as an interesting topic of linguistic research,' and D'Achille (2010–2011, p. 725; quoted in Krefeld, 2016, p. 267) suggests that the notion of *italiano popolare* should be historicized (see also Cortelazzo, 2001; Lepschy, 2002, among others).

Written *italiano popolare* is characterized by a variety of spelling mistakes. Typically, they result from the influence of the dialects, so they vary across regional areas. A few examples of the most common ones are given in (5).

(5) a.   [kʷ] <c>, <cq>, <q>: *aqua* for *acqua* 'water,' *quore* for *cuore* 'heart,' *cuesto* for *questo* 'this.'
   b.   [ʎ] <gl>: *filio* for *figlio* 'son,' and [ɲ] <gn>: *bisonio* for *bisogno* 'need'; and hypercorrections: *oglio* for *olio* 'oil,' *gnente* for *niente* 'nothing.'
   c.   Simplification of 'difficult' consonant clusters by inserting a vowel: *pisicologo* for *psicologo* 'psychologist,' *aritemetica* for *aritmetica* 'arithmetic'; or by assimilation: *arimmetica*.
   d.   Segmentation of 'definite article-noun' sequences: *l'aradio* for **la** *radio*, **lo** *rigano* for *l'origano*.
   e.   Omission or addition of 'silent' <h>: *a* for **ha** 's/he has,' *anno* for **hanno** 'they have,' **h**abbiamo for *abbiamo* 'we have.'
   f.   <n> for <m>: *banbola* for *bambola* 'doll,' *canbiare* for *cambiare*.

Some of the most prominent features of *italiano popolare* which are independent of dialectal influence are illustrated in (6).

(6) a.   Pronominal system:
   i.   Redundant pronouns: *a* **lui** **gli** *piace* 'he likes' (vs. *a* **lui** *piace*).
   ii.   Third-person singular/plural *si* for first-person plural *ci*: **si** *siamo visti* (vs. **ci** *siamo visti* 'we saw each other').
   iii.   *Ci* for third-person singular indirect object pronouns *gli* 'to them.M/F' and *le* 'to her': *ho telefonato a Claudia e* **ci** *ho chiesto se veniva con noi* 'I called Claudia and asked her if she was coming with us' (vs. **le** *ho chiesto*).

   b.   Agreement ad sensum: *tutto il paese ne* **parlavano** 'the whole town was talking about it' (vs. **parlava**), *c'era tanti bambini* 'there were a lot of children' (vs. *c'erano*).
   c.   Regularization of irregular forms:
   i.   Verbs: *dicete* 'you say' for *dite*, *facete* 'you do' for *fate*, *potiamo* 'we can' for *possiamo*.
   ii.   Masculine definite articles: **un/il** *zio* 'an uncle,' *i zii* 'the uncles'(vs. **uno/lo** *zio*, **gli** *zii*).

   d.   'Regularization' of grammatical gender (*moglia* 'wife' for *moglie*) or gender confusion (**la** *diabete* 'the diabetes' vs. **il** *diabete*).
   e.   Use of wrong and/or redundant prepositions: *è bravo* **di** *parlare* 'he's good at talking' (vs. *a parlare*), *preferisco* **di** *rimanere a casa* 'I prefer to stay home' (vs. *preferisco rimanere*).
   f.   Redundant comparative and superlative forms of adjectives: *più migliore* 'best' (vs. *migliore*), *molto bellissimo* 'very beautiful' (vs. *bellissimo* or *molto bello*); and adverbs: *più bene* 'better' (vs. *meglio*).
   g.   Redundant *che* with conjunctions: *siccome* **che** *faceva freddo* 'since it was cold,' *mentre* **che** *cucinavo* 'while I was cooking,' *quando* **che** *l'ho visto* 'when I saw him.'
   h.   Multifunctional *che*, that is, the use of *che* in contexts that would call for the relative pronoun *cui* or *quale*, often accompanied by a clitic pronoun which expresses the syntactic function of the relative pronoun: *un ragazzo* **che** *(gli) piace studiare* 'a boy

who likes to study' (vs. *a cui /al quale*), *il paesino che (ci) sono nato* 'the village where I was born' (vs. *in cui /nel quale*).

    i.   Hypothetical sentences with double subjunctive: *se non sarei ricco* **pagherei** *io* 'if I were rich, I would pay'; or double conditional: *se **fossi** ricco **pagassi** io* (vs. *se **fossi** ricco **pagherei** io*).

Finally, the vocabulary displays many regional words and expressions (as addressed in the next section) and is characterized by the use of generic terms for specific referents (*carta* 'paper' for *documento* 'document') and malapropisms (*celebre* 'famous' for *celibe* 'bachelor,' *decenza* 'decency' for *degenza* 'hospitalization,' *patè* 'pâté' for *patema* 'anxiety').

We can now move on to review the main distinctive features of neo-standard Italian which, as noted before, pertain to morphology/morphosyntax and syntax. Concerning the former domain, the most notable changes have affected the pronominal and verbal systems. The neo-standard features related to the system of personal pronouns are summarized in (7).

(7)   a.   **Subject** pronouns. The forms *egli* 'he,' *ella* 'she,' and their plural counterparts, *essi* 'they.M' and *esse* 'they.F,' are very rare and are commonly replaced by the corresponding complement forms *lui*, *lei*, and *loro* 'they.M/F,' both in the spoken and written language. Moreover, the forms *lui/lei* are also used for inanimate referents instead of *esso/essa*.

      b.   **Unstressed** (clitic) **indirect object** pronouns. The third-person masculine singular form *gli* 'to him' has ousted the plural form *loro* 'to them.M/F,' both in the spoken and written language: '*I Soldati Nato e i carnefici a tu per tu: arrestateli se li incontrate, non date**gli** la caccia*' 'NATO soldiers up against each the murderers: arrest them if you come across them, don't search for them' (*La Stampa*, November 26, 1995; from Tosi, 2001, p. 59). In spoken (informal) Italian, *gli* is often used also for feminine referents: *sono secoli che non vedo Claudia, stasera **gli** telefono* 'It's been ages since I saw Claudia, tonight I'll call her.'[13]

The system of relative pronouns has been undergoing changes as well. The relative pronoun paradigm of standard Italian includes three forms, as shown in (8).

(8)   a.   Invariable *che* 'who/that, whom,' which has two functions:

        i.   Subject: *la persona **che** sta parlando* 'the person who is speaking.'
        ii.   Direct object: *la persona **che** ho conosciuto* 'the person (whom) I met.'

      b.   Two periphrastic forms for complements other than direct object:

        i.   'Preposition + *cui*': *la persona **con/a cui** parlavo* 'the person to/with whom I was speaking.'
        ii.   'Preposition + definite article + *quale* (singular)/*quali* (plural)' with the definite article agreeing in number and gender to the pronoun referent: *il problema **del quale** ti parlavo* 'the problem I was telling you about,' *le persone **delle quali** non ricordo i nomi* 'the persons whose names I don't recall.'

In neo-standard Italian, the forms with *quale/quali* are restricted to written (highly) formal contexts; elsewhere, the forms with *cui* have taken over. Also, *che* frequently replaces *in cui* when referring to temporal complements: *l'ultima volta* **che** *sono andato in Italia* 'the last time I went to Italy.'

These changes involve expansion of the functional load of certain members of a paradigm. Some forms take over grammatical functions carried by others, eventually pushing them out from the paradigm so that the paradigm becomes more 'regular.'

The main neo-standard traits pertaining to the verb system involve expansion (or shift) of the functions of some verb tenses, as illustrated in (9).

(9) a. The imperfect indicative has acquired **modal** values.

        i. Hypothetical counterfactual value, replacing the pluperfect subjunctive and the past conditional: *se mi* **invitavi venivo** 'if you had invited me, I would have come' vs. *se mi* **avessi invitato sarei venuto**.

        ii. Attenuative value, to mitigate requests: **volevo** *chiederti un favore* 'I wanted to ask you a favor' (vs. present indicative *voglio* 'I want,' or present conditional *vorrei* 'I would like').

    b. Present indicative has gained **future** value, particularly to refer to imminent events or events that are perceived as certain: *stasera* **vado** *a teatro* 'tonight I'm going to the theater,' *quest'estate* **andiamo** *in Italia* 'This summer we are going to Italy' (vs. future **andrò** 'I will go' and **andremo** 'we will go').

    c. The future indicative has acquired **modal** value.

        i. **Epistemic** value (i.e., it conveys supposition or doubt): *sono le 11,* **starà** *dormendo* 'it's 11pm, he's probably sleeping.'

        ii. **Deontic** value (i.e., expresses duty or obligation): *il modulo* **dovrà** *essere compilato in stampatello* 'the form must (lit. will have to) be filled out in block letters.'

At the syntactic level, one of the most prominent traits of neo-standard Italian is the increased frequency of so-called **dislocated constructions**. These constructions are distinguished by a 'non-canonical' word order, in that a given constituent does not occur in the position it is found in affirmative declarative sentences (or 'canonical' sentences) and/or the presence of a superfluous pronoun. They come in two types, **left-** and **right-**dislocation.

(10) a. *Adoro i carciofi.*   Affirmative declarative
      'I love artichokes.'

    b. *I carciofi* **li** *adoro.*   Left-dislocation
      'Artichokes, I love them.'

    c. **Li** *adoro, i carciofi.*   Right-dislocation
      'I love them, artichokes.'

In the left-dislocated construction in (10b), the direct object *i carciofi* 'artichokes' occurs at the beginning of the sentence rather than in its 'expected' position (i.e., after the verb as in (10a)); also, (10b) includes the third-person plural direct object pronoun *li* 'them.ᴍ,' which refers to *carciofi* but is redundant. The right-dislocated construction in (10c), on the other hand, displays the same word order as declarative sentences, but it still includes the pronoun *li*. Both left- and right-dislocation are widely attested throughout the history of the Italian language; however, they have endured extensive and vehement censure by (prescriptive) grammars and language scholars in general and viewed as sub-standard constructions restricted to spoken (colloquial) and informal written registers. This position has finally been corrected, and it is now agreed that left-dislocation is widespread in basically any variety and register of Italian (D'Achille, 2016, p. 182), while right-dislocation is still considered by some a spoken language feature (D'Achille, 2010, p. 227; Zamora Muñoz, 2002, p. 452). Two examples from contemporary written Italian are given in (11).

(11) a. '*Il capitano si sbottona il colletto della giubba. Il berretto se lo è già tolto . . .'*
          'The captain unbuttons the collar of his jacket. His cap, he has already taken off . . .'
          (Lucarelli, 2014, p. 9)
     b. '. . . *anche se poi se li tiene i soldi o i regali che le fanno.'*
          '. . . even though then she keeps them, the money or the gifts they give her.'
          (Lucarelli, 2014, p. 3)

Two other constructions traditionally considered non-standard have also gained ground in neo-standard Italian: cleft sentences and the presentative construction with the verb *esserci* 'be there' (or *c'è presentativo* 'presentational *c'è*'). The general template of **cleft sentences** is sketched in (12a) and illustrated by a constructed example in (12a'), while (12b) shows the corresponding canonical construction. Two attested examples are given in (13).

(12) a. *essere* 'be' + pronoun/phrase/clause + [*che* + finite clause]/[*a* + non-finite clause]
     a'. *È LUI/SUO FRATELLO/STUDIARE che non mi piace.*
          'It's him/his brother/studying that I don't like.'
     b. *Lui/Suo fratello/Studiare non mi piace.*

(13) a. '*Adesso è lui che vorrebbe . . . farsi psicanalizzare.'*
          'Now it's him who would like to be psychoanalyzed.'
          (L. Romano, *Le parole tra noi leggere*, 1969)
     b. '. . . *non era la pubblicità a imitarli, erano loro che la imitavano . . .'*
          '. . . it wasn't advertising that imitated them, it was them who imitated it . . .'
          (G. Pontiggia, *La grande sera*, 1989)[14]

The main communicative function of cleft sentences is to draw attention to the constituent that follows *essere* (i.e., to mark it as focal information) and, usually, to contrast it (directly or indirectly) with another referent within a given set (*è LUI che non capisce (non io)* 'it's him who doesn't understand (not me)'); in spoken language, in fact, this constituent is also prosodically stressed (symbolized by small caps).

The structure of the presentational *c'è* construction is sketched in (14a) and illustrated by a constructed example in (14a'), and the corresponding canonical construction is given in (14b). One attested example is provided in (15).

(14) a. *esserci* + noun/pronoun + *che* + clause
     a'. *C'è Claudia/una donna/lei che ti cerca.*
          'There is Claudia/a woman/she who is looking for you.'
     b. *Claudia/una donna/lei ti cerca.*

(15) '*Certe volte* **c'è qualcosa che** *mi striscia sotto la pelle, come un animale . . .*'
'Sometimes, there is something that crawls underneath my skin, like an animal . . .'
(Lucarelli, 1999, p. 41)

The communicative function of this construction is to highlight topic constituents by 'fram-ing' them within *esserci* and *che*.

1.3 Dialects and regional varieties

This section first introduces the main groups of Italian dialects and reviews their most distinc-tive structural features, primarily as pertaining to sounds (phonetics/phonology). Next, it addresses the regional varieties of Italian (*italiani regionali*) and their status vis-à-vis the dialects. Before we start, however, a few important premises are in order.

First, we must clarify what a dialect (< late Lat. DIALECTO(N) < Gr. διάλεκτος 'discussion, language') is and how it differs from a language.[15] From a strictly linguistic perspective, dia-lects are fully developed, independent linguistic systems (i.e., they are characterized by their own structural properties); hence, they are absolutely equal to languages. The difference between a dialect and a language rests on sociolinguistic (language external) parameters rather than structural (language internal) features.

1.3.1 The dialects

The main factors commonly adopted to distinguish between languages and dialects are sum-marized in (16).

(16) a.   Geographic distribution. Dialects typically pertain to a local region, whereas lan-guages belong to countries.
b.   Political relevance. Dialects bear low/no political relevance and normally do not rise to the status of 'official' (standard) language.
c.   Modality and contexts of usage. Dialects' 'natural' modality is spoken (in fact, they tend to lack a written tradition), and they are used primarily in informal contexts (e.g., with family and friends). The written use of dialect is deliberate and usually indexical (e.g., marking narrative characters' socio-cultural status, expressing soli-darity to socio-cultural traditions and/or political views, serving ludic function, as in the language of the youth or the internet). Since dialects remain outside formal written domains, they do not develop a specialized technical lexicon.
d.   Forms of codification. Dialects usually lack normative grammars and dictionaries; when these exist, they are the aimed at dialectologists (and linguists in general) and meant specifically for research. Dialects, then, are acquired spontaneously within the family and are not taught in school.

Overall, the evaluation of dialects vis-à-vis languages along the factors in (16) points to a relationship of hegemony/subordination, which rests essentially on socio-cultural and politi-cal prestige.

Second, we must make clear that the Italian dialects are not to be understood as 'dialects of the Italian language,' that is, they are full-fledged, independent languages, not geographical varieties of Italian. (These, as we will see later, are *italiani regionali*.) Put differently, the Italian dialects are sisters of standard Italian – which, as we recall, developed from a 'dialect,' Old Florentine – born by the same mother, Latin, just like any other Romance language. So it would be more appropriate to refer to them as 'dialects of Italy' or 'Latin dialects' (Telmon, 2016, p. 302), or perhaps, even better, 'non-standard Romance varieties spoken in Italy' (Repetti, 2014, p. 221). The dialects, then, are native languages, acquired spontaneously within the family, while Italian is learned later in school. More properly, this was the 'original' scenario, because dialects and Italian have gradually been converging together, leading to the strengthening of *italiani regionali*.

Finally, we must emphasize that it isn't feasible to pin down exactly how many dialects there are in Italy, or to give them precise boundaries, because identifying precise, bounded language varieties is difficult as well as partly subjective. Therefore, it is more appropriate to speak of dialectal continua, that is, geographical areas where different dialects exist which are interconnected in 'a chain of mutual intelligibility, so that the variety of a given locality x is intelligible to the speakers of directly neighboring localities y and z' (Loporcaro, 2016, p. 277, fn. 3). Dialectal continua can be identified by means of **isoglosses**, which are lines plotted on a map delimiting a geographical area characterized by a given linguistic feature.[16] Two important isoglosses for the classification of the main dialectal areas of Italy are the La Spezia-Rimini line, which separates northern from central dialects, and the Roma-Ancona line, which separates central from southern dialects. To these three main general areas, three smaller, more constrained ones are usually added – Ladin, Friulian, and Sardinian –– though it should be noted that Ladin Friulian and Sardinian are generally classified as Romance languages in the Romance linguistic literature.[17]

The last remark to be made before we start reviewing some of the most distinctive features of each area pertains to naming practices. Technically, dialects can be named after individual cities, towns, or even villages; practically, however, they are usually named after the 20 regions which constitute the country's administrative units.

The **northern** dialectal area is enclosed between the national boundaries and the La Spezia-Rimini line and comprise two main groups: (a) Gallo-Italian (Piedmont, Liguria, Lombardy, Emilia-Romagna, western Trentino) and (b) Veneto (Veneto, eastern Trentino). A third group includes Ladin (It. *ladino*, which refers to a group of dialects spoken in the Dolomites) and Friulian.

Some distinctive features shared across all groups are given in (17).

(17) a. **Weakening** (lenition) of intervocalic consonants, in the form of voicing or even loss: Milanese [urˈtiga], Torinese [yrˈtia] 'nettle' vs. Italian [orˈtika].

   b. **Degemination** (i.e., shortening of long consonant): Piedmontese [ˈfjama] 'flame,' Bolognese [kaˈpɛl] 'hat' vs. Italian [ˈfjamma], [kapˈpɛllo].

   c. **Palatal affricates** [tʃ, dʒ] realized as fricatives [s, ʒ]: Venetian [ˈsento] 'one hundred,' [ʒeˈnotʃo] 'knee' vs. Italian [ˈtʃɛnto], [dʒiˈnɔkkjo].

   d. **Obligatory expression of subjects**, often accompanied by an unstressed (clitic) subject pronoun: Veneto /ˈ**ti te** ˈparli/ 'you.sɢ speak,' where /ti/ is the subject stressed pronoun and /te/ is the clitic one, vs. Italian /ˈparli/.

Another feature present in all groups is loss of word-final vowels other than [a], which is pervasive in the Gallo-Italian group (Lombard [nɔtʃ] 'night,' [kaˈval] 'horse' vs. Italian [ˈnɔtte] [kaˈvallo]) but occurs only after [r] and [n] in the Veneto group (Venetian [kɔr] 'heart,' [moˈliŋ] 'mill' vs. Italian [ˈkwɔre], [muˈlino]). Distinctive of the first group, on the other hand, are front rounded vowels (Milanese [ˈlyna] 'moon,' [ˈøtʃ] 'eye' vs. Italian [ˈluna], [ˈɔkkjo]).

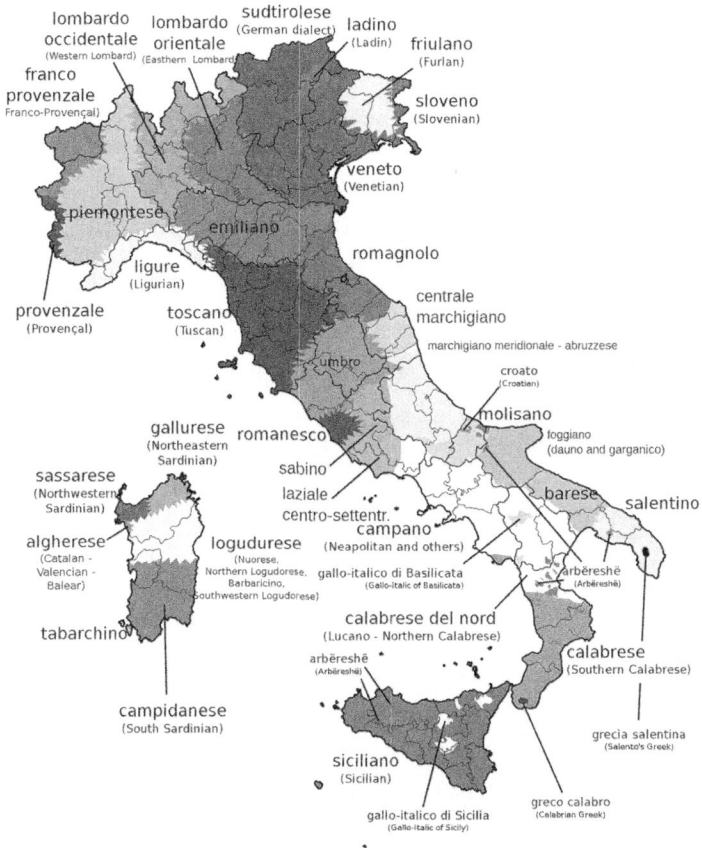

FIGURE 1.2   Dialects of Italy.

Source: Wikimedia Commons.[18]

Some of the distinguishing features of Ladin and Friulian are illustrated in (18).

(18) a. Palatalization of [k, g] before [a]: Ladin [caˈval] 'horse,' Friulian [ɟal] 'rooster' vs. Italian [kaˈvallo], [galˈlo]).

b. Retention of consonant + [l] clusters: Friulian [**fl**oːr] 'flower,' [**kl**aːf] 'key' vs. Italian [ˈ**fj**ore], [ˈ**kj**ave]).

c. Plural marked by [s]: Friulian [tʃan**s**] 'dogs' vs. Italian [ˈkani]).

Distinctive of Friulian, on the other hand, is phonemic vowel length ([pas] 'step' vs. [paːs] 'peace,' [brut] 'ugly' vs. [bruːt] 'broth').

The **central** area can be subdivided into the **Tuscan** area, which covers Tuscany and extends to some areas of the Emilia-Romagna Apennines and northern Umbria, and the **middle** (It. *mediana*) area, which embraces northern Lazio, northern-central Umbria, central Marche, and western Abruzzo.

The **Tuscan** dialectal area stands out from all other dialectal areas for the absence of metaphony, a phenomenon to be addressed shortly in the context of middle and southern dialects. Some distinctive features of Tuscan dialects which are absent in standard Italian are illustrated in (19).

(19) a. **Monophthongization** of [wɔ] in open syllable: [ˈbɔno] 'good.M.SG' [ˈnɔvo] 'new.M.SG' vs. Italian [ˈbwɔno], [ˈnwɔvo].

   b. **Weakening (spirantization)** of intervocalic stops (or Tuscan *gorgia*):

       i. /p, t, k/ realized as [ɸ, θ, h/x]: [ˈtɔɸo] 'mouse,' [ˈpɛθalo] 'petal,' [aˈmiho]/ [aˈmixo] 'friend' vs. Italian [ˈtɔpo], [ˈpɛtalo], [aˈmiko]; in the case of /k/, we can have loss: [aˈmio].

       ii. /b, d, g/ realized as [β, ð, ɣ]: [ˈliβero] 'free,' [ˈlɔðe] 'praise,' [ˈlaɣo] 'lake' vs. Italian [ˈlibero] 'free,' [ˈlɔde] 'praise,' [ˈlago].[19]

   c. **Palatal affricates** [tʃ, dʒ] realized as fricatives [ʃ, ʒ]: [ˈbaʃo] 'kiss,' [ˈfraʒile] 'fragile' vs. Italian [ˈbatʃo], [ˈfradʒile].

   d. **Obligatory expression of subjects** accompanied by clitic subject pronouns (as in northern dialects): *te tu parli* 'you speak,' where *te* and *tu* are, respectively, the stressed and clitic form of subject pronoun, vs. Italian *parli*.

   e. The construction *noi* **'we' + impersonal verb form with *si*: *noi si va* 'we go' vs. *andiamo*.

   f. Active use of the **demonstrative** *codesto* 'that (near the addressee),' lost in Italian.

The **middle** dialectal area is a fairly complex one. Its precise outline remains debated as it is characterized by numerous isoglosses which link it to the upper southern area (which is addressed next), to the extent that they can be considered as broadly matching (e.g., Vignuzzi, 1997, p. 314); in fact, these two areas are grouped together in some analyses (e.g., Loporcaro, 2013). A highly distinctive feature is retention of the original unstressed word-final [o] (< Lat. ŏ) and [u] (< Lat. ŭ) as opposed to reduction to [ə] (Marchigiano [ˈsatʃ:o] < Lat. SAPĬŎ 'I know,' [kaˈpillu] < Lat. CAPILLŬ(M) 'hair' vs. Abruzzese [ˈsatʃ:ə], [kaˈpillə]).

The **southern** area is subdivided into two areas as well: the **upper** southern area (central-southern Lazio, southern Umbria, southern Marche, Abruzzo (western area excluded), Molise, Puglia (Salento excluded), Campania, Basilicata, northern Calabria) and the **extreme** southern area (Salento, southern Calabria, and Sicily). Among the most prominent distinctive features of the upper southern area, which distinguish the middle dialectal area as well, are presented in (20).

(20) a. **Progressive assimilation** of the clusters.

       i. [nd]: Marchigiano [ˈmunnu] 'world' vs. Italian [ˈmondo].

       ii. [mb]: Marchigiano, Neapolitan [ˈgamma] 'leg' vs. Italian [ˈgamba].

       iii. [ld] (in some areas): Marchigiano [ˈkallo], Abruzzese [ˈkallə] 'warm' vs. Italian [ˈkaldo].

   b. **Voicing** of [p, t] before nasal: Abruzzese [ˈtandə] 'much,' [ˈkambə] 'field' vs. Italian [ˈtanto], [ˈkampo]).

   c. **Dental fricative** [s] realized as affricate [ts] after [n, r, l]: Abruzzese [ˈpentsə] 'I think,' [ˈbortsə] 'bag' vs. Italian [ˈpenso], [ˈborsa].

   d. **Post-nominal possessive adjective**: Abruzzese [lu ˈkanə ˈme] 'my dog' vs. Italian /il ˈmio ˈkane/; with singular nouns denoting family members, the unstressed (enclitic) form of the possessive is used: Abruzzese ['fratətə], Umbrian ['frate**tu**] 'your brother' vs. Italian /'tuo fra'tɛllo/.

Features typical of the southern area include:

(21) a. **Weakening of word-final (or all unstressed) vowels** to [ə], as seen in the Abruzzese examples in (20), or even loss: Neapolitan ['kworp] 'body,' ['vjend] 'wind' vs. Italian ['kɔrpo], ['vɛnto]. Note, however, that word-final [a] may escape reduction (Neapolitan ['gamma] 'leg' ['fatʃ:a] 'face').

   b. **Realization of [b] as [v]** (spirantization): Abruzzese ['vokkə] 'mouth,' ['varvə] 'beard' vs. Italian ['bokka], ['barba].

   c. **Palatalization of Latin** PL-, BL-: PLANGĔRE > Abruzzese ['caɲə] 'to weep' vs. Italian ['pjandʒere], ★BLASTEMARE > Abruzzese [ʝaʃte'ma] 'to curse' vs. Italian [bestem'mjare].

   d. **Prepositional accusative**, that is, marking of the direct object with the preposition *a* (also typical of extreme southern dialects): Abruzzese /so 'viʃtə **a** 'fratətə/ 'I have seen your brother' vs. Italian /'ɔ visto tuo fra'tɛllo/.

   e. **Transitive use of intransitive verbs** as *salire* 'go up,' *scendere* 'go down,' *entrare* 'enter,' *uscire* 'exit': **salire** la spesa 'bring up the groceries' (vs. *portare su*), **uscire** la spazzatura 'take out the garbage' (vs. *portare fuori*).

   f. **Reduplication** of:

      i. **Adjectives** to obtain the superlative form: Calabrese [sku'rusu sku'rusu] 'very dark' (lit. 'dark dark').

      ii. **Nouns** to form adverbs: Calabrese ['jiri ' mura ' mura] 'skirt along the walls' (lit. 'go wall wall').'

   g. *Allocuzione inversa* 'inverse allocution,' which is the use of family terms denoting the speaker with endearing, expressive function rather than referential one: *fai un boccone,* **mamma**← 'take a bite, **come on/please** (lit. Mom),' uttered by a mother to solicit a child who doesn't want to eat.

Finally, we note **metaphony**, an instance of distant regressive assimilation which, as we recall, is found extensively across Italian dialects but absent in Tuscan ones (therefore, in standard Italian). Most typically, metaphony involves raising of the front and back mid vowels triggered by a following high vowel (22a). The trigger may also change into [ə] (22b) or be lost (22c), and in these cases, metaphony is the sole marker of number or gender. Finally, metaphony can involve diphthongization of the targeted vowel (22d).

(22) a. Umbrian ['pɛde] 'foot' ~ ['pedi] 'feet.'
   b. Abruzzese ['pedə] 'foot' ~ ['pidə] 'feet'; ['sortʃə] 'mouse' ~ ['surtʃə] 'mice'; Basilicatese ['sikkə] 'dry.M.SG' ~ ['sekkə] 'dry.F.PL.'
   c. Lombard ['kʷest] 'this.M' ~ ['kʷist] 'these.M.'
   d. Piedmontese [bu'ton] 'button' ~ [bu'tojn] 'buttons'; Abruzzese ['mɔrtə] 'dead.F/PL' ~ ['mwɔrt] 'dead.M.SG/PL'; Neapolitan [peʃ] 'fish' ~ [piʃ] 'fishes.'

Cross-dialectally, the most frequent pattern is that all mid vowels except [a] are subject to metaphony, but there are several areas (e.g., Ischia, Adriatic Abruzzo, central Romagna,

Piedmont) where [a] is subject to metaphony as well (Abruzzese [ˈfratə] 'brother' ~ [ˈfrɛtə] 'brothers; [ˈgallə] 'rooster' ~ [ˈgillə] 'roosters').

The **extreme southern** dialects cover Salento (Puglia), central-southern Calabria, and Sicily. They stand out for a vocalic system comprising five stressed vowels ([a, ɛ, i, ɔ, u]) and three unstressed ones ([a, i, u]) and for retaining word-final vowels. Other notable distinctive features are given in (23):

(23) a. **Retroflex** consonants: Sicilian [ˈbɛɖɖu] 'beautiful,' [ˈpaʈɽi] 'father' vs. Italian [ˈbɛllo], [ˈpadre].

   b. Use of **synthetic past** (*passato remoto*, literally 'remote past') rather than periphrastic past (*passato prossimo*, literally 'near past'): [ˈvinni ˈɔra] 'I arrived now/I've just arrived' vs. *sono arrivato ora*.

   c. **Finite clauses** (*ku/mu, mi, ma* + finite verb form) instead of infinitival clauses: Calabrese [vɔju **mu mantʃu**] 'I want to eat (lit. that I eat)' vs. Italian *voglio* **mangiare**.

The **Sardinian** area includes five varieties: Logudorese, Nuorese, Sassarese, Campidanese, and Gallurese; the first two stand out for their noticeably conservative features, while the last one is the more innovative. Their most distinctive features are presented in (24).

(24) a. **Five-vowel** (penta-vocalic) system, like the extreme southern dialects: [a, ɛ, i, ɔ, u].

   b. **Retention of velar stops** [k, g] before front vowel in Logudorese, Nuorese, and Sassarese: [ˈkɛna] 'dinner' (< Lat. CENA(M)), [giˈrare] 'to turn' (< Late Lat. GYRARE) vs. [ˈtʃena], [dʒiˈrare].

   c. **Retention of consonant + [l] clusters**, with [l] > [r]: [ˈprɛnu] 'full' (< Latin PLENU(M)), [ˈframma] 'flame' (< Latin FLAMMA(M)) vs. [ˈpjɛno], [ˈfjamma].

   d. **Retroflex realization of [ll]**: [ˈnuɖɖa] 'nothing,' [ˈpɛɖɖɛ] 'skin' vs. [ˈnulla], [ˈpɛlle].

   e. **Weakening** of intervocalic consonants: [ˈaβɛ] 'bee,' [ˈnuðu] 'naked,' [ˈpaɣu] 'little, ADV,' [ˈnuɛ] 'cloud' vs. [ˈape] [ˈnudo], [ˈpɔko], [ˈnube].

   f. **Realization of labiovelar [kʷ, gʷ] as bilabial**: [ˈbattɔru] 'four,' [ˈlimba] 'tongue' vs. [ˈliŋgʷa], [ˈkʷattro].

   g. **Plural in <-s>**: [ˈmurɔs] 'walls' vs. It. [ˈmuri].

   h. **Definite articles from** IPSU(M) 'self' rather than from ILLU(M) 'that': [su] 'the.M.SG,' [sa] 'the.F.SG.'

   i. **Prepositional accusative**: [ˈviðo a ˈissɔs] 'I see them.'

   j. **Periphrastic future and conditional** formed by the present of [ˈaɛrɛ] 'have' + *a* 'to' + infinitive: Log. [ˈat a ˈproɛrɛ ˈkraza] 'it will rain tomorrow.'

   k. **Interrogative constructions with auxiliary inversion**: [mani ˈɣaðu ˈaza] 'have you eaten?' (lit. 'eaten have.2SG').

In assessing the status and vitality of the Italian dialects vis-à-vis standard Italian, especially from a diachronic perspective, two notions bear particular relevance: bilingualism and diglossia. **Bilingualism** denotes competency in two different linguistic systems of equal prestige, for example, two national languages (e.g., Italian and German in the Alto-Adige region), or a literary/prestigious language and a 'natural' language (e.g., Latin and the Florentine vernacular in Dante Alighieri). **Diglossia**, on the other hand, refers to the use of different linguistic systems of unequal prestige depending on communicative situation, register, style; for instance, use of the dialect in informal (spoken) communicative settings (i.e., with family and friends) and the use of Italian in formal (written and oral) ones. As we recall, when Italy became a united country (the Kingdom of Italy) in 1861, only an extremely low number of Italians were proficient in the 'standard language,' that is, the Italian taught in schools and used for all official communication, which was still under development. Since the rate of literacy was extremely low, the greatest majority of the population was monolingual in a dialect, which indicates that Italy's linguistic landscape was characterized by '**diglossia without bilingualism**.' Important changes to this scenario will start in the mid-twentieth century, leading to a situation of '**diglossia with bilingualism**.' As already noted, a considerable increase of literacy, vast migration from rural to main urban areas, and the growth of the media (particularly television) were some of the most influential factors which contributed to changing Italy's linguistic setup since it became a republic in 1946. All these factors fostered and facilitated the acquisition and everyday use of Italian in contexts previously dominated by dialects. To this we must add that the use of dialects (as well as minority languages and loanwords) was fiercely opposed and persecuted during the Fascist regime, whose language policy, in fully consistency with its radical autarchic position, aimed to control the entire linguistic repertoire by promoting the diffusion of a standard unitary variety. Moreover, a deep pro-Florentine, anti-dialect attitude persisted in the education system, and the dialects would not gain attention and appreciation until the late 1970s. Consequently, by the 1970s, the active use of Italian or of both Italian and dialect had risen considerably, whereas the use of dialect only gradually declined, dropping considerably by the end of the twentieth century.

As seen in Table 1.1, which reports the results of surveys conducted by *Istituto nazionale di statistica* ('National Institute of Statistics,' ISTAT) among Italians aged between 18 and 74, during the first decade of the new millennium, the percentage of Italians who use exclusively their dialect remains low and continues to drop.[20]

Furthermore, the use of dialect appears to be most prominent with family and friends (i.e., it is restricted to informal contexts), albeit with different dynamics across the different regions. On the whole, southern Italy shows the highest rates of use of dialect combined with Italian, the northeast registers the highest rates of exclusive use of dialect, while the lowest rates are recorded for the northwest. Also, the large urban areas show the lowest rates of use of dialect with strangers, and older speakers display a more active use of dialect more than younger ones. These two last trends are not surprising: metropolitan areas tend to be more cosmopolitan, consequently offering less chances to speak in dialect, and younger speakers are less likely to be fully proficient in their dialect.

TABLE 1.1 Use of Italian and dialect across communicative contexts

Year	Only/predominantly dialect			Only/predominantly Italian			Both Italian and dialect		
	Family	Friends	Strangers	Family	Friends	Strangers	Family	Friends	Strangers
2000	18.8	15.6	5.9	43.3	47.3	73.6	34.0	33.8	18.7
2006	15.0	12.1	4.5	44.8	48.2	73.9	34.0	34.3	19.0
2012	9.0	9.0	1.8	53.1	56.4	84.8	32.2	30.1	10.7

Source: Adapted from Palermo, 2020, p. 260.

Summarizing, the mixed use of Italian and dialect has overall been rising; Italian has been entering contexts previously restricted to the dialects, first and foremost the spoken domain, and the dialects have been conquering contexts formerly dominated by Italian. The linguistic setup of present-day Italy, then, appears to have undergone a reversal: from the original situation of 'diglossia without bilingualism' to a scenario of **'bilingualism without diglossia,'** which involves a fairly widespread proficiency in the dialects but no more distinctions as to usage contexts. In other words, in present-day Italy, Italian and dialect have come to overlap as equally functional (and equally prestigious) linguistic codes in a wider range of communicative contexts, with Italian becoming progressively confined to the (formal) written domain. Moreover, the increased mixed use of Italian and dialect, together with the decreasing rate of native dialect proficiency and radical changes to Italy's economy (primarily a major shift from agriculture to industry, commerce, and service), has led to a general process of Italianization of the dialects with consequent strengthening of the regional varieties.

This process of Italianization has affected the dialects at all levels of grammar, though its impact is most visible in the lexicon; dialectal words have been replaced by Italianized counterparts (Lombard [er'bjun] 'peas' and [pi'zej] from Italian [pi'sɛlli]), and many neologisms directly borrowed by Italian (Italian ['sito] 'internet site' has given, for example, ['situ], ['sitə], [sit]) have been adopted. Conversely, morphology and syntax, which are considered at the core of a dialect's identity, appear to be the levels of grammar most resistant to the impact of Italian. In any case, despite the many predictions of the impending death of the dialects, there is consensus that this is an improbable picture: currently, the dialect is 'alive and kicking' as a linguistic system for certain uses, and it is very likely that the present situation of coexistence of Italian and dialect will persist (Berruto, 1987, pp. 121–122).

To conclude, it should be pointed out that from about the last two decades of the twentieth century, a notable tendency to promote the revival of the dialects has emerged, spurred by new/changed dynamics, among which is a general restructuring of the Italian people's linguistic system and changes in speakers' attitudes toward native language (i.e., the dialects are no longer associated to lower education and/or social status and linguistic incompetence). As De Mauro points out:

> The relationship between Italian and its dialects is increasingly experienced as less conflictual. The cause and effect of this development are linked to the growing change in attitude among the cultured, or at least more educated, classes. The witch hunt against dialects that plagued classrooms in post-unity education has gradually subsided, and the reality of dialects has been regarded with more sympathetic attention at various levels of the intellectual scene.
>
> *(De Mauro, 2014, pp. 128–129)*

This has resulted in a fresh surge of the use of dialect by choice in a variety of media (e.g., literature, films, songs, advertising, social networks, and the internet in general) and with a diverse array of functions (e.g., expressive, ludic, transgressive).[21]

1.3.2 Regional varieties

Italiano regionale 'regional Italian' is a complex notion. Briefly put, it can be defined as the set of geographic varieties of the Italian language (Poggi Salani, 2010, p. 726), with each variety differing from both standard Italian and each other. It is important to note that 'regional' is not to be equated to the 20 administrative regions of Italy; rather, comparably to what was remarked about the dialects, it refers to a geographical area whose extension is highly variable.[22] *Italiano regionale*, then, embodies countless local varieties, which is why it is more appropriate to use the plural *italiani regionali* 'regional Italians.' Together with the dialects, *italiani regionali* form a continuum within which four main levels can be (loosely) identified: local dialect, regional dialect (or *koinè*), regional Italian, neo-standard Italian. As noted in the previous section, since about the mid-twentieth century, this continuum has been undergoing a process of gradual merging with (neo-)standard Italian. *Italiani regionali*, then, 'represent, in essence the "new dialects" of Italian, and are the product of what has been called the "**second dialectalization**" of Italy's linguistic system' (Telmon, 2016, p. 302), where 'second' dialectalization denotes the whole of different ways and circumstances in which dialect monolingual Italians acquired standard Italian after Italy's unification in 1861, as opposed to the '**first dialectalization**,' which refers to the development of the Italo-Romance vernaculars from Latin between the seventh and the tenth century (Telmon, 2016, p. 302).

Compared to the dialects, *italiani regionali* are characterized by a fairly high degree of homogeneity, hence a considerably higher degree of mutual intelligibility. But of course, they do display specific distinctive features which pertain to all levels of the language. Since they are essentially spoken varieties, however, they differ from each other primarily with respect to pronunciation, first and foremost intonation, followed by the lexicon (including idiomatic expressions). Conversely, morphology and syntax tend to remain unaffected or minimally affected by dialect interference.

The lack of linguistic atlases for regional varieties makes any areal classification loosely defined. Given the strong tendency for geographical variation to level out, three main areas are typically identified (though some linguists propose five, for example, Telmon, 2016). The phonological, morphological, and syntactic distinguishing features of these main areas are essentially the same ones used to identify the main dialectal areas in the preceding section. Therefore, we will focus on the lexicon and review first dialectal terms denoting distinctly local entities and idiomatic expressions which are no longer perceived as regional (i.e., **regionalisms** that have officially entered standard Italian), then geo-synonyms and geo-homonyms.

Many terms denoting distinctly local entities, as well as high-frequency idiomatic expressions (and proverbs), are no longer perceived as regionalisms. A few examples are listed in (25), grouped by semantic domains, and in (26), grouped by region.

(25) a. **Gastronomy**. *Bagna cauda* 'hot dish made of garlic and anchovies (lit. hot dip),' *barolo* 'Barolo wine,' *fontina* (Piedmont); *grappa, grissino* 'bread stick,' *panettone* (Lombardy), *cotechino, tagliatelle, tortellini, zampone* (Emilia-Romagna); *caciotta* (Abruzzo); *mozzarella, pizza, vongole* (Campania); *cassata* (Sicily).

   b. **Bureaucracy and military**. *Cicchetto* 'liquor shot,' *funzionario* 'officer' (< French *fonctionnaire*), *pelandrone* 'idler' (Piedmont); *scartoffia* 'paper (pejor.),' *secondino* 'prison guard' (Lombardy); *naia* 'draft,' *scontrino* 'receipt' (Veneto).

   c. **Nature and places**. *Arsenale* 'dockyard' (Venetian), *brughiera* 'moor; heath' (Lombardy); *darsena* 'dock' (Pisano), *lavagna* 'slate (mineral)' (Liguria), *slavina* 'snowslide' (Veneto).

> d. **Arts and trades**. *Gondola* 'gondola' (Venetian), *mezzadria* 'sharecropping' (Emilia-Romagna); *cinematografaro* 'somebody who works in cinema (pejorative)' (Rome), *sommozzatore* 'deep-see diver' (Neapolitan).
>
> e. **Illegality**. *Camorra* (Neapolitan); *mafia, omertà* 'conspiracy of silence,' *pizzo* 'protection money' (Sicily).

(26) a. Piedmont: *Battere la fiacca* 'to shirk.'

> b. Lombardy: *Essere una mezza calzetta* 'to be a nobody,' *far ridere i polli* 'to be utterly ridiculous,' *fare un quarantotto* 'to raise hell.'
>
> c. Veneto: *Nascere con la camicia* 'to be born with a silver spoon in the mouth' (literally, 'to be born with the shirt').
>
> d. Tuscany: *Andare in visibilio* 'to go into raptures over something,' *mandare a quel paese* 'to tell somebody to get lost.'
>
> e. Rome: *Lasciar perdere* 'to let something/someone go' (*lascia perdere* 'let it go'), *sputare l'osso* 'to cut it out' (literally, 'to spit the bone').
>
> f. Southern: *Cose da pazzi!* 'unbelievable!'

Geo-synonyms are words with the same meaning but restricted to specific geographical areas (i.e., synonyms in complementary geographical distribution). A few well-known examples are given in (27).

(27) a. 'Muscles' (seafood): *Cozze* (central, southern), *mitili* (Tuscany, central), *muscoli* (Liguria), *peoci* (Veneto).

> b. 'Watermelon': *Anguria* (northern), *cocomero* (Tuscany), *cetrone* (Abruzzo), *mel(l)one* (Sicily, south), *popone* (Tuscany).
>
> c. 'Green beans': *Cornetti* (Lombardy), *fagiolini* (Tuscany), *tegoline* (Veneto).
>
> d. 'Apron': *Bigarolo* (Lombardy), *grembiule* (Tuscany), *mantesina/o* (southern), *parannanza* and *sinale/zinale* (central), *traversa* (Veneto).
>
> e. 'Coat hanger': *Appendino* (Piedmont), *gruccia* (Tuscany), *ometto* (Lombardy).
>
> f. 'Boy; young man': *Bocia* (Veneto), *caruso* (Sicily), *fio* (Veneto), *guaglione* (Campania, Abruzzo), *mulo* (Veneto), *picciotto* (Sicily, Calabria), *pischello* (Lazio), *toso* (Lombardy, Veneto).

Geo-synonyms, too, may eventually lose their regional connotation and become established in the standard; some examples are *cozze, cocomero, fagiolini, grembiule*.

The first study on Italian geo-synonyms is by Rüegg (1956), who reports the results of a survey involving 124 Italians from 54 different provinces who were asked to provide the term/phrase for 242 common notions. Only one of these resulted to be the same for all participants, *caffè forte* 'strong coffee,' designated as *espresso*. Among the most famous (and most cited) example of the geo-homonyms reported by Rüegg is the phrase meaning 'to play hooky.'

(28) a. *Bruciare la scuola* – Four provinces: Padua and Venice (Veneto), Brescia (Lombardy), and Ravenna (Emilia-Romagna).

> b. *Bigiare* – Five provinces between Bergamo and Pavia (Lombardy).
>
> c. *Bucare* – Three provinces: Turin (Piedmont), Lucca, and Pisa (Tuscany).
>
> d. *Marinare la scuola* – 36 provinces across the entire country.

e. *Far campagnola* – Province of Messina (Sicily).
f. *Far filone* – Nine provinces between L'Aquila (Abruzzo) and Cosenza (Calabria).
g. *Far forca* – Pour provinces, primarily the province of Florence.
h. *Far schissa* – Province of Turin (Piedmont).
i. *Far Sicilia* – Provinces of Messina and Palermo (Sicily).
j. *Segare/Far sega* – Four provinces, primarily the Rome province.
k. *Salare la scuola* – 17 provinces across the country.

(Rüegg, 1956, p. 104; adapted from Telmon, 2016, p. 319)

Geo-homonyms, on the other hand, are words identical (or very similar) in form which bear different meanings in different geographical areas. A few examples are listed in (29).

(29) a. *Cocomero*: 'watermelon' (Tuscan, Italian), 'cucumber' (Sicily, south).
b. *Fregno*: 'shrewd' (Abruzzo), 'silly' (Rome) (Grassi et al., 2003, p. 156).
c. *Quartino*: 'one quarter of a liter (of wine)' (Italian), '(small) apartment' (center, south).
d. *Tovaglia*: 'tablecloth' (Italian), 'towel' (center, south).

Like dialects, *italiani regionali* used to be attributed different degrees of prestige, and typically, the northern ones were considered more prestigious than the southern ones due to the socio-cultural and economic inequality that has always divided the privileged wealthier north from the disadvantaged poorer south. In general, this attitude has now disappeared, or at least has worn off drastically, but it explains a still-lingering tendency (particularly among poorly educated speakers from the south) to lexical hypercorrection so that northern regionalisms are mistaken for standard Italian words, especially if the standard word was originally a regionalism itself (e.g., *anguria*, *ometto*, or *salvietta* instead of *tovagliolo* 'napkin' or *fazzoletto* 'handkerchief').

1.3.3 The Italian of immigrants

We will close this chapter with some notes on the fortune of the Italian language in English-speaking countries to which Italians have immigrated. This is a highly actual topic, certainly worthy of further and more up-to-date research, particularly in light of the changed dynamics and configuration of migration waves, immigration policies, and also conventional attitudes on language. Although this topic falls beyond the scope of this textbook, it is briefly addressed to draw attention to some key issues related to the linguistic practices of Italian immigrants in English-speaking countries. In consideration of space, the discussion is limited to Italian in the US and focuses only on two (interrelated) points: (a) the linguistic background of Italian immigrants and the nature of the interaction between native Italian and English – and how this has changed through time – and (b) the emergence and growth in more recent times of movements promoting the maintenance and revitalization the Italian language.[23]

Starting from the late 1800s, the United States has become one of the most sought-after countries among Italian immigrants, who have had a significant impact on their new land both at the (socio-)cultural and economic level. Research shows that compared to other major European immigrant groups, Italians assimilated into English much faster and made less attempts at maintaining their native language, which led to a steady decline in the number of US speakers of Italian. Recently, however, the decline of the Italian language in the United

States has been countered by a growing interest in the Italian language and culture due primarily to the significantly different dynamics of Italian immigration, changed views on Italy's public image, and also the more intense contact between the United States and Italy spurred by globalization.

The Italians who immigrated to the United States between the late nineteenth and early/mid-twentieth century came predominantly from southern Italy. As already noted, they were native speakers of local dialects, rather than the newly born standard Italian. These dialects varied broadly in terms of degree of mutual intelligibility; furthermore, the dialects held very low status because they were considered (under a grossly erroneous view, as we recall from the previous sections) 'corrupted,' 'degraded' versions of standard Italian. In order to communicate effectively with one another, dialect-speaking Italian immigrants (as immigrant groups in general) developed a hybrid form of speech combining English with their dialects. Conversely, the linguistic background of later Italian immigrants (i.e., starting from the mid-/late twentieth century), albeit to varying extents, did include standard Italian. Thus, the linguistic backgrounds (and practices) of these two main immigrant groups differ in a very important way: while first-wave immigrants were monolingual in their local dialect, second-wave immigrants were bilingual in their local dialect and standard Italian. Italian immigrants, then, brought with them Italy's complex linguistic history, which would influence their own linguistic practices as well as those of the following generations.

Linguistic background and practices are tightly interconnected with (if not shaped by) socio-economical status and degree of education. First-wave Italian immigrants came from the lowest working class and were basically illiterate. As common among immigrant communities of this kind, most immigrants (especially women) would learn just English to manage due to a number of interrelated factors, including isolation and tight cohesion within the immigrant community, lack of support of and resources to language education, and dire working conditions (as well as racial discrimination), which were not conducive to learning English. In contrast, Italian immigrants of the second wave – commonly referred to as *la fuga dei cervelli* 'brain drain,' lit. 'the flight of the minds' – come from upper-middle classes, hold university degrees, work in highly prestigious fields, and do not tend to remain confined within the Italian/Italo-American community. Consequently, their linguistic assimilation to the new country proceeds much faster and more easily, also because many of them come to the United States with some knowledge of English and their working environments provide both the means and the motivation to foster proficiency in English. The presence of Italian women in greater proportions than in the past facilitates language maintenance, given the historical role of migrant mothers in perpetuating the cultures of origin. Even dialect usage has been reclaimed by some Italian Americans whose parents arrived in the later twentieth century, just as Italy has begun to place new value on its dialects that are now fast disappearing.

As for the interaction between native Italian and English and how it has changed in time (i.e., native language transmission and retention), parents of both first- and second-wave Italian immigrant groups typically spoke in their native language (i.e., local dialect or standard Italian) to their children, who, in contrast, tended to use more English not only with their siblings and peers but also with their parents. Hence, second-generation Italians were bilingual, at least to some extent, while their parents were monolingual. However, second-generation Italians raised their children speaking in English, which produced the first generation of English monolingual Italians. Obviously, third-generation English monolingual Italians remain exposed to Italian through interaction with older relatives, friends and acquaintances, and the Italian community in general, but typically they do not develop any significant active competence in Italian. Rather, their Italian proficiency seems to remain restricted to a bunch of high-frequency 'familiar' expressions and idioms. Summing up, among Italian immigrant communities in the United States, language shift from native Italian to English occurred within three generations (e.g., Carnevale, 2009; De Fina & Fellin, 2010; Fellin, 2007; Haller, 1987).

Language attitudes significantly bear upon language maintenance (and, of course, language status). Despite the (comparatively) large number of Italian speakers and the fact that

> Italian ranked ninth among the second languages spoken in the United States in 2010, it is also the language that since 1980 has shown the greatest drop (55 %) among second languages spoken at home, with a precipitous decline registered in the most recent period which shows Italian at home declining at a faster rate than any other language.
>
> *(Carnevale, 2017, pp. 247–248)*

Among the major factors which contributed to the falloff of the Italian language are the overall inactive attitude of the Italian government as well as educational agencies and the Catholic Church in promoting the study of Italian abroad and providing actual means and venues to accomplish it. In fact, none of these organs pursued specific policies in this respect until quite recently. To these factors, we should also add the role played by the more complex linguistic background of Italian immigrants, more specifically the import of diglossia between the 'high-prestige' standard and the 'low-prestige.' Given that dialects were attributed low, inferior status and practically had no actual value outside the immigrant community, it is not surprising that they were not passed on to the next generation. The similar fate of standard Italian can be accounted for by the need to integrate quickly to the new country, at times also spurred by racial discrimination. In fact, until the twentieth century, Italian immigrants, particularly those from southern Italy, were subject to considerable ethnic discrimination by White Americans, which fueled fast assimilation to the American community, leading to the disregard for their ethnic traditions, including language (Carnevale, 2000, 2003). Recent changes in the perception of Italy and Italian Americans have dispelled ethnic discrimination; being Italian American and speaking Italian have become reasons of pride, fueling a rising movement toward the revitalization and maintenance of the Italian language which hopefully will keep growing.

1.4 Exercises

1. Answer the following questions, providing illustrative examples to support your claims.

    a. What are the most crucial phases of the historical development of standard Italian?

    b. Who were the *Tre Corone*? What is their relevance for the development of the Italian language?

    c. What are the main aspects of Pietro Bembo's model for a common, unitary language? What are alternative proposals put forward in the sixteenth century?

    d. What are the key points of Alessandro Manzoni's views on the linguistic unification of Italy? What strategies did he propose to achieve it? How do his views differ from those of Graziadio Isaia Ascoli?

e.   What is a language 'variety'?

f.   What are the main differences between standard, neo–standard, and sub–standard Italian?

g.   Discuss the differences between language, dialect, and regional variety. What are the main parameters used to identify them?

h.   Identify the main dialectal areas of Italy, providing their distinctive features.

i.   What is the status of dialects in contemporary Italy? What are their main uses?

j.   What are your thoughts about the circumstances of the Italian language in Italian immigrant communities in the United States as well as on the issue of immigrants' native language? Do you have any personal experience with this issue?

2.   Complete with the appropriate option. Justify your choices.

1.   The rise of the Florentine vernacular in the fourteenth century was due to

   a.   the wide success of Dante's, Petrarca's, and Boccaccio's literary works among common people.

   b.   Florence's outstanding economic, political, and cultural influence.

   c.   the fact that in his *De vulgari eloquentia*, Dante identifies it as the most distinguished among contemporary vernaculars.

   d.   its close similarity to Classic Latin.

2.   The most important factors that furthered the unification and diffusion of Italian after Italy's political unification include

   a.   immigration.

   b.   the creation of a unified administrative and bureaucratic system.

   c.   urbanization and industrialization.

   d.   the linguistic politics of the Fascist regime.

3.   Neo–standard Italian is

   a.   a synonym for *italiano popolare*.

   b.   a synonym for *italiano regionale*.

   c.   the variety of Italian spoken by the younger generation.

   d.   the variety of Italian regularly used by the majority of Italian speakers in most communicative situations.

4.   An *isogloss* is

   a.   a distinctive feature of a single dialect.

   b.   a morphological feature common to a dialectal area.

   c.   a line plotted on a map delimiting a geographical area characterized by a given linguistic feature.

   d.   a dialectal area.

5.   A dialect differs from a language because it

   a.   is only spoken, never written.

   b.   is restricted in terms of distribution and contexts of usage.

   c.   has a different phonological structure.

   d.   has an imperfect, rudimentary grammar.

6. *Italiano regionale* is a

    a.   variety of Italian spoken in one of the administrative regions.
    b.   variety of Italian spoken in a specific geographical area.
    c.   language variety spoken by a linguistic minority.
    d.   synonym for 'Italian dialect.'

3. True/false. Justify your choices.

    a.   Pietro Bembo proposed the language of Dante's *Commedia* as model for the language of poetry.
    b.   Petrarca's lyric language is distinguished by a highly composite multilingualism use of a full range of registers and styles, from the most refined to the lowest or even scurrilous.
    c.   Manzoni's proposals failed because it was opposed by the government.
    d.   Standard Italian is the native language of the Italian people.
    e.   Diglossia denotes the use of different linguistic systems of unequal prestige, depending on communicative situation, register, style.
    f.   *Italiano popolare* is the language variety used by speakers in informal communicative settings (e.g., at home or with friends).
    g.   Dialectal areas can be identified by a single primary isogloss.
    h.   Metaphony is a distinctive feature of the Tuscan dialectal area.
    i.   Prepositional accusative is a shared feature of the southern dialects.
    j.   Retroflex consonants are a distinctive feature of the Gallo-Italian dialects.
    k.   Voicing or loss of intervocalic voiceless consonants is absent in central and southern dialects.
    l.   Pronunciation and vocabulary are the components of *italiano regionale* that are least affected by the dialects' influence.
    m.   *Cocomero* and *anguria* are geo-homonyms.

Notes

1 The adjective *Romance* refers to all the languages and dialects/varieties that originated from Latin. It derives from Old French *romanz*, which derives from the Latin expression *ROMANĬCE LOQUI* '(to speak) in the Roman way,' that is, to speak the vernacular spoken in Rome, as opposed to Latin (i.e., LATINE LOQUI). An alternative term to *Romance* is *neo-Latin*, which is in fact more common in the Italian and European tradition.

2 A rather-accurate description of the schooling system in fourteenth-century Florence is found in *Nuova Cronica* by the prominent Florentine merchant and historian Giovanni Villani (1280–1348).

3 To give just a couple of examples, the banks founded by the Peruzzi and Bardi families acquired great power all over Europe, and *fiorino* (the currency of Florence) became the strongest European currency; the court of Lorenzo de Medici (Lorenzo *il magnifico*) gathered and sponsored the most prominent artists in the history of Italian (world) arts.

4 The *Scuola siciliana* was a poetic and cultural movement that flourished at the Sicilian royal court of Frederick II, King of Sicily and Holy Roman Emperor, under Giacomo da Lentini (1210–1260), a senior poet and court notary and, possibly, the creator of the sonnet. It promoted a scholarly literary community whose members authored the first lyric works in vernacular, drawing from and expanding upon the tradition of Provençal love poetry. Their works – which focus on the theme of *amore cortese* 'courtly love,' an idealized, platonic form of love revolving around the figure of the virtuous noblewoman who could guide their male poet-lovers to God's divine love – stand out for their stylistic, metrical, and linguistic experimentation and originality. The tradition quickly

reached Tuscany, where it continued with the so-called *scuola toscana* 'Tuscan school,' leading to the emergence in the second half of the thirteenth century of the literary movement *Dolce stil novo* 'Sweet new style,' which continued to pursue the *amor cortese* themes.

5 Latin was part of the middle-school core curriculum until 1979 and remains part of the high school curriculum in a *licei*.

6 Estimates about the percentage of Italians who were able to speak Italian at that time range between 2.5% (De Mauro, 1976), 9.25% (Castellani, 1982), and 12% (Serianni, 1990).

7 In 1861, illiteracy rates ranged from a highest of 90% (Sardinia) to a lowest of 54% (Piedmont, Lombardy, and Liguria); in 1951, the highest rate was registered for Calabria (32%) and the lowest for Lombardy and Liguria (4%) (De Mauro, 1976, p. 95).

8 Dante's *Commedia* is taught in all high schools, and Manzoni's *I promessi sposi* in middle school.

9 Technically, 'language **user**' is more proper than 'language **speaker**' because it encompasses both written and spoken language (as well as sign languages). However, 'speaker' is used in this textbook since the focus is on the spoken dimension.

10 Since there are no standardized orthography systems for the dialects, the International Phonetic Alphabet (IPA) is used to transcribe them. The full IPA chart is available at www.internationalpho neticassociation.org/content/full-ipa-chart.

11 Recent general works on Italian sociolinguistics are D'Agostino (2012), one/two more, and also Tosi (2001). For specialized varieties in particular, see Gualdo and Telve (2011) and also the contributions in Trifone (2009) and the references therein. Linguistic minorities are addressed in Toso (2008), Orioles (2003), and Italian abroad in Giovanardi and Trifone (2012), Vedovelli (2002, 2011).

12 The first corpus of *italiano popolare* is Spitzer (1922/1976); another well-known corpus is Rovere (1977).

13 Cortelazzo (2001) includes the use of *gli* for plural and feminine referents among the accepted features of neo-standard Italian. The use of *gli* for *loro* is also acknowledged (though usually still presented as a form to be avoided in formal settings, both written and spoken) also in more recent grammars of Italian (e.g., Dardano & Trifone, 2002; Adorno, 2003).

14 Both examples were retrieved from the corpus DiaCORIS (https://corpora.ficlit.unibo.it/DiaCORIS/).

15 Following established conventions, Latin is given in small caps, and nouns and adjectives are given in the ACC SG form, with the final -M in parentheses to indicate that it was lost early (e.g., FLORE(M) 'flower'). Graphemes (i.e., letters or combination of letters that represent sounds in orthography) are enclosed in angled brackets <>, and sounds are transcribed with the IPA (e.g., <gn> [ɲ]). Note that, on the whole, a broad phonetic transcription is adopted, and vowel length is not marked in the Italian examples.

16 Isoglosses are plotted on linguistic maps, typically collected in linguistic atlases; presently, the only complete linguistic atlas available for Italian is Jalberg and Jud's (1928–1940) *Sprach- und Sachatlas Italiens und der Südschweiz/Atlante linguistico ed etnografico dell'Italia e della Svizzera meridionale (AIS)*.

17 Ladin, Friulian, and Romansh (Grisons and Engadin, Switzerland) are classified as Rhaeto-Romansh languages (e.g., Haiman & Benincà, 1992), while Sardinian is an eastern Romance language, like Italian and Romanian.

18 https://commons.wikimedia.org/w/index.php?search=italian+dialects&title=Special:MediaSearc h&go=Go&type=image&haslicense=unrestricted.

19 The gorgia is related to consonant position precisely, posteriority: it is most common with the velar stops /k/ and /g/, less common with the dental stops /t/ and /d/, and even less common with the bilabial stops /p/ and /b/. Also, it is rather regular with voiceless stops, but more variable with the voiced ones.

20 These surveys are based on self-assessment, so they should be taken with a grain of salt.

21 Some contemporary examples are Remo Rapino (Abruzzese), whose novel *Vita, morte e miracoli di Bonfiglio Liborio* (2019) won *Premio Campiello 2020*; the rapper Clementino (Neapolitan) and the ragga band Sud Sound System (Salentino); the movies *Suburra* (Stefano Sollima, 2013, Romanesco) and *Anime nere* (Francesco Munzi, 2014, Calabrese); the *Pepsi* ad in Romanesco *Pepsi, m'hai provocato e io me te bevo. Pepsi, volemose bene* 'Pepsi, you provoked me, and I'm going to drink you up. Pepsi, let's love each other' (www.cultora.it/riscoprire-dialetti-per-imparare-meglio-linglese/, Accessed December 2021).

22 Equating *italiano regionale* to an administrative region of Italy might possibly hold for Sicily and Sardinia (Sobrero, 2012, pp. 129–130).

23 The topic of 'immigrant language/s' is closely linked to the issue of identity, that is, how immigrants convey their ethnic identity through language practices, which appears to have received more scholarly attention (e.g., Carnevale, 2000; De Fina, 2014; De Fina & Fellin, 2010, among others).

Bibliography

Adorno, C. (2003). *La grammatica italiana*. Mondadori.

Antonelli, G. (2007). *L'italiano nella società della comunicazione*. Il Mulino.

Ascoli, G. (1873). Proemio. *Archivio Glottologico Italiano*, *1*, v–xli.

Avolio, F. (1994). I dialettismi dell'italiano. In L. Serianni & P. Trifone (Eds.), *Storia della lingua italiana. Vol. 3: Le altre lingue* (pp. 561–595). Einaudi.

Avolio, F. (2009). *Lingue e dialetti d'Italia*. Carocci.

Banfi, E., & Cordin, P. (Eds.). (1990). *Storia dell'italiano e forme dell'italianizzazione: Atti del XXIII congresso internazionale della società di linguistica Italiana*. Bulzoni.

Baricco, A. (1994). *Novecento: Un monologo*. Feltrinelli.

Berruto, G. (1987). *Sociolinguistica dell'italiano contemporaneo*. Carocci.

Berruto, G. (1993). Varietà diamesiche, diastratiche, diafasiche. In A. A. Sobrero (Ed.), *Introduzione all'italiano contemporaneo: Le strutture* (pp. 37–92). Laterza.

Berruto, G. (2002a). Parlare dialetto in Italia alle soglie del Duemila. In G. L. Beccaria & C. Marello (Eds.), *La parola al testo: Scritti per Bice Mortara Garavelli* (pp. 33–49). Edizioni dell'Orso.

Berruto, G. (2002b). Quale dialetto per l'Italia del Duemila? Aspetti dell'italianizzazione e risorgenze dialettali in Piemonte (e altrove). In A. A. Sobrero & A. Miglietta (Eds.), *Lingua e dialetto nell'Italia del Duemila* (pp. 101–127). Congedo.

Berruto, G. (2005). Gli italiani e la lingua. In L. F. Piparo & G. Ruffino (Eds.), *Gli italiani e la lingua* (pp. 332–342). Sellerio.

Bonomi, I. (1996). La narrativa e l'italiano dell'uso medio. *Studi di Grammatica Italiana*, *15*, 321–338.

Carnevale, N. C. (2000). Language, race, and the new immigrants: The example of Southern Italians in the U.S. In N. Foner, R. G. Rumbaut, & S. J. Gold (Eds.), *Immigration research for a new century: Multidisciplinary perspectives* (pp. 409–422). Russell Sage Publications.

Carnevale, N. C. (2003). "No Italian spoken for the duration of the war": Language, Italian American identity, and cultural pluralism in the world war II years. *Journal of American Ethnic History*, *22*(3), 3–33.

Carnevale, N. C. (2009). *A new language, a new world: Italian immigrants in the United States, 1890–1945*. University of Illinois Press.

Carnevale, N. C. (2017). The languages of Italian Americans. In W. J. Connell & S. G. Pugliese (Eds.), *The Routledge history of Italian Americans* (pp. 239–251). Taylor & Francis Group.

Casapullo, R. (1999). *Il medioevo*. Il Mulino.

Castellani, A. (1982). Quanti erano gl'italofoni nel 1861? *Studi Linguistici Italiani*, *8*, 3–26.

Correa-Zoli, Y. (1981). The language of Italian Americans. In C. A. Ferguson & S. Brice Heath (Eds.), *Language in the USA* (pp. 239–256). Cambridge University Press.

Cortelazzo, M. A. (1972). *Avviamento critico alla dialettologia italiana. III: Lineamenti di italiano popolare*. Pacini.

Cortelazzo, M. A. (2001). L'italiano e le sue varietà: Una situazione in movimento. *Lingua e Stile*, *36*(3), 417–430.

Cravens, T. D. (2014). *Italia linguistica* and the European charter for regional or minority languages. *Forum Italicum*, *48*(2), 202–218.

D'Achille, P. (2010). *L'italiano contemporaneo* (3rd ed.). Il Mulino.

D'Achille, P. (2010–2011). Italiano popolare. In R. Simone (Ed.), *Enciclopedia dell'italiano* (Vol. 1, pp. 723–726). Istituto della Enciclopedia Italiana.

D'Achille, P. (2016). Architettura dell'italiano di oggi e line di tendenza. In S. Lubello (Ed.), *Manuale di linguistica italiana* (pp. 165–189). De Gruyter.

D'Agostino, M. (2012). *Sociolinguistica dell'Italia contemporanea*. Il Mulino.

Dardano, M., & Frenguelli, G. (2008). *L'italiano di oggi*. Aracne.

Dardano, M., & Trifone, P. (2002). *Grammatica italiana modulare*. Zanichelli.

De Blasi, N. (2014). *Geografia e storia dell'italiano regionale*. Il Mulino.

De Fina, A. (2014). Language and identities in US communities of Italian origin. *Forum Italicum, 48*(2), 253–267.

De Fina, A., & Fellin, L. (2010). Italian in the US. In K. Potowski (Ed.), *Language diversity in the USA* (pp. 195–205). Cambridge University Press.

De Mauro, T. (1970). Per lo studio dell'italiano popolare unitario. In A. Rossi (Ed.), *Lettere da una tarantata* (pp. 43–75). De Donato.

De Mauro, T. (1976). *Storia linguistica dell'Italia Unita*. Laterza.

De Mauro, T. (2014). *Storia linguistica dell'Italia repubblicana dal 1946 ai nostri giorni*. Laterza.

Devoto, G., & Giacomelli, G. (1991). *I dialetti delle regioni d'Italia* (5th ed.). Sansoni.

Fanciullo, F. (2015). *Prima lezione di dialettologia*. Laterza.

Fellin, L. (2007). Lost tongues and reinvented repertoires: Ideologies of language and creative communicative practices among third generation Italian Americans. *Studi Italiani di Linguistica Teorica e Applicata, 36*(3), 443–462.

Francioni, G., & Romagnoli, S. (Eds.). (1998). *Il Caffè: 1764–1766* (2nd ed.). Bollati Boringhieri.

Giovanardi, C., & Trifone, P. (2012). *L'italiano nel mondo*. Carocci.

Grassi, C. (1993). Italiano e dialetti. In A. A. Sobrero (Ed.), *Introduzione all'italiano contemporaneo: La variazione e gli usi* (pp. 279–311). Laterza.

Grassi, C. (2002). Note sull'italiano regionale. In F. Fusco & C. Marcato (Eds.), *L'italiano e le regioni: Atti del convegno di studi (Udine, 15–16 giugno 2002)*. Universita Degli Studi Di Udine (Special Issue: *Plurilinguismo, 8*, 21–28).

Grassi, C., Sobrero, A. A., & Telmon, T. (2003). *Introduzione alla dialettologia italiana*. Laterza.

Gualdo, R., & Telve, S. (2011). *Linguaggi specialistici dell'italiano*. Carocci.

Haiman, J., & Benincà, P. (1992). *The Rhaeto-Romance languages*. Routledge.

Hall, R. A. Jr. (1960). Statistica grammaticale: L'uso di *gli* e *loro* come regime indiretto. *Lingua Nostra, 21*, 58–65.

Haller, H. W. (1981). Between standard Italian and creole: An interim report on language patterns in an Italian-American community. *Word, 32*(3), 181–191.

Haller, H. W. (1987). Italian speech varieties in the United States and the Italian American lingua franca. *Italica, 64*(3), 393–409.

Haller, H. W. (2014). Evolving linguistic identities among the Italian-American youth: Perceptions from linguistic autobiographies. *Forum Italicum, 48*(2), 245–249.

Katzner, K., & Miller, K. (2002). *The languages of the world* (3rd ed.). Routledge.

Krefeld, T. (2016). Profilo sociolinguistico. In S. Lubello (Ed.), *Manuale di linguistica italiana* (pp. 262–274). De Gruyter.

Ledgeway, A., & Lepschy, A. L. (Eds.). (2008). *Into Italy and out of Italy: Lingua e cultura nella migrazione italiana*. Guerra.

Lepschy, G. C. (2002). *Mother tongues and other reflections on the Italian language*. University of Toronto Press.

Loporcaro, M. (2013). *Profilo linguistico dei dialetti italiani* (2nd ed.). Laterza.

Loporcaro, M. (2016). L'Italia dialettale. In S. Lubello (Ed.), *Manuale di linguistica italiana* (pp. 275–300). De Gruyter.

Lucarelli, C. (1999). *Almost blue*. Einaudi.

Lucarelli, C. (2014). *Albergo italia*. Einaudi.

Maiden, M., & Parry, M. (Eds.). (1997). *The dialects of Italy*. Routledge.

Marazzini, C. (2002). *La lingua italiana: Profilo storico* (3rd ed.). Il Mulino.

Marazzini, C. (2004). *Breve storia della lingua italiana*. Il Mulino.

Marcato, C. (2007). *Dialetto, dialetti e italiano*. Il Mulino.

Marcato, C. (2011). *Guida allo studio dei dialetti*. CLEUP.

Marcato, C. (2014). Italiano e dialetto oggi. In S. Lubello (Ed.), *Lezioni d'italiano: Riflessioni sulla lingua del nuovo millennio* (pp. 37–61). Il Mulino.

Milione, V., & Gambino, C. (2009). *Sì, parliamo italiano: Globalization of the Italian culture in the United States*. Calandra Institute.

Orioles, V. (Ed.). (2003). *Le minoranze linguistiche: Profili sociolinguistici e quadro dei documenti di tutela*. Il Calamo.

Palermo, M. (2020). *Linguistica italiana* (2nd ed.). Il Mulino.

Pellegrini, G. B. (1977). *Carta dei dialetti d'Italia*. Pacini.

Poggi Salani, T. (2010). Italiano regionale. In R. Simone (Ed.), *Enciclopedia dell'italiano* (Vol. 1, pp. 726–729). Istituto della Enciclopedia italiana.

Renzi, L. (2012). *Come cambia la lingua: L'italiano in movimento*. Il Mulino.

Repetti, L. (2014). Where did all the dialects go? Aspects of the influence of Italian on dialects. *Forum Italicum, 48*(2), 219–226.

Rohlfs, G. (1990). *Studi e ricerche su lingua e dialetti d'Italia* (2nd ed.). Sansoni.

Rovere, G. (1977). *Testi di italiano popolare: Autobiografie di lavoratori e figli di lavoratori emigrati*. Centro Studi Emigrazione.

Rüegg, R. (1956). *Zur Wortgeographie der italienischen Umgangssprache*. Romanisches Seminar der Universität Köln.

Sabatini, F. (1985). L'italiano dell'uso medio: Una realtà tra le varietà linguistiche italiane. In G. Holtus & E. Radtke (Eds.), *Gesprochenes Italienisch in geschichte und gegenwart* (pp. 154–184). Narr.

Serianni, L. (1990). *Storia della lingua italiana: Il secondo ottocento*. Il Mulino.

Sobrero, A. A. (Ed.). (1993). *Introduzione all'italiano contemporaneo*. Laterza.

Sobrero, A. A. (1997). Italianization of the dialects. In M. Maiden & M. Parry (Eds.), *The dialects of Italy* (pp. 412–418). Routledge.

Sobrero, A. A. (2012). Italiano regionale: Fra tendenze unitarie, risorgive dialettali e derive postalfabetiche. In T. Telmon, G. Raimondi, & L. Revelli (Eds.), *Coesistenze linguistiche nell'Italia pre- e postunitaria* (pp. 129–145). Bulzoni.

Spitzer, L. (1976). *Lettere di prigionieri di Guerra italiani 1915–1918* (R. Solmi, Trans.). Boringhieri (Original work published 1922).

Telmon, T. (2016). Gli italiani regionali. In S. Lubello (Ed.), *Manuale di linguistica italiana* (pp. 301–327). De Gruyter.

Tesi, R. (2001). *Storia dell'italiano: La formazione della lingua comune dalle fasi iniziali al Rinascimento*. Zanichelli.

Tesi, R. (2005). *La lingua moderna e contemporanea*. Zanichelli.

Tesi, R. (2007). *La formazione della lingua italiana*. Zanichelli.

Tosi, A. (2001). *Language and society in a changing Italy*. Multilingual Matters.

Toso, F. (2008). *Le minoranze linguistiche in Italia*. Il Mulino.

Trask, L. R. (2014). *A student's dictionary of language and linguistics*. Routledge/Taylor & Francis.

Trifone, P. (Ed.). (2009). *Lingua e identità: Una storia sociale dell'italiano*. Carocci.

Vedovelli, M. (2002). *L'italiano degli stranieri: Storia, attualità e prospettive*. Carocci.

Vedovelli, M. (Ed.). (2011). *Storia linguistica dell'emigrazione italiana nel mondo*. Carocci.

Vignuzzi, U. (1988). Chi parla ancora in dialetto? *Italiano e Oltre, 5*, 241–245.

Vignuzzi, U. (1997). Lazio, Umbria and the Marche. In M. Martin & M. Parry (Eds.), *The dialects of Italy* (pp. 311–320). Routledge.

Vincent, N. (2018). Italian. In B. Comrie (Ed.), *The world's major languages* (3rd ed., pp. 240–259). Routledge.

Zamora Muñoz, P. (2002). Dislocazioni a destra e sinistra nell'italiano e nello spagnolo colloquiale parlato: Frequenza d'uso, funzioni e parametri linguistici. *Studi Italiani di Linguistica Teorica e Applicata, 31*(3), 447–470.

2

SOUNDS

The main goal of this chapter is to present the sounds of Italian and their patterns of organization. First, however, some preliminary key notions and technical terminology will be introduced, which are essential to achieve a proper characterization of the Italian sound system. Among the most important of these foundational concepts and terms are the difference between phonetics and phonology, the notions of phone, phoneme, and allophone; how speech sounds are to be represented graphically; and how they are categorized in terms of the way they are produced.

2.1 Phonetics and phonology

Phonetics and phonology are two correlated subfields of linguistics that study the sounds of languages. **Phonetics** studies the physical characteristics of the sounds, or **phones**, of the world's languages. It comprises three main areas: **articulatory** phonetics, which deals with the description and categorization of speech sounds according to the way they are produced by the speech organs; **acoustic** phonetics, which focuses on the physical characteristics of speech sounds as sound waves examining features like duration and intensity; and **auditory** phonetics, which studies how speech sounds are perceived by the auditory system. Our survey of the sounds of Italian target articulatory phonetics, including occasional remarks on acoustic phonetics; auditory phonetics is not addressed, because it falls outside the scope of this introductory textbook.

   Phonology, on the other hand, examines how languages arrange phones into structured systems, that is, it is concerned with how phones combine together to form words and which combination patterns are allowed or disallowed in a given language. Unlike phonetics, which examines the concrete, physical dimension of all speech sounds, phonology deals with abstract patterns of speech sounds and is language-specific. The central structural unit in phonology is the **phoneme**. Phonemes are sound units which bear distinctive property in the sense that they change the meaning of words; for example, the English words *pit* and *kit* differ from each other only in their initial sound, while the words *pit* and *pot* contrast only in the second sound. Word pairs of this kind are called **minimal pairs**. Phonemes, then, are

DOI: 10.4324/9781003057536-2

abstract linguistics units rather than actual phones. A sound unit that does not bear distinctive properties is called **allophone**. Allophones are different realizations of a phoneme in particular contexts; in English, for example, the *p* in *spit* sounds differently from both the *p* in *pit* and the *p* in *tip*, but these three different pronunciations depend exclusively on the context in which the sound occurs, namely, if *s* precedes *p* or it is at the beginning or end of the word. In technical terms, sounds that receive different pronunciations in specific contexts are said to be in **complementary distribution**. Different allophones of a phoneme may also occur in the same context; in casual speech, *p* could be (in fact, most likely is) pronounced in the same way in *pit*, *spit*, and *tip*. This type of alternation is called **free variation**.

2.2 Representation, production, and classification of speech sounds

2.2.1 Orthography and the international phonetic alphabet

Before examining how speech sounds are defined and categorized according to the way they are articulated, it is important to address the issue of their graphic representation. Using **orthography**, a standardized system used for writing a given language (i.e., a prescribed spelling), to transcribe speech sounds is problematic for at least three main reasons. First, there are languages that have not developed a standard written form used by their native speakers. Second, there are languages that do not have an alphabet (i.e., a set of letters arranged in a conventional order used in a given writing system) but use a **logographic** system where a single character or sign represents a complete word; an example of such language is Chinese. Third, and perhaps most importantly, orthography cannot achieve an unequivocal representation of speech sounds because, although to different degrees, written languages lack a one-to-one correspondence between the individual letters/symbols of their alphabet and the phones they employ.

The smallest functional unit of a writing system (i.e., letters or a combination of letters that stands for a certain sound) is called **grapheme** and is written in angled brackets (<p>). The same grapheme, however, can actually correspond to different sounds, as in the case of <th> in *thing* and *this*, and different graphemes can express the same sound, as in the case of <f> in *font*, <ph> in *phone*, and <gh> in *rough*. These shortcomings are easily resolved by using the *International Phonetic Alphabet* (IPA) devised by the *International Phonetics Association*, which provides a set of symbols to unequivocally transcribe the sounds of all the languages of the world. As we will see later in this section, the IPA symbols include a number of familiar letters from the Latin and Greek alphabets and other marks or signs called **diacritics**, which are added to symbols to provide additional, more detailed information about the sounds they represent, that is, to achieve a **narrow** phonetic transcription, as opposed to a **broad** transcription which contains less details. IPA symbols are used to transcribe both phones and phonemes; phones are enclosed in square brackets ([p]), and phonemes in oblique slashes (/p/). Currently, the IPA is the preferred, most commonly used transcription system worldwide. When we examine the sound system of Italian in the next section, we will see that Italian is characterized by an almost one-to-one correspondence between the letters of its alphabet and the sounds they represent; it is this close match that has promoted the popular belief that Italian is a 'phonetic' language, in the sense that in Italian 'you write how you speak.'

2.2.2 The speech organs

The production of speech sounds involves a number of body parts that are referred to as **speech organs**, **vocal organs**, or **organs of speech**. As Figures 2.1 and 2.2 illustrate, the vocal organs are typically divided into three subsystems on the basis of their functions in speech production.

First, we distinguish the **subglottal** or **respiratory system**, which comprises the lungs and the trachea. Second, we have the **larynx** (or **voice box**), a cartilaginous organ that sits on top of the trachea and encloses the **vocal folds**, the twin infoldings of mucous membrane stretching horizontally across the larynx. Finally, we have the **supra-glottal system**,

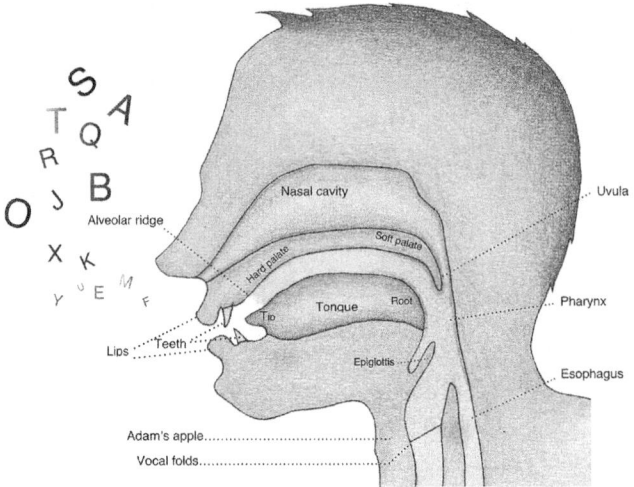

FIGURE 2.1   The speech organs.

Source: Courtesy of Claudia Seccia.

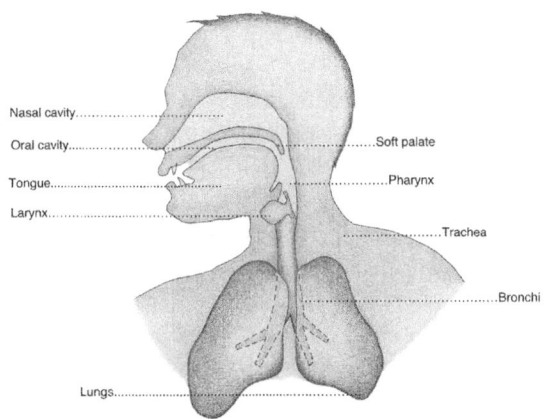

FIGURE 2.2   The vocal tract.

Source: Courtesy of Claudia Seccia.

commonly referred to as the **vocal tract**, which includes the **articulators**, the movable organs in the mouth which are used to produce the speech sounds. The process of speech production starts with the lungs pushing air upwards, then the flow or air passes through the larynx and is shaped into sounds by the articulators.

2.2.3 Speech sounds

In producing speech, the articulators modify the shape of the vocal tracts so that it alternates between relatively open and relatively (or completely) closed configurations. On the basis of the different configurations of the vocal tract, speech sounds can be divided into two main types of sound units, called **segments**: vowels and consonants.

2.2.4 Vowels

Vowels are sounds produced with no major constriction in the vocal tract, so that the air can escape from the mouth without encountering obstructions, and with the vocal folds vibrating. Traditionally, vowels are categorized based on the shape and position of the tongue in a hypothetical bidimensional space within the oral cavity and on the shape of the lips. The first fundamental parameter for classifying vowels is the **height** of the tongue. In producing a vowel, the tongue can be in a high, mid, or low position inside the oral cavity, and tongue height is also determined by the opening of the mouth. In the articulation of **high** vowels, the mouth is slightly open and the body of the tongue is close to the roof of the mouth; two examples are the vowel in *bead*, which is transcribed as [i], and the vowel in *bid*, transcribed as [ɪ]. **Mid** vowels, on the other hand, are produced with the mouth halfway open and the body of the tongue positioned midway in the oral cavity, as for example the vowel in *bed*, transcribed as [ɛ]. Finally, in the articulation of **low** vowels, the mouth is wide open and the lower jaw is dropped down so that the body of the tongue is far from the roof of the mouth; an example of low vowel is the vowel in *bad*, transcribed as [æ].

Vowels can also be classified in terms of the position of the high point of the tongue with respect to the front and back areas of the oral cavity, a parameter called **backness**. In the articulation of **front** vowels, the high point of the tongue is in the front of the mouth; thus, [i], [ɪ], [ɛ], and [æ] are all front vowels. Conversely, when producing a **back** vowel, the high point of the tongue is in the back of the mouth; an example of back vowel is the vowel in the word *balm*, transcribed as [ɑ], which is also low because in its articulation the mouth is fully open, the lower jaw is down, and the body of the tongue is far from the roof of the mouth. On the other hand, the vowel in *fought*, transcribed as [ɔ], is a mid-back vowel, while the vowels in *food* (IPA symbol [u]) and *foot* (IPA symbol [ʊ]) are high back vowels. Vowels produced with the high point of the tongue in midway between the front and the back of the mouth are called **central**. Two examples of central vowels are the low vowel in *bud*, transcribed as [ʌ], and the first vowel of *about*, commonly known as **schwa** and transcribed as [ə].

Strictly correlated to **height** dimension (i.e., the front vs. back distinction) is the dimension of **closeness**, which refers to the gradient closed–open status of the lower jaw and distinguishes between **close** vowels, produced with the tongue as close as possible to the roof of the mouth as not to create a constriction (hence high), and **open** vowels, produced with the tongue as far as possible from the roof of the mouth (hence low). The IPA adopts the close-ness dimension and posits a four-level distinction, as shown in Figure 2.3, which reproduces the full IPA vowel chart.

Another relevant parameter in classifying vowels is **lip rounding**, which refers to the shape of the lips: vowels whose articulation involves pursing the lips are called **rounded**, while vowels articulated with spread or neutral lips are called **unrounded**. Thus, [u], [ʊ], and [ɔ] are back rounded vowels, while [ʌ] and [ɑ] are back unrounded vowels. The front vowels introduced above, [i], [ɪ], [ɛ], and [æ], are all unrounded. English (as standard Italian) does not have front rounded vowels, but they are found in French; for example, <u> in *lune* 'moon,' transcribed as [y], is a high front rounded vowel (i.e., the 'equivalent' of [i] produced adding rounding and protrusion of the lips).

An important parameter for the classification of speech sounds in general is **nasality**: if the articulation of a sound involves lowering the **soft palate** (or **velum**, which is the upper part of the mouth, whose surface is soft and movable) so that the airflow can pass through the nose, it is **nasal**. If the soft palate is raised, the airflow escapes through the mouth; the sound is **oral**. Thus, vowels produced with a lowered velum are called nasal vowels, and the IPA diacritic mark used for transcribing them is the tilde placed above the vowel, [˜]. Like English, Italian doesn't have nasal vowels, but they are found in two other Romance languages: French (<o> in *monde* 'world' is [ɔ̃]) and Portuguese (<u> in *mundo* 'world' is [ũ]).

One last point to address before moving on to the classification of consonants is the difference between monophthong and diphthong. Briefly put, a **monophthong** is a single vowel, that is, a steady-state vowel produced by movement of the articulators toward a single point in the oral cavity with no noticeable change in its phonetic quality. All the vowels we have introduced so far are monophthongs. In contrast, a **diphthong** is a composite vowel articulation characterized by a noticeable change from one vowel quality to another; some examples of diphthongs in English are <i> (IPA /aj/) as in *file*, <ou> (IPA /aw/) as in *foul*, and <oi> (IPA /ɔj/) as in *foil*. As we will see in the next section, in Italian there are also vowel articulations where three distinct vowel qualities can be perceived; these are called **triphthongs**. Diphthong (and triphthongs) must be part of the same syllable. The notions of syllable and stress will be introduced properly in the next section; for now, let's think of the syllable as a phonological unit consisting of one or more segments that all languages use to organize sounds into types of segments, which in turn make up words.

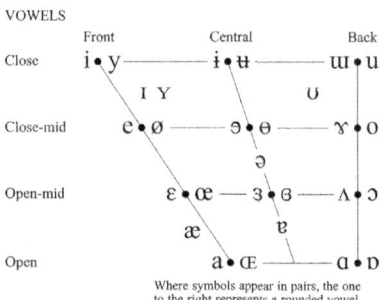

FIGURE 2.3   The IPA vowel chart.[1]

2.2.4.1 Consonants

Unlike vowels, **consonants** are articulated with a complete or partial constriction of the vocal tract and can be categorized in terms of three main parameters. The first is **place of articulation**, which indicates where the constriction occurs – that is, it refers to the articulators involved in the production of the sound. The second parameter is **manner of articulation**, which pertains to the differences in the constriction of the vocal tract. The last parameter is **voicing**, which refers to the vibration of the vocal folds, the two small multi-layered folds of tissue situated in the larynx. In producing sounds, the vocal folds can either remain open or they can draw closely together so that the outgoing airflow will cause them to vibrate, creating a buzzing sound that resonates through the rest of the vocal tract. Consonants articulated with the vocal folds drawn together are called **voiced** (/[b] in *bill*, <d>/[d] in *dill*), whereas consonants produced with the vocal folds staying open are called **voiceless** (<p>/[p] in *pack*, <t>/[t] in *tack*).

With respect to place of articulation, consonants are typically divided into 11 main groups, as indicated in (1).

(1) a. **Bilabial**: articulated by bringing together the upper and lower lips (<p>/[p] in *pan*, / [b] in *ban*, <m>/[m] in *man*).
  b. **Labiodental**: articulated by bringing the lower lip to the upper front teeth (<f>/ [f] in *fan*, <v>[v] in *van*).
  c. **Dental**: produced by bringing the tip of the tongue to the upper front teeth (<th>/ [θ] in *thick*, <th>/[ð] in *this*).
  d. **Alveolar**: articulation involves bringing the tip or blade of the tongue to the **alveolar ridge**, the bony ridge of the mouth immediately behind the upper teeth (<d>/ [d] in *dig*, <s>/[s] in *sip*, <n>/[n] in *nap*).
  e. **Postalveolar** (or **pre-palatal**): articulation involves bringing the tip or blade of the tongue to the area bordering the alveolar ridge and the palate (<sh>/[ʃ] in *ship*, <s>/ [ʒ] in *treasure*).
  f. **Retroflex**: produced with the tip or blade of the tongue curled back and articulating with the back of the alveolar ridge. Retroflex consonants are fairly uncommon in European languages, but they are found in southern Italian dialects.
  g. **Palatal**: articulated by raising the front of the tongue to the hard palate (<y>/[j] in *young*, or <ñ>/[ɲ] in Spanish *niño* 'child').
  h. **Velar**: produced by raising the back of the tongue toward the soft palate (<ck>/[k] in *tick*, <g>/[g] in *tag*).
  i. **Uvular**: produced with the back of the tongue articulating with the **uvula**, the small appendage hanging down at the back of the soft palate (<r>/[ʁ] or [ʀ] in French).
  j. **Pharyngeal**: articulated by moving the root of the tongue back toward the rear wall of the pharynx, or the **pharyngeal wall**. Pharyngeal consonants are found mainly in Semitic languages (e.g., Arabic and Hebrew), Berber and Cushitic languages (spoken in Africa), Northeast and Northwest Caucasian languages (spoken in the Caucasus), and some native languages of the Pacific Northwest of North America (e.g., Wakashan languages, spoken on and around Vancouver Island in British Columbia, and in the northwestern corner of the Olympic Peninsula of Washington State).

k.   **Glottal**: made in the larynx and involves closure or narrowing of the space between the vocal folds, called the **glottis** (<h>/[h] in *hot*).

In terms of manner of articulation, four main types of consonants are distinguished, as shown in (2).

(2) a.   **Stops** (or **plosives**): articulation involves a complete closure somewhere in the vocal tract (i.e., at some place of articulation), blocking the air from escaping through the mouth (<p>/[p] in *tip* is a bilabial stop, while <ck>/[k] in *tick* is a velar stop). If the articulation of a stop involves lowering the soft palate so that the air flows through the nose rather than through the mouth, we have a **nasal** stop (<m>/[m] in *map* is a bilabial nasal, <n>/[n] in *nap* is an alveolar nasal, <ng>/[ŋ] in *fang* is a velar nasal).

b.   **Fricatives**: articulation involves a constriction at some place in the vocal tract through which air is pushed through, producing an audible turbulent noise (<s>/[s] in *sip* and <z>[z] in *zip* are alveolar fricatives, while <sh>/[ʃ] in *ship* and <s>/[ʒ] in *treasure* are post-alveolar fricatives).

c.   **Affricates**: composite sounds consisting of a stop immediately followed by a fricative produced at the same place of articulation (<ch>/[tʃ] in *chin* and <g>/[dʒ] in *gin* are palato-alveolar affricates).

d.   **Approximants**: articulation involves only a slight narrowing of the articulators; the constriction is greater than in the articulation of a vowel and less than in the articulation of fricative, and there is no audible noise made by the air flowing out through the mouth. Two examples of approximants present in English are <l>[l] in *lip*, which is called **lateral** because during articulation the air flows along one or both sides of the tongue, and <tt> in *letter* in American pronunciation, which is transcribed as [ɾ] and commonly known as **tap** because its articulation involves the tip of the tongue lightly and quickly touching the alveolar ridge. Another common type of approximant is the **trill**, whose articulation involves the active articulator striking the passive articulator with a series of very quick, percussive movements. The most common types of trill are the alveolar [r] (or dental [r̪]) trill, with the tip of the tongue against the alveolar region (or the upper front teeth) (<rr> in Spanish *perro* 'dog'), and the uvular [ʀ] trill, articulated with the uvula tapping against the dorsum of the tongue (<r> in French *père* 'father').

Consonants are further divided into **obstruents**, which include oral stops, fricatives, and affricates, and **sonorants**, which comprise nasals and approximants.

2.3 The sounds of Italian

Now that we have become familiar with the basic concepts and terminology pertaining to the production and categorization of speech sounds, we can move to examining the sound system of Italian.

2.3.1 Vowels

The full vowel system of Italian comprises seven phonemes symmetrically plotted in a trilateral rather than quadrilateral diagram: specifically, three front unrounded vowels, three back rounded vowels, and a central vowel. They are listed in (4), where they are given in both their orthographic representation and IPA transcription and accompanied by examples of minimal pairs that attest to their phonemic status.

(3) The Italian vowels chart

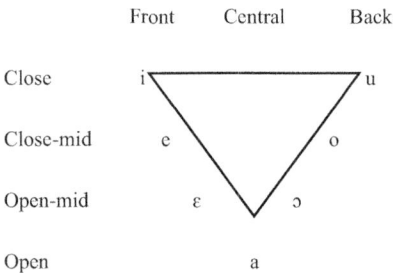

(4) a. High front <i>, /i/: *figlio* 'son' ~ *foglio* 'sheet,' *miglio* 'miles' ~ *maglio* 'mallet.'
      b. High back <u>, /u/: *luna* 'moon' ~ *lana* 'wool,' *fune* 'rope' ~ *fine* 'thin, fine.'
      c. Close-mid front <e>, /e/: *pera* 'pear' ~ *pira* 'pyre,' *cero* 'candle' ~ *coro* 'chorus; choir.'
      d. Close-mid back <o>, /o/: *coni* 'cones' ~ *cani* 'dogs,' *sole* 'sun' ~ *sale* 'salt.'
      e. Open-mid front <e>, /ɛ/: *pelle* 'skin' ~ *palle* 'balls,' *cento* 'one hundred' ~ *conto* 'account; bill.'
      f. Open-mid back <o>, /ɔ/: *cosa* 'thing' ~ *casa* 'house,' *rosa* 'rose; pink' ~ *risa* 'laughs.'
      g. Low central <a>, /a/: *faro* 'lighthouse' ~ *foro* 'hole,' *nave* 'ship' ~ *neve* 'snow.'

The examples in (4) show that Italian uses five letters of the alphabet to spell seven sounds. Specifically, the two sets of close-mid and open-mid vowels are both represented by the same grapheme: <e> for the front set and <o> for the back one. In writing, close-mid and open-mid vowels can be distinguished by means of a diacritic accent mark: the acute accent marks close-mid [e] and [o] are marked (<é> and <ó>), while the grave accent marks open-mid [ɛ] and [ɔ] (<è> and <ò>). However, accent marking is actually not a widespread practice; essentially, it is used only in dictionaries and other technical texts, such as grammar/language manuals. More details on accent marking will be given in the sections that examine Italian syllables, stress, and intonation patterns.

Some important details about close-mid and open-mid vowels should be addressed. First, in standard Italian, the phonemic contrast between close-mid and open-mid occurs only if the vowel is **stressed** (or **tonic**), while **unstressed** (or **atonic**) mid vowels are always realized as close, with **stress** referring to the degree of prominence of a syllable within a word in terms of duration and intensity (see section that follows for a more detailed account of stress). In other words, the phonemic contrast is neutralized in the environment of atonic/unstressed vowels. Thus, we have minimal pairs, like *vènti* 'winds' vs. *vénti* 'twenty or *pèsca* 'peach' vs. *pésca* 'fishing,' but the first and last <e> of *settèmbre* 'September' are always realized as [e] because they are unstressed. Similarly, for the set of back vowels, we have minimal pairs like *bòtti* 'bang; thuds' vs. *bótti* 'barrels,' but the final <o> of the singular form *bòtto* 'bang' is closed. In general, the number of minimal pairs is not very large. The system of Italian unstressed vowels, then, comprises five phonemes: /i/, /e/, /a/, /o/, and /u/.

Close- and open-mid vowels originate from different Latin vowels. In principle, then, if we know the Latin word that is at the source of the Italian word (its **etymon)**, we know the quality of the vowel. In reality, however, it is quite unlikely that 'normal,' average speakers are aware of the history of words. Therefore, the distinction between close and open vowels is subject to considerable variation among speakers. Excluding some professional categories as, for instance, actors, dubbers, and of course, linguists (particularly phoneticians, phonologists, and historical linguists) and language instructors, the number of speakers who actively and systematically maintain the distinction between [e]/[ɛ] and [o]/[ɔ] is relatively small. The most typical scenario involves retaining the contrast for high-frequency words; if the contrast is lost, the vowel that takes over (i.e., the outcome of the contrast neutralization) varies, mainly depending on the speaker's geographical origins. To give a brief illustration, I pronounce *dènte* 'tooth' 'correctly' but 'mis-pronounce' *bène* 'well' since I use [e] rather than [ɛ]; also, I keep the distinction between *vénti* 'twenty' and *vènti* 'winds' but no longer distinguish between *pèsca* 'peach' and *pésca* 'fishing' and use [e] for both. As for the back vowels, I retain somewhat consistently the contrast between *fòsse* 'pits; holes' and *fósse* 'be 1/2sg.is' but use [o], not [ɔ], for *còsa* 'thing,' *ròsa* 'rose; pink,' and [ɔ] not [o] for *pósto* 'place.'

All seven Italian vowels can be long or short, with length depending on the position they occupy within the word and on whether they are stressed or unstressed. We will take a closer look at vowel length in the next section; for now, let's just note that vowel length is characterized as a gradient and the following generalizations can be drawn: (a) stressed vowels are longer than unstressed ones; (b) vowels that occur at the beginning of a word (word-initial vowels) and in an open syllable (i.e., a syllable that ends in a vowel) are long; (c) vowels in closed syllables (i.e., syllables ending in a consonant) are short; and (d) vowels that occur at the end of a word (word-final vowels) are never long independently of whether they are stressed or unstressed. Thus, vowel length, which in IPA transcription is notated by a colon [:], depends on the position vowels occupy within words, which means that it is not phonemic: there are no minimal pairs in Italian which contrast only in terms of short vs. long vowel, as for instance Latin pŏpulus /populus/ 'people' vs. pōpulus /po:pulus/ 'poplar.'[2]

Along with the seven vowels we have just reviewed, Italian has a number of diphthongs. As we recall, a *diphthong* is a complex vowel sound that functions as a single unit even though is made of two vocalic segments with different articulatory targets, hence characterized by a perceptible difference in both quality and prominence (or **sonority**). Diphthongs are traditionally divided into two main types, depending on the sonority degree of the two components. Diphthongs where the first component is more prominent are called **falling** diphthongs since they involve a decrease of sonority from the first to the second part. Falling diphthongs may also be referred to as **closing** diphthongs because the second segment is a high or close vowel, while the first segment is most commonly lower or more open, so that the articulatory movement goes from a relatively open mouth to a more closed mouth position. Diphthongs characterized by the opposite sonority pattern, that is, diphthongs involving an increase of sonority from the first to the second component, are called **rising**, or **opening,** since in this case the articulatory movement goes from a relatively close mouth position to a more open one.

Italian has both types of diphthongs, and in both types, the less vocalic element is either the palatal approximant [j] or the labiovelar approximant [w]. As defined earlier, approximants are sounds articulated with a constriction in the vocal tract that is greater than in the articulation of a vowel but smaller than in the articulation of fricative so that the airflow produces no audible noise in escaping through the mouth. Note that [j] and [w] are often referred to as **glides**; other terminologies commonly used, which highlight their dual status in between vowels and consonants, are **semi-consonant** (for rising diphthongs) and **semi-vowel** (for falling diphthongs).[3]

The set of Italian falling diphthongs is smaller than the set of rising diphthongs; some illustrating examples are given in (5), with [j], and (6), with [w].

(5) a. [aj]: *baita* 'mountain hut,' *laico* 'lay; secular,' *mai* 'never,' *zaino* 'backpack.'
     b. [ɛj]: *lei* 'she,' *sei* 'six.'
     c. [ej]: *potei* 'I could.'
     d. [ɔj]: *poi* 'then; later.'
     e. [oj]: *noi* 'we,' *voi* 'you, pl.'
     f. [uj]: *lui* 'he.'

(6) a. [aw]: *auto* 'car,' *cauto* 'cautious,' *flauto* 'flute,' *lauto* 'lavish.'
     b. [ɛw]: *feudo* 'fief,' *neutro* 'neuter,' *reuma* 'rheum.'
     c. [ew]: *pneumatico* 'tire,' *europeo* 'European.'

The examples in (5) and (6) point out four unattested diphthongs: [ij], [uw], [iw], [ɔw], and [ow]. These gaps are accounted for by phonetics: the two segments are too similar in terms of their articulation and auditory properties to be perceived as separate sounds. The disparity in the number of examples provided for each diphthong shows that some falling diphthongs are rather rare; also, falling diphthongs involving /w/ do not occur in word-final position, except in a few onomatopoeic words (e.g., *bau bau*, which is how Italian expresses dog barking, or *babau* 'boogeyman').

The rising diphthongs found in Italian are listed and illustrated in (7), with [j], and (8), with [w].

(7) a. [ja]: *bianco* 'white,' *chiave* 'key,' *fiala* 'phial,' *piastra* 'slab,' *tiara* 'tiara.'
     b. [jɛ]: *dieci* 'ten,' *fieno* 'hay,' *piede* 'foot,' *siero* 'serum.'
     c. [je]: *fienile* 'hayloft,' *piegare* 'fold V,' *soffietto* 'bellows.
     d. [jɔ]: *chiodo* 'nail,' *fiocco* 'flake; bow,' *pioggia* 'rain,' *piovra* 'octopus.
     e. [jo]: *biondo* 'blond,' *fionda* 'sling,' *fiore* 'flower.'
     f. [ju]: *chiuso* 'closed,' *fiume* 'river,' *piuma* 'feather,' *schiuma* 'foam.

(8) a. [wa]: *guado* 'ford,' *guardia* 'guard,' *quando* 'when,' *quadro* 'painting.'
     b. [wɛ]: *guerra* 'war,' *quercia* 'oak,' *questua* 'collection of alms.
     c. [we]: *quello* 'that,' *questo* 'this.'
     d. [wi]: *acquisto* 'purchase,' *guida* 'guide,' *quindi* 'therefore.'
     e. [wɔ]: *cuore* 'heart,' *fuoco* 'fire,' *nuora* 'daughter-in-law,' *ruota* 'wheel.'
     f. [wo]: *acquoso* 'watery.'

The only missing segments in this case are [ji] and [wu], which are gaps that are accounted for by the same articulatory and auditory constraints that block the falling diphthongs [ij] and [uw].

Italian also has some **triphthongs**, which can be distinguished into two main types. As illustrated in (9), the first type comprises the two approximants [j] and [w], followed by a vowel (9a), while the second type involves [j] or [w], followed by a vowel then [j] (9b).

(9) a. [j] + [w] or [w] + [j] + vowel: *aiuola* 'flower bed,' *quiete* 'quietness.'
     b. [j] or [w] + vowel + [j]: *miei* 'my, mine,' *cambiai* 'I changed,' *tuoi* 'your, yours,' *guai* 'troubles.'

As already noted, diphthongs and triphthongs must belong to the same syllable. A sequence of vowels that does not belong to the same syllable is called a **hiatus** (e.g., *spia* 'spy' or *leone* 'lion'), where the two vowels are articulated as separate segments).

2.3.2 Consonants

Table 2.1 gives the full inventory of standard Italian consonant phonemes ordered in terms of place of articulation (rows) and manner of articulation (columns).

Table 2.1 shows that the consonant system of Italian includes 23 phonemes, distributed in seven manners and six places of articulation. Note that the affricates /tʃ/ and /dʒ/ and the fricative /ʃ/ are alternatively categorized as pre-palatal, and the nasal /n/ as alveolar (e.g., Maturi, 2014; Palermo, 2020).

Before examining more closely each set of phonemes, we must point out that the majority of Italian consonants can be **short** or **long** (also **geminate**). In writing, consonant length is indicated by doubling the consonant, except in a few cases that we will address shortly. In IPA, consonant length is transcribed either with the colon diacritic [ː], as in the case of vowels, or by reduplication of the consonant symbol, mirroring spelling (e.g., *notte* [nɔtːe] or [nɔtte] 'night'). This variable notation stems from an enduring debate among phoneticians and phonologists on whether geminates should be analyzed as single or double segments, that is, whether they should be viewed as mono- or bi-phonetic units. Following the more commonly held position, we will consider geminates as one phonetically long segment. The exceptions to this general trend will be addressed next as we present the individual sets. Note that consonant length is a distinctive feature of Italian absent in the other main European languages. (Remember that spelling cannot be trusted: <tt> in *petty*, for example, is [t] not [tː].) Let's now take a closer look at each group of consonants to get a clearer, more precise understanding of their phonetic and phonological features and to see how they are represented orthographically. We start with oral stops, then continue downward to the next manner of articulation.

2.3.2.1 Oral stops

Italian displays three sets of oral stops, voiceless and voiced, in three places of articulation: labial, dental, and velar. When we introduced the notion of allophone, we illustrated it with examples from English, noting that the pronunciation of <p> differs depending on its

TABLE 2.1 The Italian consonants

	Labial	Labiodental	Dental	Alveolar	Palatal	Velar
Oral stop	p b		t d			k g
Nasal stop	m		n		ɲ	
Affricate				ts dz	tʃ dʒ	
Fricative		f v		s z	ʃ	
Approximant					j	w
Lateral approximant				l	ʎ	
Trill				r		

position within the word (or syllable). If <p> occurs in word-/syllable-initial position, its articulation involves a brief burst of air when the closure of the lips is released. You can test this by placing your hands in front of your mouth and saying words like *pit*, *pet*, *pat*. Stops articulated with this small puff are called **aspirated**, and the IPA notation for aspiration is a superscript [ʰ], so the <p> in *pit* is transcribed as [pʰ]. On the other hand, if <p> occurs after <s>, it is produced without aspiration (again, you can test uttering words like *spit*, *spat*, *spot*); the <p> in this case is **unaspirated** and is transcribed simply as [p]. Finally, if <p> occurs in word-/syllable-final position, as for instance in *sip* or *sap*, it is articulated in yet a different way: the occlusion may be held for some time so that there is no audible indication of its release. Stops with inaudible release are also known as **unreleased** stops and are marked by the raised corner diacritic [˺] in IPA transcription, so the <p> in *sip* is transcribed as [p˺]. Summing up, then, in English the phoneme /p/ has three allophones: [pʰ], [p], and [p˺]. The same holds for all English voiceless stops, so we have *tin* [tʰɪn] and *kin* [kʰɪn], *still* [stɪl] and *skill* [skɪl], and *sit* [sɪt˺] and *sick* [sɪk˺].

Italian oral voiceless stops, instead, are always unaspirated. Also, Italian /t/ and /d/ are articulated with the tip of the tongue pushed against the upper front teeth; hence, they are dental rather than alveolar, as English /t/ and /d/. The IPA uses the same symbol for dental, alveolar, and postalveolar; if needed (i.e., in the case of languages that have two or all three segments either as phonemes or as allophones), the exact place of articulation is specified by adding a diacritic. The diacritic for dental is the subscript bridge ([t̪]), but we won't use it because Italian dental stops do not contrast with alveolar or postalveolar stops either at the phonemic or allophonic level. As we will see in more detail when we address the syllable, Italian does not allow stops (and consonants in general) in word-final position.

The orthographic symbols used for the sets of labial and dental stops are the same as the IPA symbols: *pane* /pane/ 'bread,' *bara* /bara/ 'coffin,' *toro* /tɔro/ 'bull,' *dono* /dono/ 'gift'; and consonant length is reflected in writing by doubling: *doppio* /dop:jo/ 'double' (vs. *dopo* /dopo/ 'after'), *fibbia* /fib:ja/ 'buckle' (vs. *tibia* 'shinbone' /tibja/), *fatto* 'fact' (vs. *fato* 'fate'), *cadde* 's/he fell' (vs. *cade* 's/he falls'). The consonant sequences involving stops allowed in Italian are addressed next in the context of syllable structure.

The orthographic representation of Italian velar stops is slightly more complex, as we see in (10).

(10) a. The voiceless velar stop /k/ is written:

    i. <c> before /a/ (*casa* /kasa/ 'house, home,' *duca* /duka/ 'duke'), back vowels (*collo* /kɔl:o/ 'neck,' *fico* /fiko/ 'fig,' *cubo* /kubo/ 'cube'), and another consonant (*crepa* /krɛpa/ 'crack').

    ii. <ch> before front vowels and rising diphthongs with /j/: *chela* /kɛla/ 'nipper,' *chilo* //kilo/ 'kilo,' *chiave* /kjave/ 'key,' *chiodo* /kjɔdo/ 'nail,' *richiesta* /rikjɛsta/ 'request.'

    iii. <q> or <cq> before rising diphthongs with /w/: *quadro* /kwadro/ 'painting,' *quindi* /kwindi/ 'then; therefore,' *liquore* /likwore/ 'liqueur,' *acqua* /akwa/ 'water'; but note that before /wo/ /k/ may also be written <c> (e.g., *cuoco* /kwɔko/ 'cook,' *cuore* /kwɔre/ 'heart').

b. The voiced velar stop /g/ is written:

  i. <g> before /a/ (*gatto* /gat:o/ 'cat,' *ruga* /ruga/ 'wrinkle'), back vowels (*gola* /gola/ 'throat,' *gusto* /gusto/ 'taste; flavor,' *regola* /rɛgola/ 'rule,' *figura* 'figura/ 'figure; picture'), another consonant (*grano* /grano/ 'grain; wheat,' *segreto* /segreto/ 'secret'), and rising diphthongs with /w/ (*guardia* /gwardja/ 'guard,' *guerra* /gwɛ r:a/ 'war,' *gui*da /gwida/ 'guide').

  ii. <gh> before front vowels and rising diphthongs with /j/: *ghepardo* /gepardo/ 'cheetah,' *ghirlanda* /girlanda/ 'garland; wreath,' *ghianda* /gjanda/ 'acorn,' *ghiotto* /gjot:o/ 'greedy (for); appetizing.'

In sequences consisting of a velar stop and /i/ or /j/ (i.e., /ki/, /kj/, /gi/, /gj/), the articulation of the stop is actually fronted and takes place in the palatal rather than the velar region. In this environment, then, /k/ and /g/ have a palatal allophone transcribed as [kʲ] [gʲ], respectively, with the diacritic superscript [ʲ] indicating palatalization, or also as [c] and [ɟ], which are the IPA symbols for the voiceless and voiced palatal stops.

2.3.2.2 Nasal stops

We find three nasal stops in the phonemic inventory of Italian, all voiced. The first is the labial /m/, spelled <m>: *mare* /mare/ 'sea,' *fame* /fame/ 'hunger,' *somma* /som:a/ 'sum; amount,' *gamba* '/gamba/ 'leg.'

Then, we have the dental /n/, spelled <n>: *nave* /nave/ 'ship,' *cane* /kane/ 'dog,' *panna* /pan:a/ 'cream.' The dental nasal has two allophones: when it is followed by the labiodental fricatives, it is articulated as labiodental [ɱ] (*inferno* [iɱferno] 'hell,' *confine* [koɱfine] 'border'; *inverno* [iɱverno] 'winter,' *invalido* [iɱvalido] 'invalid'); and when it occurs before a velar stop, it is articulated as velar [ŋ] (*banca* [baŋka] 'bank,' *bianco* [bjaŋko] 'white'; *fungo* [fuŋgo] 'mushroom,' *sangue* [saŋgwe] 'blood'). Some scholars prefer to classify /n/ as alveolar rather than dental; within this view, /n/ would have a third dental allophone [n̪] when it occurs before dental obstruents (i.e., oral stops, fricatives, and affricates): *dente* [dɛn̪t̪e] 'tooth,' *fondo* [fon̪d̪o] 'bottom,' *pensiero* [pen̪sjɛro] 'thought,' *senza* [sɛn̪t̪sa], *danza* [dan̪t̪sa]).

The third nasal phoneme is the palatal /ɲ/, spelled <gn>. This phoneme is quite rare in word-initial position, where it is found only in a handful of words which, except for *gnocchi* /ɲɔk:i/ 'potato dumplings' and possibly *gnomo* /ɲɔmo/ 'gnome,' are not high-frequency words and essentially amount to technical, specialized terms of Greek origin (e.g., *gnostico* /ɲɔstiko/ 'gnostic,' *gnoseologia* /ɲɔseolodʒja/ 'gnoseology'). Also, /ɲ/ is always realized as geminate when it occurs in intervocalic position (*bagno* /baɲ:o/ 'bath; bathroom,' *cigno* /tʃiɲ:o/ 'swan,' *ragno* /raɲ:o/ 'spider,' *sogno* /soɲ:o/ 'dream').

2.3.2.3 Fricatives

Italian has two sets of voiceless/voiced fricatives: labiodental /f/ and /v/, spelled <f> and <v>, respectively (*fico* /fiko/ 'fig,' *cofano* /kɔfano/ 'coffer,' *soffio* /sof:jo/ 'breath'), and alveolar /s/ and /z/, both spelled <s> (*sera* /sera/ 'evening,' *casa* /kasa/ 'house; home,' *masso* /mas:o/ 'rock; boulder'; *base* /baze/ 'base,' *rosa* /rɔza/ 'rose; pink'). Since /z/ never occurs at the beginning of a word, the voiceless and voiced alveolar fricative stand in phonemic contrast only in intervocalic position, though there are very few minimal pairs (e.g., *chiese* /kjɛze/ 'churches' ~ *chiese* /kjɛse/ 's/he asked,' *fuso* /fuzo/ 'spindle' ~ *fuso* /fuso/ 'melted'). On the whole, however, the contrast between /s/ and /z/ is rather weak and appears to be declining. As in the case of the mid vowels, both the strength of the opposition between /s/ and /z/ and which of the two segments takes over if the opposition is neutralized depends on geographic factors. Generally, intervocalic <s> is realized as /z/ by northern speakers and as /s/ by speakers from central-southern Italy. Also, /z/ is never realized as geminate. Finally, when /s/ and /z/ occur before a consonant, they are in complementary distribution (i.e., they have allophonic status), with /s/ before voiceless consonant (*spada* /spada/ 'sword,' *stella* /stel:a/ 'star,' *scatola* /skatola/ 'box,' *sfida* /sfida/ 'challenge') and /z/ before voiced consonant (*sbarra* [zbar:a] 'bar; barrier,' *sdentato* [zden̪tato] 'toothless,' *sguardo* [zgwardo] 'look,' *svenire* [zvenire] 'faint V,' *smeraldo* [zmeraldo] 'emerald,' *snello* [znɛl:o] 'slender').

The fifth (and last) fricative of Italian is the voiceless palatal /ʃ/; like the velar stops /k/ and /g/, /ʃ/ has multiple orthographic representations, as shown in (11).

(11) a. <sc> before front vowels: *scena* /ʃɛna/ 'scene,' *scempio* /ʃempjo/ 'massacre'; slaughter,' *scivolo* /ʃivolo/ 'slide.'
      b. <sci> before <a> and back vowels: *sciarpa* /ʃarpa/ 'scarf,' *sciocco* /ʃɔk:o/ 'silly; foolish,' *sciupare* /ʃupare/ 'ruin; to spoil.'

The voiceless palatal fricative is always geminate in intervocalic position, though consonant length is not reflected in the orthography (*ascella* /aʃ:ɛl:a/ 'armpit,' *nascita* /naʃ:ita/ 'birth,' *coscia* /kɔʃ:a/ 'thigh,' *asciugamano* /aʃ:ugamano/ 'towel'). As you will have guessed by the phonemic transcriptions, the <i> of <sci> is simply a diacritic to indicate palatal place of articulation and has no phonetic value – that is, it does not correspond to [j] (if it were, its transcription would have been /kɔʃ:ja/).

2.3.2.4 Affricates

Italian has two sets of voiceless and voiced affricate phonemes: alveolar /ts/ and /dz/ and palatal /tʃ/ and /dʒ/. The presence of four affricate phonemes is considered a distinctive phonological feature of Italian since all the main European languages have at most two.

We have seen so far that the opposition between voiced and voiceless consonants is quite robust in Italian, as attested by an overall sizable number of minimal pairs. In the case of alveolar affricates, however, the opposition is more problematic, and the scenario that emerges resembles the one observed for the alveolar fricative /s/ and /z/ and the mid vowels.

The two alveolar affricates, voiceless /tz/ and voiced /dz/, are both written <z>: *zampa* /tsampa/ 'leg (of animal); paw,' *zio* /tsio/ 'uncle,' *zucchero* /tsuk:ero/ 'sugar,' *fazzoletto* /fats:olet:o/ 'handkerchief,' *pizza* /pits:a/ 'pizza,' *polizia* /polits:ia/ 'police'; *zaino* /dzajno/ 'backpack,' *zero* /dɛzro/ 'zero,' *mezzo* /mɛdz:o/ 'means; way.' As the examples show, /ts/ and /dz/ are always geminate in intervocalic position, but consonant length is not necessarily reflected by spelling. As already noted, the phonemic contrast between /ts/ and /dz/ is rather weak, basically limited to one minimal pair, *razza* /rats:a/ 'race, people' ~ *razza* /radz:a/ 'ray fish,' and the realization of <z> as /ts/ or /dz/ varies considerably across regions, as well as among speakers.

The two palatal affricates, voiceless /tʃ/ and voiced /dʒ/, also have different spelling, depending on the following segment, as we see in (12).

(12) a. Before front vowels, /tʃ/ is written <c> and /dʒ/ is written <g>:
  i. *cena* /tʃena/ 'dinner,' *cibo* /tʃibo/ 'food,' *voce* /votʃe/ 'voice,' *bacino* /batʃino/ 'pelvis,' *faccenda* /fatʃ:ɛnda/ 'matter,' *vaccino* /va tʃ:ino/ 'vaccine.'
  ii. *gelo* /dʒɛlo/ 'frost,' *gita* /dʒita/ 'outing; trip,' *vagito* /vadʒito/ 'crying, of a new-born,' *logica* /lɔdʒika/ 'logic,' *oggetto* /odʒ:ɛt:o/ 'object,' *muggito* /mudʒ:ito/ 'lowing.'
  b. Before /a/ and back vowels, /tʃ/ is spelled <ci> and /dʒ/ is spelled <gi>:
  i. *cialda* /tʃalda/ 'wafer,' *ciocca* /tʃɔk:a/ 'lock of hair,' *ciuffo* /tʃuf:o/ 'tuft,' *baciare* /batʃare/ 'kiss V,' *bacio* /batʃo/ 'kiss N,' *faccia* /fatʃ:a/ 'face,' *braccio* /bratʃ:o/ 'arm,' *cocciuto* /kotʃ:uto/ 'stubborn.'
  ii. *giacca* /dʒak:a/ 'jacket,' *giocare* /dʒokare/ 'play V,' *giuramento* /dʒuramento/ 'oath,' *fagiano* /fadʒano/ 'pheasant,' *stagione* /stadʒone/ 'season,' *assaggiare* /as:adʒ:are/ 'taste V,' *peggiore* /pedʒ:ore/ 'worse,' *raggiungere* /radʒ:ungere/ 'reach V.'

The examples in (12) show that, unlike their dental counterparts, the palatal affricate can be either short or long in intervocalic position, and consonant length is not always reflected in the spelling. As in the case of the voiceless palatal /ʃ/, the <i> of <ci> and <gi> is simply a diacritic <i>, and there is no [j] sound involved.

2.3.2.5 Approximants

Along with palatal [j] and velar [w] (more properly labio-velar, since in its articulation the lips round), Italian has two lateral approximants, alveolar /l/ and palatal /ʎ/, and the trill /r/. The alveolar lateral is spelled <l>: (*luna* /luna/ 'moon,' *sole* /sole/ 'sun,' *colla* /kɔl:a/ 'glue.'

The palatal lateral /ʎ/, spelled <gli>, is quite rare in word-initial position, even rarer than the palatal nasal /ɲ/; indeed, it occurs only in the word *gli*, which is both one of the masculine plural forms of the definite article (*gli studenti* 'the students') and the form of the third-person pronoun meaning 'to him/them.' Like the alveolar affricates /ts/ and /dz/, the palatal nasal /ɲ/, and the palatal fricative /ʃ/, /ʎ/ is always geminate in inter-vocalic position, though consonant length is not reflected in the spelling: *ciglia* /tʃiʎ:a/ 'eyelashes,' *foglia* /fɔʎ:a/ 'leaf,' *giglio* /dʒiʎ:o/ 'lily.' And once again, <i> has simply dia-critic value.

The last consonant phoneme of Italian we must introduce is the alveolar trill [r]: *rana* /rana/ 'frog,' *poro* /poro/ 'pore,' *porro* /por:o/ 'leek.' In spontaneous speech, the trill may be realized as a tap [ɾ] when it occurs in intervocalic position.

2.4 Syllables, stress, and intonation

2.4.1 Syllables

A **syllable** is the smallest unit of sound sequences, typically consisting of one vowel, with or without surrounding consonants. A syllable can form a whole word by itself or be just one part of a word. All languages of the world organize their sound inventories in terms of syllables. In more technical terms, then, a syllable is the minimal phonological unit of organization of languages. Speakers have quite clear and largely shared intuitions on how to count how many syllables are in a word. For instance, any English speaker would agree that *word* is made of one syllable, *wordy* of two, and *wordiness* of three. Conversely, breaking down words into syllables (i.e., identifying exactly which segments form one syllable) may be less straightforward. Although all English speakers most likely agree that *lady* has two syllables, there will most likely be disagreement on their shape: are the syllables *la* and *dy*, or *lad* and *y*? We will not deal with the issue of 'proper' syllabification, because it is closely related to the specific theoretical approach adopted for analysis, while our main objective is to provide a descriptive sketch of the Italian sound system.

Syllables are subdivided into three main components: the nucleus, the onset, and the coda. The **nucleus** is usually a vowel and constitutes the most prominent part, the **peak**; in Italian, the nucleus is always a vowel. The **onset** is a consonant (or more than one) that precedes the nucleus, whereas the **coda** is the consonant that follows it. The sequence of nucleus and coda is called **rhyme**. Depending on whether they have a coda or not, syllables are characterized as **open**, which don't have a coda, and **closed**, which do. The IPA symbol to represent a syllable boundary is a period [.].

Let's now examine the general structure of Italian syllables. First, only vowels and diphthongs can be a syllable nucleus. As for the onset, it can be lacking (e.g., *ala* /a.la/ 'wing'), or it can consist of a maximum of three consonants (e.g., *tela* /te.la/ 'cloth,' *treno* /trɛ.no/ 'train,' *strage* /stra.dʒe/ 'massacre; slaughter'). The allowed onsets are listed in (13).

(13) a. One-consonant onsets. With the exception of [z] and geminate consonants, all consonants can form a syllable onset, although, as seen earlier, word-initial syllables beginning with the palatal nasal /ɲ/ are very rare, and word-initial syllables beginning with the palatal lateral /ʎ/ are even rarer.

b. Two-consonant onsets.

  i. Stop or voiceless labiodental fricative /f/ followed by /r/: *prato* /**pra**.to/ 'meadow; lawn,' *brivido* /**bri**.vi.do/ 'shiver,' *trono* /**trɔ**.no/ 'throne,' *drago* 'dragon,' *cratere* /**kra**.tɛ.re/ 'crater,' *gracile* /**gra**.tʃi.le/ 'frail,' *frana* /**fra**.na/ 'landslide.'

  ii. Stop or voiceless labiodental fricative /f/ followed by /l/: *plico* /**pli**.ko/ 'parcel,' *blando* /**bla**n.do/ 'mild, bland,' *clava* /**kla**va/ 'club,' *glaciale* /**gla**.tʃ ja.le/ 'icy,' *flebile* /**flɛ**.bi.le/ 'feeble.'

  iii. Voiceless alveolar fricative /s/ followed by:
   • Stop: *spada* /**spa**.da/ 'sword,' *sbadato* /**sba**.da.to/ 'careless,' *studio* /**stu**.djo/ 'study,' *sdentato* /**sde**n.ta.to/ 'toothless,' *scatola* /**ska**.to.la/ 'box,' *sguardo* /**sgwa**r.do/ 'look.'
   • Nasal: *smania* /**sma**.nja/ 'restlessness,' *snaturato* /**sna**.tu.ra.to/ 'heartless.'
   • Fricative: *sfera* /**sfɛ**.ra/ 'sphere,' *svago* /**sva**.go/ 'relaxation; pastime), or approximant: *slegato* /**sle**.ga.to/ 'untied; loose,' *sradicare* /**sra**.di.ka.re/ 'uproot.'

  iv. Other possible two-consonant onsets (which, as the examples show, are restricted to technical/scientific words of Greek origin) are:
   • /pt/: *pterodattilo* /**pte**.ro.dat.ti.lo/ 'pterodactyl.'
   • /pn/: *pneumatico* /**pne**u.ma.ti.ko/ 'tire,' *pneumologia* /**pne**u.mo.lo.dʒja/ 'pneumology.'

- /ps/: *psichiatria* /**psi**.kja.tri.a/ 'psychiatry,' *psicololologia* /**psi**.ko.lo.dʒja/ 'psychology.'
- /tm/: *tmesi* /**tm**e.zi/ 'tmesis.'
- /kn/: *ctenodattilo* /**kt**e.no.dat.ti.lo/ 'ctenodactyl.'
- /ft/ (*ftaleina* /**ft**a.lej.na/ 'phthalein.'

  c. Three-consonant onsets.

    i. /s/ followed by either a stop or /f/ followed by /r/: *spreco* /**spr**ɛ.ko/ 'waste,' *sbranare* /**sbr**a.na.re/ 'tear to pieces,' *strada* /**str**a.da/ 'street,' *sdrucito* /**sdr**u.tʃi.to/ 'thorn,' *screpolato* /**skr**e.po.la.to/ 'chapped; cracked,' *sgradevole* /**sgr**a.de.vo.le/ 'unpleasant,' *sfrigolare* /**sfr**i.go.la.re/ 'sizzle.'

    ii. /s/ followed by /p, b, k/ by followed /l/: *splendore* /splendore/ 'splendor,' *sbloccare* /sblok:are/ 'unblock,' *sclerosi* /sklerɔzi/ 'sclerosis.'

There are much stricter constraints as for the types of admissible syllable coda. Word-internal codas typically consist of only one of the following consonants: /m/, /n/, /r/, and /l/ (*campo* /kam.po/ 'field,' *tenda* /tɛn.da/ 'tent,' *porta* /pɔr.ta/ 'door,' *colpa* /kol.pa/ 'fault; guilt'), or the first part of a geminate. As noted in the preceding text, in IPA transcription, consonant length can be marked by either [ː] or doubling the consonant: *latte* 'milk' /latːe/ or /latte/. However, in analyses that refer to syllabic structure (or phenomena pertaining to the syllable domain), the latter notation is preferred since the former does not actually allow for the representation of the split of a geminate consonant into coda of the preceding syllable and onset of the second one (*palla* /pal.la/ 'ball').

Word-final syllables typically lack a coda since there is just a handful of autochthonous Italian words that end with a consonant (*per* 'for,' *in* 'in; at; to,' *con* 'with,' *non* 'not,' *il* 'the,' mas. sg.'). Other words ending with a consonant are words that Italian borrowed from other languages (English *bar*, *cocktail*).

There is an ongoing debate among Italian phonologists on the status of /s/ in word-internal syllables (*bosco* /bɔsko/ 'wood,' *finestra* /fi.nɛ.**str**a/ 'window'). In one view, which is supported by evidence from historical data, /s/ and the following consonant(s) do not belong to the same syllable (i.e., they are **heterosyllabic**): /s/ forms the coda of the preceding syllable, and the following consonant(s) form the onset of the following syllable. Within this position, then, *bosco* is to be syllabified as /bɔs.ko/ and *finestra* as /fi.nɛs.tra/. Yet other scholars embrace the opposite view and propose that, although the heterosyllabic status of /s/ undoubtedly holds for Old Italian, it is no longer viable for contemporary Italian. Therefore, they maintain that /s/ and the following consonant(s) belong to the same syllable (i.e., they are **tautosyllabic**) so that the right syllabification would be /bɔ.sko/ and /fi.nes.tra/. In spelling, <s> forms a cluster with the following consonant(s): *te-sta* /tɛ.sta/ 'head,' *ce-sto* /tʃe.sto/ 'basket,' *di-sgrazia* /di.**sgr**atsja/ 'misfortune,' *pale-stra* /pa.lɛ.stra/ 'gym' (as opposed to *con-to* /kon.to/ 'bill,' *cen-tro* /tʃɛn.tro/ 'center,' *com-plice* /kɔm.pli.tʃe/ 'accomplice').

2.4.2 Stress and intonation patterns

Stress and intonation are known as **suprasegmental** features because rather than pertaining to individual sounds (i.e., segments), they apply to a level above the segments, that is, they concern strings of segments (syllables and words) and of words (phrases and sentences). Suprasegmental properties relate to **prosody**, which refers to variations along four different dimensions of sounds. The first is **pitch**, which is the attribute of auditory sensation in terms of which a sound may be ordered on a scale form 'low' to 'high.' Pitch correlates to **fundamental frequency,** which, in speech sounds, is based on the number of complete cycles of vibration made by the vocal folds. The second dimension is **intensity** (or volume), which is the strength of a sound wave and is perceived as loudness. The third is **speech timing**, which refers to the distribution of speech units through time in terms of acceleration, deceleration, and pausing. The last dimension of sounds concerning prosody is **voice quality**, which indicates the range of changes a normal speaking voice goes through during speech (e.g., harsh/soft, whispering).

2.4.2.1 Stress

Stress refers to the relative prominence of different syllables in a word; in other words, stress makes one syllable (more accurately, the syllable nucleus) stand out from the other syllables that make up a given word. Stressed (or **tonic**) syllables are distinguished from unstressed (or **atonic**) syllables by having longer duration, greater intensity, or differences in pitch (or more likely a combination thereof). In Italian, the most salient feature of word stress is intensity. In words consisting of three or more syllables, another syllable besides the tonic one seems to bear some degree of stress as well. This indicates that a third level of stress, intermediate between stressed and unstressed, may be needed, which is referred to as **secondary** stress, as opposed to **primary** stress. The IPA notation for primary stress is ['] placed before the stressed syllable, while secondary stress is marked with [ˌ], also placed before the relevant syllable. Thus, in the six-syllable word *ar-ti-co-la-zio-ne* /ar.ˌti.ko.lats.ˈtsjo.ne/ 'articulation,' the primary stress falls on the fifth syllable, –*zio*-, and the secondary stress falls on the second syllable, –*ti*-.

There is a correlation in Italian between word stress and vowel length: stressed vowels in word-initial open syllable are long (*pala* /ˈpaːla/ 'shovel' vs. *palla* /palˈla/ 'ball' and *parola* /paˈrola/ 'word'), whereas stressed vowels in word-final position are always short (*caffè* /kafˈfɛ/ 'coffee'). Unstressed vowels are always short, and the only unstressed vowel that cannot occur in word-final position is /u/.

As you may have guessed from the examples given so far, stress does not have a fixed position in Italian (as in French, for instance, where stress always falls on the last syllable). The three main positions of word stress in Italian are summarized in (14).

(14) a. **Last** syllable: *verbosità* [ver.bo.si.ˈta] 'verbosity,' *caffè* [kaf.ˈfɛ] 'coffee,' *affinché* [af.fin.ˈke] 'so that,' *colibrì* [ko.li.ˈbri] 'hummingbird,' *parlò* [par.ˈlɔ] 's/he spoke,' *virtù* [vir.ˈtu] 'virtue. All vowels except /o/ can be stressed in word-final position; stressed /o/ occurs only in foreign words (e.g., the French city (or wine) *Bordeaux* [bor.ˈdo]; note, though, that the word for the color is pronounced [bor.ˈdɔ], often spelled *bordò* instead of *bordeaux*, which indicates that this word has fully assimilated into the phonological patterns of Italian, that is, it is no longer perceived as foreign). Words stressed on the last syllable are known as **oxytone** words.

   b. **Penultimate** (second to last) syllable: *mattìna* [mat.ˈti.na] 'morning,' *colóre* [ko.ˈlo.re] 'color,' *genitóre* [dʒe.ni.ˈto.re] 'parent.' This is the most common word stress pattern. Words stressed on the penultimate syllable are called **paroxytone**.

   c. **Antepenultimate** (third to last) syllable: *tàvolo* [ˈta:.vo.lo] 'table,' *cèlebre* [tʃɛ:ˈle.bre] 'famous; celebrated,' *scìvolo* [ˈʃi:.vo.lo] 'slide,' *gòmito* [ˈgo:.mi.to] 'elbow,' *sùbito* [ˈsu:.bi.to] 'at once.' Words stressed on the antepenultimate syllable are **proparoxytone**.

Stress can also occur farther back in the word and fall on the fourth-to-last syllable (e.g., in third-person plural forms of verbs like *àbitano* [ˈaː.bi.ta.no] 'they live').

Word stress has phonemic value in Italian, as shown by minimal pairs like *àncora* /ˈan.ko.ra/ 'anchor' ~ *ancóra* /an.ˈko.ra/ 'still, yet,' *prìncipi* /ˈprin.tʃi.pi/ 'princes' ~ *princìpi* /prin.ˈtʃi.pi/ 'principles,' *méta* /ˈme.ta/ 'aim'~ *metà* /me.ˈta/ 'half,' *papa* /ˈpa.pa/ 'pope' ~ *papà* /pa.ˈpa/ 'dad.'

Let's conclude our survey of word stress with some remarks on how stress is represented orthographically. Marking stress in spelling is obligatory only for two classes of words. The first comprises **pluri-syllabic oxytone** words, that is, words consisting of two or more syllables stressed on the last syllable, as in (13a). The second class consists of a small group of **monosyllabic** words (*già* 'already,' *giù* 'down,' *più* 'more; plus'); some of these words have **homonyms** (i.e., words that are written and pronounced in the same way, for instance, the verb *bear* vs. the noun of the animal), and stress allows one to disambiguate between them (i.e., it bears phonemic function). Among the most common are *dà* 's/he gives' ~ *da* 'from,' *è* 's/he is' ~ *e* 'and,' *là* 'there' ~ *la* 'the.F.SG,' *lì* 'there' ~ *li* 'them.M. PL,' *sì* 'yes' ~ *si* 'reflexive pronoun.'

In pluri-syllabic words that are not stressed on the last syllable, stress may be marked orthographically if it is phonemic, as we saw earlier. On the whole, however, orthographic marking of stress in this case is very uncommon and, as already mentioned, practically restricted to dictionaries and texts dealing with language/linguistics. We know from our discussion of mid vowels that the acute and grave accents may be used to differentiate between close-mid and open-mid vowels, respectively. For the other three vowels, /a/, /i/, and /u/, the more widespread tendency is to mark stress always with the grave accent (<à>, <ì>, <ù>). Using the acute accent for high vowels (<í>, <ú>) and the grave for the low vowel (<à>) is also possible, but this practice is much less common.

2.4.2.2 Intonation patterns

When we speak, we don't utter flat, evenly timed strings of sounds (at least not in normal circumstances); rather, our speech displays a series of variations along the prosodic dimensions we introduced earlier. The variation in pitch that conveys meaning distinctions at the level of phrases and sentences is referred to as **intonation**; in other words, intonation marks differences in meaning that are not conveyed by differences at the segmental level (i.e., at the level of sounds). To give a brief example, the sentence *Mary is coming to dinner* can be uttered with a pitch fall at the end, in which case it indicates that the speaker is simply making a statement, that is, they are just communicating to the listener(s) that Mary will join them for dinner. In contrast, if the sentence is uttered with a pitch rise at the end, it denotes that the speaker is repeating a statement made by the interlocutor to express that they are doubtful of or surprised by this piece of information.

Intonation also accomplishes important communicative functions. It serves to guide the interlocutors through the conversation by signaling, for example, that the speaker has finished talking. And it also serves to mark emphasis on specific aspects of the information the speaker wants to communicate, as well as to express emotions and attitudes (e.g., doubt, politeness, irritation, etc.). A given pattern of intonation is called **intonation contour**. All languages make use of intonation to express differences in meaning, though intonation patterns and the functions of intonation contours vary both across languages and within the same language.

In Italian, intonation can be the only means to differentiate among sentence types. An important distinction carried out exclusively by intonation is the one between statements (**declarative** sentences) and questions (**interrogative** sentences). As shown in (15), there is no structural difference between the declarative (15a), the yes/no interrogative (or **polar** interrogative) (15b), and (15c), that is, they are perfectly identical as for the words they are made of. (Remember that punctuation – that is, the question mark – is irrelevant since we are dealing with speech, not writing.) These sentence types, however, have noticeably different intonation contours.

(15) a. *Hai   comprato   la   frutta.*
          you.have   bought   the fruit
          'You bought fruit.'
      b. *Hai comprato la frutta?*
          'Did you buy fruit?'
      c. *Hai comprato la frutta!*
          'You bought pasta!'

It's generally agreed that in standard Italian, declarative sentences are characterized by a falling contour, whereas yes/no interrogative sentences are distinguished by an intonation fall followed by a steep rise (i.e., falling–rising contour). It should be noted, though, that regional varieties of Italian may employ different intonation contours to mark declarative and interrogative sentences. In fact, intonation patterns vary considerably across varieties and provide significant cues to identifying the geographical origins of speakers.

2.5 Exercises

1. Give the IPA symbol for each of the following sounds. Illustrate with two examples.

    a. Palatal nasal _____ as in _____, or _____.
    b. Voiceless velar stop _____ as in _____, or _____.
    c. Low central vowel _____ as in _____, or _____.
    d. Voiced palatal affricate _____ as in _____, or _____.
    e. Open-mid back vowel _____ as in _____, or _____.
    f. Voiceless labiodental fricative _____ as in _____, or _____.
    g. Voiced labial stop _____ as in _____, or _____.
    h. Close-mid front vowel _____ as in _____, or _____.
    i. Lateral palatal _____ as in _____, or _____.
    j. High back vowel _____ as in _____, or _____.

2. Give the orthographic transcription of the following words.

    a. ['tsukkero]
    b. ['ʃarpa]
    c. [maʎ'ʎone]
    d. [iɱfets'tsione]
    e. ['viʃʃido]
    f. [pɛska]
    g. [zvil'uppo]

    h.   ['baɲɲo]

    i.   ['dʒɛːo]

    j.   [vir'tu]

    k.   [aŋ'gwilla]

3.   Provide the phonemic transcription of the following words.

    a.   *ingegnosità* 'ingenuity'

    b.   *glicine* 'wisteria'

    c.   *soggezione* 'uneasiness; subjection'

    d.   *zucchine*

    e.   *tovagliolo* 'napkin'

    f.   *bruschetta*

    g.   *inferno*

    h.   *ciliegia* 'cherry'

4.   Each of the following transcriptions contains one mistake; identify it and explain what it consists of.

    a.   *sogno* ['soɲo] 'dream'

    b.   *ciliegia* [tʃi'ljedʒja] 'cherry'

    c.   *fango* ['fango] 'mug'

    d.   *caviglia* [ka'viʎa] 'ankle'

    e.   *vènti* [ven'ti] 'winds'

    f.   *manifestazione* [manifesta'tsione] 'manifestation'

5.   Which of the following are minimal pairs? Why?

    a.   *cane* 'dog' ~ *carne* 'meat'

    b.   *sono* 'I am' ~ *sogno* 'dream'

    c.   *àncora* 'anchor' ~ *ancóra* 'still; again'

    d.   *pala* 'shovel' ~ *palla* 'ball'

    e.   *ha* 'she/he/it has' ~ *a* 'at; to'

    f.   *capélli* 'hair' ~ *cappèlli* 'hats'

6.   Provide concise but complete answers to the following questions, illustrating with examples.

    a.   Explain the main differences between phonetics and phonology.

    b.   Define the notions of phoneme and allophone.

    c.   What type of sound is a vowel? What are the main parameters considered in the categorization of vowels?

    d.   How many vowel phonemes does Italian have?

    e.   What type of sound is a consonant? What are the main parameters considered in the categorization of consonants?

    f.   What is a geminate consonant? Are Italian geminates phonemes or allophones?

    g.   What is a syllable? How many subparts does it include? How many types of syllables are distinguished?

    h.   What are the most important characteristics of word stress in Italian? How are Italian words classified in terms of word stress?

    i.   What is intonation? What functions does intonation carry in Italian?

Notes

1 IPA Chart, www.internationalphoneticassociation.org/content/ipa-chart, available under a Creative Commons Attribution-Sharealike 3.0 Unported License. Copyright © 2015 International Phonetic Association.
2 Latin words are conventionally given in small capitals.
3 Semi-vowels are sometimes transcribed as [ii] and [ui].

Bibliography

Albano Leoni, F., & Maturi, P. (2010). *Manuale di fonetica*. Carocci.

Benincà, P., Mioni, A., & Vanelli, L. (Eds.). (1999). *Fonologia e morphologia dell'italiano e dei dialetti d'Italia*. Bulzoni.

Canepari, L. (1999). *Manuale di pronuncia italiana*. Zanichelli.

Canepari, L. (2000). *Dizionario di pronuncia italiana*. Zanichelli.

Canepari, L. (2003). *Manuale di fonetica*. Lincom Europa.

Ladefoged, P. (2006). *A course in phonetics* (5th ed.). Harcourt Brace Jovanovich.

Ladefoged, P., & Maddison, I. (1996). *The sounds of world's languages*. Blackwell.

Leoni, F. A., & Maturi, P. (2018). *Manuale di fonetica* (3rd ed.). Carocci.

Marotta, G., & Vanelli, L. (2021). *Fonologia e prosodia dell'italiano*. Carocci.

Maturi, P. (2014). *I suoni delle lingue, i suoni dell'italiano: Nuova introduzione alla fonetica* (2nd ed.). Il Mulino.

Muljačić, Ž. (1972). *Fonologia della lingua italiana*. Il Mulino.

Palermo, M. (2020). *Linguistica italiana* (2nd ed.). Il Mulino.

Schmid, S. (1999). *Fonetica e fonologia dell'italiano*. Paravia.

Sorianello, P. (2006). *Prosodia: Modelli e ricerca empirica*. Carocci.

3

WORDS

This chapter examines how words are broken down into smaller units; in other words, it inspects the internal structure of words. First, key background notions and terminology pertaining to morphology and the tightly related field of morphosyntax are introduced. Then, some important issues pertaining to the characterization of the concept of 'word' are addressed, followed by a discussion on how words can be categorized into different classes. Next, the notion of morpheme is surveyed in more depth by addressing how they are classified according to the structural functions they fulfill and the types of meaning they convey. Finally, the core morphological properties of Italian nouns (and other words that are related to nouns, that is, adjectives and determiners), pronouns, and verbs are analyzed.

3.1 Morphology and morphosyntax

Linguistics borrowed the term 'morphology' from biology, where it refers to the study of the forms of plants and animals. In contemporary linguistics, **morphology** denotes the subdiscipline that studies the internal structure of words (i.e., how words can be subdivided into smaller parts) and the systematic correspondences between forms and meanings that hold among words. However, the term *morphology* is also used to refer to what we could call 'the grammar of words,' the specific component of the grammar of any language that comprises the set of rules which govern the construction of words.

The basic element of morphological analysis (i.e., the core morphological building block of words) is called **morpheme**. It can be defined as the smallest linguistic unit to which meaning can be attributed; in other words, a *morpheme* is a sequence of segments that cannot be further broken down into smaller parts and expresses some kind of meaning. Generally, speakers have rather strong intuitions on how to divide words into separate morphemes and characterize the type of meaning they express. Let's illustrate with a few examples from English. Take the word *desk*; we would agree that this is a quite straightforward case: *desk* cannot be divided up into meaningful parts, so it is made of one single morpheme {desk}. (Traditionally, morphemes are enclosed in curly brackets.) Now let's take the word *desktop*, which the *Oxford English Dictionary* (online version, https://www-oed-com) defines as '[t]he

DOI: 10.4324/9781003057536-3

top or working surface of a desk.' It is quite safe to assume that any English speaker (including linguistically naïve ones) would split *desktop* into two morphemes, {desk} and {top}, and attribute each a meaning, respectively: 'a sort of table, board, or the like, which is typically found in specific places (school, office, library) and is intended for specific functions (placing items like books, manuscripts, computers and performing activities that require these items),' and 'the higher or uppermost part of something.'

Let's now consider the word *walker*. In this case, too, we can be fairly confident that speakers will identify two morphemes, {walk} and {er}, and if asked to describe the meaning of {er}, a very likely answer would be 'someone or something that does (or helps doing) some kind of action/function.' What allows us to formulate this definition is the meaning of *walker* (i.e., 'a person (or animal) that walks' and 'something that assists or enables walking') and the association to a network of words (*runner*, *jogger*, *swimmer*, etc.) which are comparable to *walker* both in their composition (they consist of a verb and {er}) and their meaning (they denote a person or thing that performs/assists in performing an action/function).

Finally, let's look at the word *walkers*. Again, we can be fairly confident that speakers will divide it into three morphemes, {walk}, {er}, and {s}, and associate {s} to the notion of 'more than one instance of something' (i.e., the grammatical category 'plural'). As in the case of {er}, the 'meaning' of {s} is derived by the identification of a systematic pattern observed in the English language, namely, word pairs like *apple/apples*, which express the contrast 'one'/'more than one.'

Now, what about the word *candor*? Does it comprise two morphemes or only one? We would most likely agree that *candor* can be segmented into two parts: *cand-or* or *can-dor*. In this case, however, in contrast to what's observed for *desktop*, neither of the two parts contributes to determine the meaning of *candor*, nor can they be associated to systematic patterns of the kind we just discussed. In this case, then, the two units are syllables and *candor* is a **disyllabic** word (i.e., made of two syllables) but comprises one morpheme only.

Determining whether or not a given part of a word constitutes a morpheme, then, requires a systematic and extensive comparison across words that display it.

Words made of more than one morpheme are called **complex** (or **polymorphemic**), whereas words that are made of a single morpheme are called **simplex** (or **monomorphemic**) words. In contrast to simplex words, complex words are not entirely arbitrary, neither in terms of their internal structure nor with respect to their meaning. Rather, complex words are motivated by the parts they are made of and associate with structurally comparable words to form different networks based on their shared components. These networks play an important role in the creation of new words.

Different categories of morphemes can be distinguished based on their structural properties (e.g., in terms of acceptable vs. unacceptable combination of morphemes and the position they occupy in words), as well as the type of meaning they express. The classification of morphemes into distinct categories and the different domains and scopes of morphological analysis are addressed in more detail later in the chapter.

Morphemes can have sentence-level functions, that is, they can affect other words in the sentence, or the structure of the sentence itself (i.e., word order). This is the case, for instance, of the plural morpheme {s}, since its presence/absence determines the forms of the verb and the demonstrative, as shown by *This/That book is interesting* vs. *These/Those books are interesting*.

The domain of morphology can be outlined from two different viewpoints. Under the view that conceives morphology as the study of systematic correspondence between form and meaning observed across words in a given language, the starting point of morphological analyses will be properties and/or features of certain types of words, which are then used to identify sets of linguistic items that display them. This type of approach is called **paradigmatic** since it includes in its scope (and gives importance to) **paradigms**, to be understood as sets of linguistic elements that share some properties/features. For example, English *this*, *these*, *that*, and *those* form the paradigm of demonstrative determiners; the properties that link the four forms are that they can all occur with a noun (which they must precede) and can never occur together (e.g., *★this that desk*). Similarly, the set *walker, jogger, runner, swimmer, player*, etc. forms a paradigm because all the members share the morpheme {er}. The paradigmatic approach, thus, is **word-based**, since the word is considered the basic unit of analysis.

If, on the other hand, morphology is conceived as the study of the internal structure of words, morphological analyses will take as starting point the **syntagm**, a linguistic unit comprising a set of forms which are in a sequential relationship with each other when they combine to form a larger linguistic unit. The analysis, in this case, will focus on the characterization of sequential relationships between linguistic units. Within a **syntagmatic** approach, then, a form like *desks* is divided into two morphemes, {desk} and {s}, and the analysis will aim at uncovering the patterns of distribution of both morphemes in the language, taking into account both the relationship they have with each other (i.e., that {s} makes the noun plural) and the relationship that they have with other elements in phrases or sentences (e.g., that *desks* can be modified by *these/those* and not by *this/that* and cannot occur with a verb form like *is*). The syntagmatic perspective, then, is **morpheme-based**, because it takes the morpheme as the fundamental unit of analysis. It is more closely related to **syntax**, which is the subdiscipline of linguistics that deals with the structure of sentences, so the term **morphosyntax** is used to capture the tight relation between morphology and syntax.

To conclude, the syntagmatic (morpheme-based) and the paradigmatic (word-based) approaches represent two complementary perspectives from which the domain of morphology can be appraised. The relative significance accorded to either the syntagmatic or the paradigmatic dimension mainly depends on whether we choose the morpheme or the word as the central unit of language. If we choose the morpheme, it would be hardly possible not to focus on syntagmatic relationships, and vice versa, if we choose the word, it would be quite difficult not to focus on paradigmatic relationships. Since morphological analyses of a given language and/or linguistic item or phenomenon may obtain (in fact, often do) different results, depending on which of the two approaches is adopted, and since any language/language unit displays both syntagmatic and paradigmatic relationships, an analysis that incorporates both the syntagmatic and the paradigmatic approach would be preferable.

3.2 Words and word classes

3.2.1 Words

We defined *morphology* as the study of the internal structure of words. Hence, understanding morphology entails a clear understanding of what words are. We would probably agree (or at least don't strongly disagree) that words are the kind of linguistic unit speakers are most likely to have a good awareness of and to be able to characterize to some extent. But what are 'words' exactly? What would be a clear, basic definition of the notion 'word'? And how would we come up with it? Formulating an adequate and uncontroversial definition of the concept 'word' is by no means an easy task, as it runs into a number of hurdles, and although an impressive body of research has been conducted on this matter, the notion 'word' remains controversial and no fully satisfactory definition of 'word' has been put forward yet.

One of the reasons (possibly the weightiest one) that determining what is meant by 'word' is problematic is that the notion 'word' can be examined from a number of different perspectives, each focusing on or prioritizing specific facets. For our present purposes, we can characterize 'word' as a linguistic unit that is independent and intelligible at the phonological level, that is, a sequence of phones (segments) that conforms to the phonological system of the language, contains one or more morphemes, and can occur in a sentence.

It is necessary, however, to distinguish between a concrete and an abstract sense of the notion 'word.' In a concrete sense, the words *walk, walks, walked,* and *walking* are all instances of 'actual words' in that all of them can occur as such in a sentence. The technical term for this 'type' of words is **word form**. In an abstract sense, the word forms *walk, walks, walked,* and *walking* are directly connected to each other by having in common the content meaning 'moving on foot,' though they differ from each other in terms of their individual grammatical functions. In other words, *walk, walks, walked,* and *walking* form a set of grammatical forms (a paradigm) sharing the same content meaning, that is, they are different 'physical' materializations of the same word, each bearing a specific grammatical value. This abstract notion of 'word' is referred to as **lexeme**.

Summing up, word forms represent the same vocabulary unit, while lexemes correspond to dictionary entry forms. To avoid confusion between the concrete word form and the abstract lexeme, lexemes are traditionally written in small capitals, so *walk, walks, walked, walking* are word forms of the lexeme WALK.

3.2.2 Word classes

Words can be grouped into separate categories, **word classes**, or **lexical categories**, both based on the kind of notions they convey (their meaning) and in terms of their morphological properties and the position/s they can occupy within a sentence (their grammatical function and placement). For example, in terms of meaning, words denoting 'things' (entities) typically belong to the class of **nouns** (*book, student, shape, hope*); words designating events are commonly classified as **verbs** (*to walk, to yawn, to ponder*); and words expressing properties of nouns usually fall within the class of **adjectives** (*long, lean, smart, dull*).

In terms of morphology/morphosyntax, words like *book, student, shape, hope* would fit together in the category of nouns because they display a number of common morphosyntactic behaviors, such as that they take the plural morpheme {s} (*book**s**, student**s**, shape**s**, hope**s***) and that they can be preceded but not followed by an article (*a/the book, a/the student, a/the shape, a/the hope*). Similarly, words like *long, short, smart, dull* would be assigned to the class of adjectives because they all have the forms *long-**er/est**, lean-**er/est**, smart-**er/est**, dull-**er/est**.* And words like *to walk, to yawn, to ponder* would be assigned to the class of verbs because they share a number of forms (*walk**s**, walk**ed**, walk**ing***).

Word classes can also be further divided into subcategories, in which case the members of one subcategory will show properties that are, to some degree, distinct from the properties of the members of other subcategories. An example of a possible subcategory of the word class verb in English could be the set of verbs that have the past tense form *-ed* (*ponder**ed**, talk**ed**, walk**ed**,* etc.). Word classes can also be merged into larger super-categories. A distinction commonly made is that between 'content' (**lexical**) word classes, whose members refer to types of entities (nouns, verbs, adjectives, adverbs), and **grammatical** (or **functional**) word classes, whose members carry primarily 'grammatical' meaning (articles and prepositions).

However, the categorization of word classes appears to be a rather-problematic matter. Two main types of problems have been pointed out. First, a member of a given class may lack some properties associated with the class to which it has been assigned. Second, a member of a class possesses properties associated with a different class. For example, we saw earlier that words denoting entities typically belong to the class noun, yet we would include in this class also words like *explosion* or *destruction*, which denote events, and also words like *length* or *thinness*, which denote properties. Likewise, given that one of the morphosyntactic properties of nouns is that they can be modified by articles and take -*s* to form the plural, we would have to classify verb forms as *reading* (e.g., *the readings assigned for next class*) as nouns.

Moreover, although all languages have word classes, extensive variation has been observed across languages regarding the number of word classes they have, their internal composition and structure, the properties associated with them, and their size. These divergences hinder the identification of a set of word classes with cross-linguistic validity. We will come back to this issue at the end of next subsection, after we examine different types of morphemes.

These problems are related to the fact that determining a language's set of word classes essentially involves arbitrary and inconsistent choices whose legitimacy may be disputed for empirical and/or theoretical reasons. More recently, the methodology of identifying word classes on the basis of the types of meaning they denote and/or the morphological and morphosyntactic properties they display has frequently fallen under attack since research has shown that any given word class is likely to include members which, in some way or another, do not behave like the members commonly associated with the class (Carstairs-McCarthy, 1999; Baker, 2003; among others).

Another parameter commonly used to define word classes is their propensity to accept new members, which distinguishes between open and closed classes. **Open** classes can add new members at any time and in a variety of ways so that (in theory) they are indefinitely large. **Closed** classes, in contrast, are usually smaller; moreover, they typically resist including new members, and when they do, they impose more rigid constraints on the types of items they welcome.

3.3 Types of morphemes

3.3.1 Classifying morphemes

Morphemes can be classified into different categories according to their structural properties and the kind of meaning they express. The first distinction to be made pertains to the possibility for a morpheme to form a word by itself. Morphemes that constitute words on their own are called **free**, whereas morphemes that cannot occur as words are called **bound**. Thus, the word *walkers* is composed of the free morpheme {walk} and the bound morphemes {er} and {s}.

A second distinction commonly made (which is related to the 'free vs. bound' distinction) is that between **lexical** morphemes, which express a 'concrete' meaning ({walk} conveys the meaning 'movement on foot'), and **grammatical** (or **functional**) morphemes, which carry a grammatical meaning or express meanings that fall in between the lexical-grammatical continuum ({s} in *walkers* expresses the grammatical category 'plural,' while {er} conveys the notion 'someone or something that does (or helps doing) some kind of action/function'). While lexical morphemes can be free, grammatical morphemes are always bound. The distinction between lexical and grammatical morphemes is relevant to the two basic functions of morphological operations: creating new words and deriving the appropriate grammatical form of a word in a given structural context.

Bound morphemes involved in word-formation are called **derivational**, and the creation of new words by means of derivational morphemes is termed **derivation**. Bound morphemes that distinguish different grammatical forms of the same word, on the other hand, are called **inflectional**, and **inflection** refers to the morphological expression of grammatical information and categories. The distinction between inflection and derivation are addressed in more detail in the next section.

A third important distinction is that between root and affix. As hinted by the word itself, **roots** are the true foundations of the word: a root is a morpheme that cannot be analyzed further, either in terms of derivation or inflection. Put differently, the root is what remains of a word after it is stripped of all the inflectional and derivational material. Roots can be either bound or free. An example of bound root in English is {dent}, as in *dentists*, where it combines with the derivational morpheme {ist} and the grammatical morpheme {s}, while {walk} would be an example of free root. A free root is also referred to as **base**. Roots that combine with another derivational morpheme are known as **stems**; for instance, both in *dentistry* and *dentists*, the stem is {dentist} (i.e., the root {dent} plus derivational {ist}), which then combines with the derivational {ry} or the inflectional affix {s}. The **stem** of a word, then, is the form stripped of any inflectional affix, and it is the stem that serves as the basis for word-formation.

While roots and stems can be either free or bound, affixes are always bound. **Affix** is a cover term for four different subtypes, **prefix**, **suffix**, **infix**, and **circumfix**, depending on the position they occupy with respect to the root (or stem). Likewise, the term **affixation** subsumes four different subtypes of morphological processes, **prefixation**, **suffixation**, **infixation**, and **circumfixation**, depending on the type of affix involved. Prefixes and suffixes are considerably more widespread than infixes and circumfixes across the world languages.

(1) Affixes

    a.   **Prefixes** appear **before** the root/stem: {dis} (***dis**believe*, ***dis**appear*), {un} (***un**believable*, ***un**certain*), {re} (***re**charged*, ***re**duplicate*).

    b.   **Suffixes** appear **after** the root/stem: {ity} (*productiv**ity**, futil**ity***), {ness} (*false**ness**, bold**ness***), {less} (*tooth**less**, spine**less**ness*).

    c.   **Infixes** appear **inside** the root/stem: *-in-* in Hoava (Solomon Islands), which combines with verbs to form nouns, *hiva* 'to want' > *h-**in**-iva* 'wishes' (Blevins, 2014, p. 138).

    d.   **Circumfixes** appear **around** root/stem: *ke- . . . -an* 'be like . . .' in Malay, ***ke**-cina-cina-**an*** 'be like a Chinese,' ***ke**-anak-anak-**an*** 'be like a doll' (Mel'čuk, 2000, p. 528).

Words can take more than one affix of different types, as shown by words like *spine-less-ness*, *un-believ-able*, *im-mortal-s*.

The last distinction to address is that between morpheme and **allomorph**. As you may guess, *allomorphs* are the counterpart of allophones in morphology. That is, allomorphs are contextually determined phonological realizations (phonetic variants) of a single morpheme, which occur in complementary distribution. For example, the plural morpheme {s} has three different realizations, which are dictated by the final sound of the word they attach to: /s/ in words like *caps* /kæps/, *cats* /kæts/, *snacks* /snæks/, *puffs* /pʌfs/; /z/ in works like *cabs* /kæbz/, *bags* /bægz/, *beds* /bɛdz/, *bins* /bɪnz/; and /əz/ or /ɪz/ in words like *voices* /ˈvɔɪsəz/, *bushes* /ˈbʊʃəz/, *ditches* /ˈdɪtʃəz/, *judges* /ˈdʒʌdʒəz/.

3.3.2 Inflectional and derivational morphology

As noted in the preceding text, morphological operations fulfill two basic functions: they create new words, and they form the appropriate grammatical form of a word in a given structural context. The first function, known as derivation, is achieved by derivational affixes, whereas the second function, known as inflection, is carried out by inflectional affixes.

Several different criteria have been employed to set apart inflectional and derivational affixes. Among the parameters most commonly used is the type of meaning the affix expresses. In theory, derivational affixes are assumed to convey meanings that pertain to the level of the lexeme, while inflectional affixes are supposed to carry meanings that apply at the level of word forms. Put differently, the meanings expressed by inflectional affixes constitute additional information in the sense that they do not alter mental representations evoked by lexemes; for example, the plural morpheme {s} in *legs* does not actually play a role in our construal of the entity denoted by the word *leg*, since both singular *leg* and plural *legs* evoke precisely the same mental image as far as the entity concerned: 'lower limb of the human body; something similar to a leg in terms of shape, appearance, function.' The information added by {s} relates to the number of tokens of the entity evoked, which does not concern any of the intrinsic, specific aspects of representation of the entity. Summing up, establishing whether an affix is derivational or inflectional based on its meaning involves assessing how the affix alters the meaning of the base.

Two correlated parameters additionally taken into consideration when differentiating between derivational and inflectional affixes are **semantic transparency** and **semantic compositionality**, which measure to what degree the meaning of an affixed form can be read off the 'sum' of the meanings of the base and the affix(es). Inflectional affixes are expected to exhibit a high degree of semantic transparency and semantic compositionality so that the meaning of the affixed form can straightforwardly and consistently be derived by 'adding' together the meanings of the base and the affixes, as in the case of *legs*. Conversely, derivational affixes are frequently characterized by semantic opacity and display a low degree of compositionality because it is often the case that the meaning of the affixed form cannot be obtained by simply 'adding up' the meanings of the base of the affix(es).

Several other factors have consistently been used to distinguish between inflectional and derivational affixes; in the interest of space, we will review only the most established ones. One criterion is considering whether affixes are **optional** or **obligatory** components. Derivational affixes are assumed to be optional, in the sense that their absence does not compromise the grammatical integrity of the linguistic unit; for instance, the English prefix *un-* is optional because omitting it does not result in an ungrammatical unit (*it is acceptable/**un**acceptable*). Inflectional affixes, in contrast, are expected to be obligatory, in the sense that their absence does compromise the grammatical integrity of the linguistic unit; the plural suffix -*s*, for example, is obligatory: if it is omitted, we end up with ungrammatical units (**the chair are comfortable*).

Another frequently used criterion concerns the **relative order** affixes display with respect to the base they attach to. It is based on the generalization put forward by Joseph H. Greenberg in his seminal research on linguistic universals, which are patterns observed systematically across languages and potentially true for all languages (Greenberg, 1963). Under *Universal 28*, Greenberg proposes that when inflectional and derivational affixes co-occur, either before or after the root, derivational affixes always occur between the root and inflectional affixes. Thus, derivational affixes are expected to occur closer to the root, whereas inflectional affixes are assumed to appear in a more peripheral position, typically at the end of the word (e.g., in *engagements*, the derivational suffix -*ment* precedes the inflectional suffix -*s*). The closer proximity of derivational affixes to the root would result from the fact that derivation pertains to word-formation: since they are expected to express more 'concrete,' conceptual meanings than inflectional affixes, derivational affixes are 'more intimately connected with the root' (Greenberg, 1963, p. 93), and this more intimate connection is metaphorically reflected in the position they occupy relative to the root.

Productivity is another parameter often used to classify affixes as derivational or inflectional. Briefly put, **productivity** refers to the extent to which a morpheme can be used to create new words. Thus, a morpheme is productive if it is recurrently used to create new instances of the same type of word, that is, if it instantiates a morphological pattern that can be systematically extended. Inflectional processes are assumed to be highly productive, whereas derivational processes are supposed to be less productive because they are characterized by a number of phonological, morphological, and semantic restrictions. For example, the plural (inflectional) morpheme {s} is highly productive since there are very few cases in which the plural form of a noun is not obtain by adding it. Conversely, the derivational morpheme {en}, which attaches to adjectives to form verbs (*deepen*, *moisten*, *whiten*, etc.) is not as productive since forms like *shallowen, *greenen, *vividen are not possible words. But even though the higher productivity of inflectional patterns has been shown to be a strong tendency across languages, exceptions are not that uncommon, and some derivational morphemes may be highly productive (e.g., {er} of *walker*).

Inflection and derivation have also been evaluated with respect to **recursiveness**, that is, whether or not they can apply more than once. Typically, inflectional morphemes cannot be reapplied (plural {s} cannot mark a noun twice), while derivational processes can (*engage*, *disengage*, *disengagement*).

The last distinguishing criterion we should mention is whether or not affixes lead to change of word class. Inflectional affixes are expected not to do so because they provide predictable meanings (e.g., number), while derivational affixes typically do (*speak* is a verb, and *speaker* is a noun; *sweet* is an adjective, and *sweeten* is a verb).

Table 3.1 summarizes the criteria typically used to distinguish between derivational and inflectional affixes.

In reality, however, establishing unequivocally whether an affix is inflectional or derivational turns out to be a rather taxing task, and multiple alternative (equally viable) interpretations of a given affix can be proposed depending on the distinguishing parameters selected for the analysis, the theoretical framework adopted, and the language under investigation. Just like the categorization and demarcation of word classes, the distinction between

TABLE 3.1 Differentiating features of derivational and inflectional affixes

	Derivational	*Inflectional*
Semantic transparency/semantic compositionality	Low degree	High degree
Necessity	Optional	Obligatory
Relative order with respect to base	Central	Peripheral
Productivity	Unproductive	Highly productive
Recursiveness	High	Low
Change in word class	High	Low

derivation and inflection is a highly controversial issue in morphology, and '[w]hether a sharp demarcation of inflection with respect to derivation is possible, is a classical problem in morphological theory' (Booij, 2000, p. 361). Controversy and skepticism about positing a clear-cut separation between inflection and derivation arise from the fact that, although there are many examples that clearly attest to the fundamental opposition between inflection and derivation, there are also many cases in which delineating the exact boundary between the two categories is challenging at best. Therefore, there has been a growing tendency in current research in morphology to view inflection and derivation as forming a continuum rather than considering them two dichotomous phenomena (Bybee, 1985; Dressler, 1989; Haspelmath,1996; van Marle, 1996; among others). Within this type of approach, the central distinction to be made is between core (prototypical) properties and peripheral (less- or non-prototypical) properties of derivation and inflection (Dressler, 1989; Scalise, 1984, 1988, 1994; among others).

In very general terms, we can conclude that inflectional morphology deals with elements and processes pertaining to the production of word forms (*writes, wrote, written, writing*); thus, inflectional morphology falls within the domain of morphosyntax. Conversely, derivational morphology deals with elements and processes involved in the creation of new words, which falls within the domain of 'vocabulary' (i.e., lexemes). Nonetheless, it appears that although there are many cases in which the contrast is straightforward, there are also many instances in which the contrast is less obvious. Therefore, setting a clear-cut division between inflection and derivation is untenable, and an approach that relies on prototypical (best vs. worst) cases is preferable because in the end it seems that '[m]orphology is a challenge for any theory of language that is focused on discreteness and regularity, because so much of morphology is neither' (Aronoff & Mark, 2014, p. 69).

The analysis of the morphological properties of the nominal and verbal system of Italian in the next two sections will give us a clearer illustration of the challenges that teasing apart inflection and derivation can present.

3.4 Nominal morphology

In this section we examine the most important morphological and morphosyntactic properties of Italian nouns and of those word classes that are related to nouns by sharing the same or comparable morphological and morphosyntactic patters, namely, adjectives, determiners (i.e., articles and demonstrative), and personal pronouns. Concerning inflection, the grammatical features that bear relevance to the morphological/morphosyntactic structure of the Italian nominal system are number (singular and plural) and gender (masculine and feminine).

While number is, in some sense, 'concretely' motivated, gender is an inherent and, on the whole, arbitrary category because even though the grammatical gender of nouns that have animate referents tends to correspond to biological sex (i.e., nouns denoting male individuals are masculine, and nouns denoting female individuals are feminine), the grammatical gender of nouns that have inanimate referents is unpredictable. The arbitrariness of gender is also evidenced by the fact that the gender of words with the same referent varies across languages (e.g., the Italian nouns *latte* 'milk,' *sale* 'salt' are masculine, whereas Spanish *leche* and *sal* are feminine). In Italian, masculine is the unmarked gender, meaning, that neologisms that are not created through derivation and borrowings are assigned masculine gender, though there are some exceptions, as we will see next.

3.4.1 Nouns, adjectives, and determiners

3.4.1.1 Nouns

Italian nouns can be classified into different groups, or **inflectional classes**, according to the specific types of morphological patterns they instantiate. Traditionally, they are divided into six main inflectional classes, as illustrated in Table 3.2.

The data in Table 3.2 shows that gender and number are expressed together by a single inflectional suffix in classes 1, 2, 4, and 5. Class 3, on the other hand, is only marked for number, and class 6 shows no inflectional marking since it includes invariable nouns. Let's now take a closer look at each inflectional class.

Classes 1 and 2 are the most stable and most productive because they consistently accept underived neologisms and borrowings ending in *-o* (*gazebo, gazpacho*) and *-a* (*bandana, rumba, samba*). Concerning gender, both classes evidence a fairly consistent correspondence between grammatical gender and biological sex, particularly for nouns with human referents. For nouns denoting animals, the correspondence is more erratic; although we find a number of perfect matches (*asino* 'donkey'/*asina, cavallo* 'horse'/*cavalla, gatto* 'cat'/*gatta, mulo* 'mule'/*mula*), there are also many cases in which different words denote the female and the male (*gallina* 'hen'/*gallo* 'rooster,' *mucca* 'cow'/*toro* 'bull,' *pecora* 'sheep'/*montone* 'ram'). Also, there are many cases in which only one form is available, and if gender must be specified, the adjectives *maschio* 'male' and *femmina* 'female' are used (*oca maschio* 'gander'). Two quite important (because of their high frequency) irregular nouns found in class 1 are *mano* 'hand'/*mani*, which is feminine, although it displays the masculine suffixes *-o/-i*, and *uomo* 'man,' whose plural is *uomini* (not *uomi*).

Class 3 remains productive thanks to nouns derived by means of the suffixes *-tore* (masculine) and *-trice* (feminine) (*scrittore/scrittrice* 'writer') and *-zione* (feminine) (*osservazione* 'observation'). Moreover, it includes all nouns in *-ante* (*insegnante* 'teacher'), which, as we will see in the next subsection, are nominal (or adjectival) forms of present participle verb forms. From the perspective of grammar, nouns of this type are ambigender; they can be either masculine of feminine, and the referents' gender is specified by means of adjectives and/or determiners (see following). The gender of non-derived words with animate referents is totally arbitrary (f. *volpe* 'fox' vs. m. *pavone* 'peacock'). If required, the distinction between masculine and feminine is achieved by means of the adjectives *femmina* 'female'/*maschio* 'male' (as for *oca* 'goose,' etc.) or, for some names, by the derivational suffix *-essa*.

TABLE 3.2 Italian inflectional noun classes

Class	Inflectional suffix	Gender	Examples	
1	SG -*o*	masculine	animate	*ragazzo* 'boy'/*ragazzi, orso* 'male bear'/*orsi*
	PL -*i*		inanimate	*albero* 'tree'/*alberi, libro* 'book'/*libri*
2	SG -*a*	feminine	animate	*ragazza* 'girl'/*ragazze, orsa* 'female bear'/*orse*
	PL -*e*		inanimate	*matita* 'pencil'/*matite, pianta* 'plant'/*piante*
3	SG -*e*	masculine	animate	*prete* 'priest'/*preti, leone* 'lion'/*leoni*
	PL -*i*		inanimate	*cuore* 'heart'/*cuori, fiume* 'river'/*fiumi, piede* 'foot'/*piedi*
		feminine	animate	*tigre* 'tiger'/*tigri, volpe* 'fox'/*volpi*
			inanimate	*notte* 'night'/*notti, voce* 'voice'/*voci*
		ambigender	animate	*nipote* 'niece/nephew; grandchild'/*nipoti, insegnante* 'teacher'/*insegnanti*
4	SG -*a*	masculine	animate	*eremita* 'hermit'/*eremiti, papa* 'pope'/*papi, poeta* 'poet'/*poeti*
	PL -*i*			
5	SG -*o*	sg. masculine,	inanimate	*dito* 'finger'/*dita*
	PL -*a*	pl. feminine		
6	invariable	masculine		*re* 'king/s', *caffè* 'coffee/s', *boia* 'executioner/s', *film* 'film/s'
		feminine		*città* 'city/ies', *specie* 'kind/s; species', *crisi* 'crisis/es', *radio* 'radio'

Source: Based on D'Achille, 2010; Lorenzetti, 2002; Palermo, 2020).

Class 4 is essentially unproductive; it survives by addition of sporadic underived neologisms (*acrobata* 'acrobat') and, most of all, by derived words in -*ista* (*artista* 'artist'), -*cida* (*insetticida* 'insecticide'), -*ma* (*fonema* 'phoneme,' *linfoma* 'lymphoma'), -*gramma* (*telegramma* 'telegram').

Class 5 is no longer productive and very small (consisting only of a few dozen words in all), but it includes many core-vocabulary nouns (i.e., nouns that denote everyday life entities), including several body parts terms (*braccio* 'arm'/*braccia, ginocchio* 'knee'/*ginocchia, labbro* 'lip'/*labbra*). This class is the result of language change phenomena.

Class 6 is highly productive because, since it lacks inflectional marking, it absorbs three main groups of nouns: nouns that have lost inflection (i.e., all oxytones, like *virtù* 'virtue'), which are actually truncated forms of variants found in older stages of Italian; monosyllabic words like *re* 'king'; and shortened words like *moto* 'motorcycle' (from *motocicletta*), *cinema* 'movies; movie theatre' (from *cinematografo*), which keep the gender of the original word so that *moto* is feminine but *cinema* is masculine. Furthermore, this class takes in borrowings ending in consonants (*computer, film, sport*), as well as learned words in -*e* (*serie* 'series,' *specie* 'species'), and words of Greek origin ending in -*i* (*ipotesi* 'hypothesis,' *tesi* 'thesis'). Finally, it is enlarged by nouns derived by means of the suffix -*ità* (*celebrità* 'fame; celebrity,' *maternità* 'motherhood; maternity'), which are all feminine, and by some borrowing in -*a* (*mascara, panda, puma*, which are masculine) and in -*o* (*dinamo* 'dynamo,' *radio*, which are feminine).

Before moving to examining adjectives, two issues should be addressed. The first is the stem allomorphy displayed by class 1 nouns with stems ending in a velar stop, as *fuoco* 'fire' and *rogo* 'pyre.' According to the general grammatical rule, paroxytone nouns retain the velar stop (*imbàrco* 'boarding'/*imbar**chi**, dittóngo* 'diphthong'/*ditton**ghi***), while in proparoxytone nouns, the velar becomes a palatal affricate (*mèdico* 'physician'/*medici, asparago* 'asparagus'/*aspàragi*). However, there are exceptions (*amìco* 'friend'/*amici, òbbligo* 'obligation'/*obblighi*); moreover, in the case of nouns derived by means of the affixes –*logo* and -*fago*, many have a double plural (*archeòlogo* 'archeologist'/*archeologi, archeologhi, sarcòfago* 'sarcophagus'/*sarcofagi, sarcofaghi*), while others have opted for the plural in -*ghi* (*catàlogo* 'catalogue'/*cataloghi*).

The last issue to address pertains to the spelling of the plural forms of feminine nouns ending in -*cia*/-*gia*. The general rule is that <i> is kept in the spelling when it is preceded by a vowel (or diphthong) (e.g., *camicia* 'shirt'/*camicie, ciliegia* 'cherry'/*ciliegie* but *pancia* 'belly'/*pance, frangia* 'fringe'/*frange*).

3.4.1.2 Adjectives

Qualitative adjectives typically denote attributes or states of nouns, as opposed, for instance, to **possessive** adjectives, which denote belonging/ownership (*my, your*, etc.), or **quantitative** adjectives (or quantifiers), which refer to amounts (*much, many, little, a few*, etc.). They can be attributive or predicate: **attributive** adjectives modify nouns directly on their own – that is, they are adjacent to the noun (*beautiful girl*) – whereas **predicate** adjectives modify nouns with the help of a verb, usually verbs like 'be' (*she is beautiful*).

Italian adjectives are divided into three primary inflectional classes, as summarized in Table 3.3.

Class 1 adjectives are marked for gender and number by the same inflectional endings of the nominal inflectional classes 1 and 2; class 2 adjectives are unmarked for gender, and their inflectional pattern matches that of nominal class 3; and class 3 adjectives are marked for gender only in the plural. Thus, adjectives agree in gender and number with the nouns they modify.[1] If the referent of the noun includes both masculine and feminine referents, the adjective takes masculine gender (*libri* [m. pl.] *e riviste* [f. pl.] *costosi* [m. pl.] 'expensive books and magazines).

Qualitative adjectives denote gradable notions and usually distinguish three degrees: **positive** (neutral, 'normal,' i.e., the forms in Table 3.3); **comparative**, which involves the comparison between two entities in terms of 'more,' 'less,' 'same'; and **superlative**, which expresses a higher-level comparison ('the most/least') involving three or more entities, or one entity against a group. **Absolute superlative** is another type of superlative which does not involve a comparison but highlights exceptional properties ('very,' 'extremely,' etc.). The comparative and superlative forms of adjectives consist of multiple items (i.e., they are **periphrastic**), as illustrated in (2).

(2) a. ***Più*/*meno** famoso* 'More/less famous.'
  b. ***Tanto** famoso **quanto; così** famoso **come*** 'As famous as.'
  c. ***Il più*/*meno** famoso* 'The most/least famous.'

TABLE 3.3 Italian adjective inflectional classes

Class	SG	PL	Examples
1	-*o*, -*a*	-*i*, -*e*	*freddo* 'cold,' *caldo* 'warm'
2	-*e*	-*i*	*dolce* 'sweet,' *sensibile* 'sensitive'
3	-*a*	-*i*, -*e*	*entusiasta* 'enthusiastic'

TABLE 3.4 Irregular comparative and superlative adjectives

Positive	Comparative	Absolute superlative
buono	migliore 'better; the best'	ottimo 'very good'
cattivo	peggiore 'worse; the worst'	pessimo 'very bad'
grande	maggiore 'greater, bigger; the greater, the biggest'	massimo 'very great, very big'
piccolo	minore 'smaller; the smallest'	minimo 'very small'

The examples in (2) show that the comparative form is realized by means of the adverbs *più* 'more,' *meno* 'less,' and *tanto . . . quanto/così . . . come* 'as' briefly, and the superlative form includes the definite article *il* in (2c), a form that we will examine shortly.

In contrast, absolute superlative forms are formed by the inflectional suffix *-issimo/a*, so they are class 1 adjectives (*muro altissimo* 'very tall walls'/*muri altissimi, libro interessante* 'interesting book'/*libri interessantissimi*). However, periphrastic variants consisting of a number of words meaning 'very; much,' such as *molto, tanto, assai* (or words as *estremamente* 'extremely,' 'incredibly,' etc.), are also quite common. A more recent tendency, which seems to be gaining increased acceptance, is to derive superlative forms by prefixation.

Four high-frequency adjectives, *buono* 'good,' *cattivo* 'bad,' *grande* 'big,' and *piccolo* 'small,' have comparative and superlative forms which do not conform to the pattern we just described, as shown in Table 3.4.

These irregular comparative and superlative forms (which Italian inherited from Latin) have been declining, and they are often replaced by the periphrastic comparative and superlative forms (*più buono, il più cattivo*) and the absolute superlative in *-issimo*.

3.4.1.3 Determiners

The word class of determiners comprises words that precede (or introduce) nouns and typically provide information pertaining to reference, quantity, proximity, and gender. The main subclasses of determiners are articles, demonstratives, quantifiers, and possessives. **Articles** primarily convey information related to definiteness and identifiability (more precisely, the speaker's assumptions about whether or not the referent of the noun modified by the article is identifiable by the addressee). Thus, **indefinite** articles typically introduce into the discourse a referent supposed to be unidentifiable by the addressee, that is, indefinite articles mark nouns which stand for the 'type' of entity they denote. For instance, if we say *A dog is barking*, we don't expect our addressee to be able to identify the referent of 'dog.' Conversely, **definite** articles mark nouns that have a 'uniquely identifiable' referent, which the speaker assumes to be identifiable by the addressee so that if we say *The dog is barking*, we do assume that our addressee will know which dog we are talking about.

Just like English, Italian has both definite and indefinite articles. Of course, Italian articles must agree with the nouns they modify in gender and number; the forms of the Italian definite and indefinite articles are given in Table 3.5.

Table 3.5 shows that indefinite articles have only singular forms; plural indefinite nouns are introduced by indefinite adjectives (e.g., *alcuni/alcune* 'some; a few') or, more commonly, by the preposition *di* 'of' combined with definite articles (*dei ragazzi* 'some boys,' *delle ragazze* 'some girls,' *degli studenti* 'some students').[2] Moreover, we notice that, except for the feminine

TABLE 3.5 Italian definite and indefinite articles

	Masculine		Feminine	
	SG	PL	SG	PL
Definite	il, lo, l'	i, gli	la, l'	le
Indefinite	un, uno		una, un'	

TABLE 3.6 Modern Standard Italian masculine definite article allomorphs and their distribution

Environments	Example	Allomorphs
Single consonant except /ʃ/ and /ɲ/	cane 'dog'	
/tʃ/, /dʒ/	cerbiatto 'fawn,' genitore 'parent	un, il, i
Consonant clusters: stop, /f/ + /r, l/	bruco 'caterpillar,' flauto 'flute'	
Consonant clusters: /s/+ C	scoiattolo 'squirrel'	
/ts/, /dz/	zio 'uncle,' zaino 'backpack'	uno, lo, gli
j/, /ʃ/, /ɲ/	ione 'ion,' scialle 'shawl,' gnomo 'elf'	
/ps/, /pn/, /pt/, /ks/, /kt/	psichiatra 'psychiatrist,' pneumatico 'tire,' pterodattilo 'pterodactyl,' xilofono 'xylophone,' ctenodattilo 'ctenodactylus'	
Vowels and diphthongs	amico 'friend,' uovo 'egg'	un, l', gli

Source: Based on Russi, 2006, p. 585).

plural definite article, all other articles have allomorphs. The feminine indefinite and singular definite articles have each two allomorphs: the full forms *una* and *la* for nouns beginning with a consonant/consonant cluster (*una/la farfalla* 'a/the butterfly,' *una/la fragola* 'a/the strawberry'), and a shorter form, *un,' l,'* for nouns beginning with a vowel/diphthong (*un'/l'isola* 'a/the island,' *un'/l'automobile* 'a/the automobile'). But there is only one form for the plural definite (*le farfalle, le fragole, le isole*).

The masculine articles exhibit a more complex allomorphy, with a total of seven variants: two for the indefinite article, three for the definite singular article, and two for the definite plural article, as summarized in Table 3.6. The definite and indefinite masculine article allomorphs are the outcome of morpho-phonological changes whose precise dynamics remain a matter of debate among scholars.

Demonstratives convey **deictic** meaning (from Greek *deixis* (δεῖξις) 'demonstration') since they point to the place, time, or situation of the discourse, that is, they specify how 'near' (concretely or metaphorically) the referent they modify is to a discourse event in terms of where, when, and how it occurs from the speaker's perspective. Italian has two sets of demonstratives: **proximal**, denoting 'near to the speaker,' and **distal**, denoting 'close to the addressee; away from the speaker and addressee'; their full paradigm is given in Table 3.7.[3]

We see in Table 3.7 that the final parts (in bold) of the distal demonstrative forms is the definite article; hence, they display the same distribution pattern as the definite article allomorphs.

The category of **possessives** comprises items that denote possession relationships in general. Here, we limit our discussion to possessive adjectives (or determiners), which

TABLE 3.7 Italian demonstratives

	Proximal		Distal	
	Masculine	*Feminine*	*Masculine*	*Feminine*
SG	*questo, quest'*	*questa, quest'*	*quel, quell', quello*	*quella, quell'*
PL	*questi*	*queste*	*quei, quegli*	*quelle*

TABLE 3.8 Italian possessives

	Possessed masculine		*Possessed feminine*	
Possessor	SG	PL	SG	PL
1SG 'my'	*mio*	*miei*	*mia*	*mie*
2SG 'your'	*tuo*	*tuoi*	*tua*	*tue*
3SG 'his/her'	*suo*	*suoi*	*sua*	*sue*
1PL 'our'	*nostro*	*nostri*	*nostra*	*nostre*
2PL 'your'	*vostro*	*vostri*	*vostra*	*vostre*
3PL 'their'	*loro*			

denote the possessor (*my, your,* etc.) and can also function as pronouns. Two important distinctive properties of Italian possessives deserve attention. First, they agree in gender and number with the possessed entity rather than with the possessor so that the phrase *la sua penna* means 'his/her pen.' Thus, Italian possessive adjectives are inflected for person and number of the possessor, and gender and number of the possessed entity, as summarized in Table 3.8.

Except for third-person plural *loro,* which is invariable, the paradigm of Italian possessives is highly regular and falls into the inflectional class 1 of adjectives.

The second distinctive property of Italian possessive adjectives is that they co-occur with definite articles (3a), except when the possessed entity denotes a singular family member/relation (3b) and is not modified by adjectives (3c) or evaluative suffixes (3d).

(3) a. SG: ***il*** *mio libro* 'my book'; PL: ***i*** *miei libri.*
  b. SG: *mio padre* 'my father,' *mia madre* 'my mother,' *tua sorella* 'your sister'; PL: ***i*** *miei genitori* 'my parents,' *le tue sorelle.*
  c. SG: ***la*** *sua sorella minore* 'his/her younger sister'; PL: *le sue sorelle minori* 'his/her younger sisters.'
  d. SG: ***la*** *nostra sorellina* 'our little sister'; PL: ***le*** *nostre sorelline* 'our little sisters.'

Note that the family relations involved in this phenomenon include blood and acquired relations, that is, *marito* 'husband'/*moglie* 'wife,' *suocero/suocera* 'father-/mother-in-law,' *genero/nuora* 'son-/daughter-in law,' *cognato/cognata* 'brother-/sister-in-law' but not *fidanzato* 'fiancé' and *fidanzata* 'fiancée.'

Determiners hold an important place in morphosyntax since they may be the only cue to identify gender and/or number of nouns lacking overt gender/number specification (*questa/questo artista* 'this artist' *la/le virtù* 'the virtue/s).

3.4.2 Pronouns

Conventionally, the term **pronoun** is defined as a word that can replace a noun or noun phrase (i.e., a noun plus modifiers, as *un libro interessante*). Like demonstratives, pronouns are deictic elements because they index the role that entities have in the speech act. **Personal** pronouns are pronouns which refer to the discourse participants: the speaker/writer (first person), the listener/reader (second person), and other participants (third person). They are the most basic subcategory of pronouns. Other types of pronouns commonly found across languages are reflexive/reciprocal, indefinite, interrogative, and relative pronouns. Also, as already noted, demonstratives and possessives typically have pronominal function as well. Although pronouns function as nouns, they do not co-occur with modifiers (adjectives, determiners, quantifiers).

3.4.2.1 Personal pronouns

Italian distinguishes two basic groups of pronouns according to their grammatical function: subject and complement pronouns. The paradigm of subject pronouns is given in Table 3.9, which shows that only the third-person forms are inflected for number and gender.

The system of Italian complement pronouns is more complex. As shown in Table 3.10, it comprises two subsets, stressed (tonic) and unstressed (atonic, clitic) pronouns, and unstressed pronouns are further divided into **direct** and **indirect** object complement forms.

Like subject pronouns, object pronouns are inflected for gender and number only in the third person, with the exception of plural stressed *loro* and plural unstressed indirect object *gli*. The forms *egli*, *ella*, *essi*, and *esse* are quite rare, both in the spoken and written language; in the spoken language, the third-person singular indirect object *gli* is frequently extended to feminine referents.

TABLE 3.9 Subject pronouns

Person	Singular	Plural
1	*io* 'I'	*noi* 'we'
2	*tu* 'you'	*voi* 'you'
3M	*egli, lui* 'he'; *esso* 'it'	*essi, loro* 'they'
3F	*ella, lei* 'she'; *essa* 'it'	*esse, loro* 'they'

TABLE 3.10 Complement pronouns

Person	Stressed	Unstressed	
		DO	*IO*
1SG	*me* 'me'	*mi* 'me'	*mi* 'to me'
2SG	*te* 'you'	*ti* 'you'	*ti* 'to you'
3SG	*lui* 'him,' *lei* 'her'	*lo* 'him; it.M,' *la* 'her; it.F'	*gli* 'to him,' *le* 'to her'
1PL	*noi* 'us'	*ci* 'us'	*ci* 'to us'
2PL	*voi* 'you'	*vi* 'you'	*vi* 'to you'
3PL	*loro* 'them.M/F'	*li* 'them.M,' *le* 'them.F'	*gli* 'to them.M/F'

Stressed pronouns always follow the verb; moreover, they are used to express grammatical relations other than direct object accompanied by prepositions, for example, benefactive (*lo faccio **per te*** 'I do it for you'), comitative (*vengo **con lui*** 'I come with him'), locative (*vieni **da noi*** 'come to us [to our place]'). In the case of direct and indirect object complements, stressed and unstressed forms bear different functions at the level of discourse information structure, that is, how interlocutors' mental representations of meaning and their corresponding linguistic utterances interface. For instance, the stressed forms are used to convey contrast, as illustrated in (4).

(4)   a.   Direct object: ***la*** *vedo* 'I see her' vs. *vedo **lei**, non lui* 'I see her, not him.'
     b.   Indirect object: ***ti*** *presto il libro* 'I lend you the book' vs. *presto il libro **a te** ma non a lui* 'I lend the book to you but not to him.'

3.4.2.2 Relative, indefinite, and interrogative pronouns

Relative pronouns introduce relative clauses (*that, who, whom, which*, etc.), so they refer to the noun heading the relative clause (e.g., in *the man who came*, the relative pronoun *who* refers to *the man*). Italian has three forms of relative pronouns: invariable *che*, and two periphrastic forms, the first consisting of a preposition (which expresses the grammatical function of the pronoun) and invariable *cui*, and the second formed by the definite article (which agrees in gender and number with the pronoun referent) and *quale* (which inflects for number only). As shown in (5), these three forms fulfill different grammatical functions: *che* carries subject and direct object function; 'preposition' + *cui* serves for all other types of complements; and 'definite article' + *quale* theoretically covers all functions, though in present-day standard Italian, it is rarely used as subject and direct object.

(5)   a.   Subject: *La persona **che** è arrivata* 'The person who arrived.'
     b.   Direct object: *La persona **che** ho conosciuto* 'The person whom I met.'
     c.   Indirect object: *La persona **a cui**/**al quale** ho scritto* 'The person to whom I wrote.'
     d.   Comitative: *La persona **con cui**/**con la quale** ho cenato* 'The person with whom I dined.'
     e.   Instrument: *Il coltello **con cui**/**con il quale** affetto il pane* 'The knife with which I slice bread.'
     f.   Other complements: *La persona **per cui**/**per la quale** lavoro* 'The person for whom I work'; *Il problema **di cui**/**del quale** ti ho parlato* 'The problem I talked to you about.'

Personal and relative pronouns have unique referents (antecedents); they refer to participants present or previously introduced into the discourse event, and the latter can also refer to entities. **Indefinite pronouns**, on the other hand, refer to non-uniquely identified members of a set and are divided into two main subclasses: **universal** pronouns, which refer to all members of the set either individually (*ognuno, ciascuno* 'each one') or collectively (*tutti/tutte* 'all'), and **partitive** pronouns, which refer to single members (*qualcuno* 'somebody,' *nessuno* 'nobody,' *qualcosa* 'something,' *alcuni/alcune* 'some; a few').

Interrogative pronouns are used in questions, both direct and indirect, and have the function of identifying referents unknown by the speaker (who is posing the question to the addressee). The Italian interrogative pronouns are *chi* 'who' (*Chi ha parlato?* 'Who has spoken?'), *che cosa* 'what' (*Che cosa hai detto?* 'What have you said?'), and *quale/quali* 'which (one/s)' (*Quale/Quali hai comprato?* 'Which one/ones have you bought?').

We have seen that determiners and pronouns are deictic elements. In fact, in many languages determiners and pronouns can overlap to some extent; for example, in Indonesian, demonstratives also mark definiteness (e.g., *buku itu* 'that/the book'; Evans, 2000, p. 716). Syntactically, articles are often equivalent to demonstrative in terms of distribution since they usually occur in the outermost position within the noun phrase (*the/that old book*); also, demonstratives and possessives can have determiner or pronominal function. Lastly, demonstratives and pronouns (as in the case of Italian) are common diachronic sources for definite articles.

3.5 Verbal morphology

3.5.1 Types of verbs

Before delving into the specific morphological features of Italian verbs, a brief overview of this word class may be helpful. Morphologically, verbs are typically more complex than nouns. Specifically, they can host clause-level morphemes expressing, for instance, **tense**, which establishes temporal relations between the state of affair denoted by the verb and the time of the utterance; **evidentiality**, which conveys the speaker's evidence or source of information about the utterance (expressed lexically in English, for example, *I heard you graduated*; *I saw you sneaking in*); **aspect**, which specifies how the state of affairs denoted by a verb extends over time, hence is tightly related to tense; **mood/modality**, which refers to the speaker's attitude toward the factual content of the utterance (e.g., certainty, possibility, probability, necessity, obligation); **voice** (active vs. passive); and **valence** (transitive vs. intransitive). Cross-linguistically, the most common verbal inflections are for tense, aspect, mood, and person and number. Person and number tend to be marked jointly by a single indivisible morpheme; this is the case for Italian, as we will see shortly.

An important distinction is the one between lexical verbs and auxiliaries. From a semantic perspective, **lexical** (or content) verbs can be defined as words describing events, actions, and in some languages, states. That is, lexical verbs can be defined as verbs denoting 'processes' understood as existing relations, which can be stable and unchanging or inherently dynamic (Langacker, 1987). Prototypical lexical verbs refer to concrete, dynamic, visible, and effective actions, for instance, *to build*, *to eat*, etc. However, since verbs often denote non-prototypical percepts (i.e., abstract, stable situations, for example, *to see*, *to think*), the term **state of affairs** more aptly covers the range of meanings verbs can express.

Conversely, **auxiliaries** convey grammatical meaning; they typically carry a broad range of temporal, aspectual, and modal (i.e., mood-related) functions, as well as voice. Diachronically, auxiliaries commonly derive from lexical verbs but have reached a stage when they function as 'helping' verbs, forming periphrastic constructions with non-finite forms of lexical (main) verbs to supply them grammatical specifications. Italian has two primary auxiliaries, *essere* 'be' and *avere* 'have'; they both express tense/aspect, and *essere* also expresses passive voice. A third auxiliary is *stare* 'stay,' which marks progressive aspect. The main auxiliaries expressing modality (or simply modals) are *dovere*, *potere*, *volere*. *Dovere* conveys obligation (*devono studiare* 'they must/have to study') or possibility/probability (*devono essere a casa* '(I think/assume) they are home'); *potere* expresses permission (*puoi andare al cinema* 'you can/ are allowed to go to the movies'); and *volere* denotes volition (*voglio andare al cinema* 'I want to go to the movies'). Morphologically, Italian auxiliaries and modals behave like lexical verbs, that is, they share the same inflectional markers as lexical verbs, though they may lack some forms.

3.5.2 Inflectional classes and categories

Italian verbs are divided into three inflectional classes, or **conjugations**, according to the **thematic** vowel, the vowel that occurs after the root, as seen in Table 3.11. They have both **finite** forms inflected for person/number, tense, mood, and **non-finite** forms, which may be inflected for number and gender but never for person. Verbal inflectional suffixes attach either to the root or the stem (i.e., the root plus the thematic vowel).

Past participle forms inflect for gender and number, following the pattern of class 1 nouns (m. *amato*/-*i*, f. *amata*/-*e*). A fourth non-finite form is the present participle, marked by the suffix -*nte* (hence, inflected for number only), which presently functions only as a noun (*amante* 'lover') or adjective (*divertente* 'funny; entertaining').

The first conjugation is the most regular and most productive. Verbs of the second conjugation can be stressed on the thematic vowel (*vedére* 'see,' *temére* 'fear') or on the root (*lèggere* 'read,' *rìdere* 'laugh'). This conjugation is no longer productive and is characterized by numerous irregular paradigms. The third conjugation comprises a rather-large subclass characterized by the infix -*isc*-, which marks the first-, second-, and third-person singular and the third-person plural forms of the present indicative and present subjunctive (*finisco, finisci, finisce, finiscono* 'I, you (sg.), she/he, they understand; pres. ind.' vs. *finiamo, finite* 'we, you (pl.) finish; pres. ind.') and the second-person singular imperative (*Finisci!*). This infix is a historical 'residue' from Latin, where it expressed the beginning of an event, a function it no longer has in Italian.

Italian finite verb forms are inflected for person/number, tense/aspect, and mood, and inflectional marking of these categories is usually fused in a single suffix. Three persons and two numbers are distinguished, resulting in six forms.

Three main tenses are then distinguished, present, future, and past: **present** tense signals that the state of affairs denoted by the verb takes place at the same time as the utterance (i.e., it expresses contemporaneity); **future** tense situates states of affairs in a time after the utterance (i.e., it marks posteriority); and **past** tense places them in a time before the utterance (i.e., it denotes anteriority). The past tense is linked to the aspectual distinction between perfective and imperfective. **Perfective** aspect gives states of affairs an endpoint so that they are viewed as unified and complete, rather than viewing them from a perspective that makes reference to their internal temporal structure and is expressed by the **preterite** (It. *passato remoto*, lit. 'remote past'). Conversely, **imperfective** aspect assigns internal temporal structure; it includes several subcategories, such as progressive, habitual, and iterative, and is expressed by the **imperfect**, a form that indicates the durative nature of the state of affairs denoted by the verb. While perfective is marked together with person/number (and mood), imperfective is marked separately by the affix -*v*- (*amavo* 'I used to love').

Mood includes four subcategories. **Indicative** is associated with statements the speaker believes to be true. **Subjunctive** is related to uncertainty, unreality, or desire and occurs primarily in subordinate sentences (*credo che (non) sia vero* 'I think that it is (not) true,' *voglio*

TABLE 3.11 Italian conjugation classes: non-finite forms

Class	Thematic vowel	Infinitive	Past participle	Gerund
1	-*a*-	*ama-re* 'love'	*ama-to* 'loved'	*ama-ndo* 'loving'
2	-*e*-	*cade-re* 'fall'	*cadu-to* 'fallen'	*cade-ndo* 'falling'
3	-*i*-	*dormi-re* 'sleep'	*dormi-to* 'slept'	*dorme-ndo*

TABLE 3.12 Inflectional paradigms of indicative, subjunctive, and conditional simple forms: *amare*

	Indicative				Subjunctive		Conditional
	Present	*Future*	*Preterite*	*Imperfect*	*Present*	*Imperfect*	*Present*
1SG	*àm-o*	*am-er-ò*	*am-à-i*	*am-à-v-o*	*àm-i*	*am-à-ss-i*	*am-er-éi*
2SG	*àm-i*	*am-er-ài*	*am-àsti*	*am-à-v-i*	*àm-i*	*am-à-ss-e*	*am-er-ésti*
3SG	*àm-a*	*am-er-à*	*am-ò*	*am-à-v-a*	*àm-i*	*am-à-ss-e*	*am-er-èbbe*
1PL	*am-iàmo*	*am-er-émo*	*am-à-mmo*	*am-a-v-àmo*	*am-iàmo*	*am-a-ss-ìmo*	*am-er-émmo*
2PL	*am-à-te*	*am-er-éte*	*am-à-ste*	*am-a-v-àte*	*am-iàte*	*am-à-s-te*	*am-er-éste*
3PL	*àm-a-no*	*am-er-ànno*	*am-à-rono*	*am-à-v-ano*	*àm-ino*	*am-à-ss-ero*	*am-er-èbbero*

TABLE 3.13 Indicative, subjunctive, and conditional periphrastic forms: 1SG *camminare* 'walk' and *andare* 'go'

Tense	Indicative	
Present perfect	**ho** *camminato*	**sono** *andato/a*
Pluperfect	**avevo** *camminato*	**ero** *andato/a*
Past perfect	**ebbi** *camminato*	**fui** *andato/a*
Future perfect	**avrò** *camminato*	**sarò** *andato/a*
	Subjunctive	
Past	**abbia** *camminato*	**sia** *andato/a*
Pluperfect	**avessi** *camminato*	**fossi** *andato/a*
	Conditional	
Past	**avrei** *camminato*	**sarei** *andato/a*

che tu **venga** *con me* 'I want that you come with me'). **Conditional** conveys implied conditions, suppositions, or approximations that states of affairs are contingent upon. **Imperative** is used to impart commands and thus has only the second-person singular and plural forms (*Studia!/Studiate!* 'Study!') and the first plural form with exhortative value (*Andiamo!* 'Let's go!'). Indicative, subjunctive, and conditional are also marked for tense.

Table 3.12 illustrates the inflectional paradigms of the simple forms through the first conjugation verb *amare*. Periphrastic (compound) forms are addressed in the next section.

Note that the imperfect subjunctive displays the temporal/mood/aspect infix *-ss-*, inserted between the thematic vowel and the person/number suffix (like the imperfect infix *-v-*), and the future and present conditional show the temporal/mood infix *-er-* which attaches between the base and the person/number suffix.

Italian has a plethora of irregular verbs, many of which are, in fact, high-frequency verbs, such as the two auxiliaries *avere* and *essere* (see Table 3.13 below), *andare* 'go,' *dare* 'give,' *fare* 'do; make,' *venire* 'go.'

3.5.3 Periphrastic forms

As shown in Table 3.13, Italian has seven main periphrastic verb forms: four for the indicative (present perfect, past perfect, pluperfect, and future perfect/anterior), two for the subjunctive (past and pluperfect), and one for the conditional (past). These are perfective forms and consist of the conjugated forms of the auxiliary verbs *avere* (for transitive verbs and a subclass of intransitive verbs) or *essere* (for the subclass of intransitive verbs known as **unaccusatives**, and for the passive voice) followed by the past participle of the main verb.[4]

The periphrastic forms express secondary temporal relations because they involve another temporal dimension in addition to utterance time and event time, as illustrated in (6–10). Theoretically, the **present perfect** stands in opposition to the preterit since it refers to states of affairs that took place in the past but are related to the utterance time either at a factual (6a) or a psychological/affective level (6b). As noted earlier, however, the preterit holds a rather marginal place in the spoken language of central and northern speakers.

(6)   a.   **Ho studiato** *italiano tanti anni fa ma lo parlo ancora.*
          'I studied Italian many years ago, but I can still speak it.'
      b.   *Questa è la casa in cui* **ha vissuto**, *Giacomo Leopardi, il mio scrittore preferito.*
          'This is the house where my favorite writer, Giacomo Leopardi lived.'

The **pluperfect** (7a) and the **past perfect** indicative (7b) refer to events that occurred prior to other past events, though in contemporary Italian, the use of the past perfect is rather marginal (in fact, practically absent in the spoken language).

(7)   a.   **Avevo** *appena* **finito** *di cenare, quando mi hai telefonato.*
          'I had just finished to have dinner when you phoned me.'
      b.   *Non appena* **ebbe finito** *di cenare, andò a dormire.*
          'As soon as he finished eating dinner, he went to sleep.'

The **future perfect** denotes events that occur before another future event, so it is a sort of 'past in the future' (8a); like the simple future, it can have modal value (8b).

(8)   a.   *Quando* **avrò finito** *i compiti, farò una passeggiata.*
          'When I finish my homework, I'll take a walk.'
      b.   **Avrà piovuto**, *la strada è tutta bagnata.*
          'It must have rained; the road is all wet.'

The **past subjunctive** denotes events that the speaker assumes to have occurred before the utterance time (9a), while the **pluperfect subjunctive** is used in subordinate clauses when the verb of the main clause is in the imperfect (9b).

(9)   a.   *Credo che tu* **abbia fatto** *un grosso errore.*
          'I think that you made a big mistake.'
      b.   *Credevo che tu* **avessi capito**.
          'I thought you had understood.'

Finally, the **past conditional** expresses unrealized past events.

(10)   **Avrei voluto** *andare in Italia l'estate scorsa.*
        'I would have liked to go to Italy last summer.'

Another verbal periphrasis to note is the progressive, which is inherently imperfective. It is formed by the auxiliary verb *stare* 'stay' and the gerund (*sto pensando* 'I am thinking') and can occur in all mood and tenses, except, of course, the imperative.

3.6 Exercises

1. Provide concise but complete answers to the following questions, illustrating with examples.

   a. Define the notions of phoneme and allophone.
   b. What is the difference between bound and free morpheme?
   c. Define the notions of word form and lexeme.
   d. What is a complex word?
   e. Explain the contrast between paradigmatic and syntagmatic approach to morphological analysis.
   f. What is a word class? What are the major word classes identified in the literature? What are some of the main problems related to the classification of word classes?
   g. What is the difference between tense and aspect?

2. Are the following statements correct or incorrect? Explain your answer, providing illustrative examples.

   a. Grammatical gender is arbitrary.
   b. All Italian nouns and adjectives are inflected for number and gender.
   c. The paradigm of the masculine definite article comprises two forms.
   d. Italian personal pronouns are marked for gender, number, and case.
   e. Italian lacks synthetic absolute superlative forms of adjectives.
   f. The verb system of Italian lacks periphrastic forms.

3. Determine whether the following sets of words are word forms of a single lexeme or different lexemes. Justify your answers.

   a. *Sorrido* 'I smile,' *sorriderebbero* 'they would smile,' *sta sorridendo* 's/he is smiling,' *avete sorriso* 'you.PL (have) smiled,' *sorridere* 'to smile.'
   b. *Folle* 'mad,' *follia* 'madness,' *follemente* 'madly.'
   c. *Braccio* 'arm,' *braccia* 'arms,' *bracci* 'arms.'
   d. *Brodo* 'broth,' *brodino* 'light broth,' *brodetto* 'fish soup.'
   e. *Pieno* 'full,' *pienissimo* very full,' *piena* 'flood.'
   f. *Fronte* 'forehead,' *fronte* 'front,' *frontale* 'frontal' *frontino* 'headband,' *frontone* 'pediment.'

4. Divide the following words into their constituent morphemes, then identify each morpheme (root/affix, free/bound, lexical/grammatical, etc.) and the function they express.

   a. *Labbra* 'lips.'
   b. *Ballavo* 'I danced.'
   c. *Puliscono* 'they clean.'
   d. *Irresponsabilmente* 'irresponsibly.'
   e. *Intelligentissimo* 'very intelligent.'
   f. *Ricominciare* 'to start again.'

5. The following phrases are incorrect. Explain why, then provide the correct versions.

   a. *Mia macchina* 'my car.'
   b. *La mia sorella* 'my sister.'
   c. *Un zaino nuovo* 'a new backpack.'

d.   *Magliette viole* 'Purple t-shirts.'
e.   *Sciarpe e cappelli nere* 'Black scarfs and hats.'
f.   *Il libro cui ho letto* 'The book I read.'
g.   *Il libro cui ho letto* 'The book I read.'
h.   *Non ho mai andato in Italia* 'I have never gone to Italy.'

6.   Identify and label all the pronouns in the following excerpt from *Le avventure di Pinocchio. Storia di un burattino* by (Collodi, 1983, p. 11).

Il carabiniere, senza punto smuoversi, lo acciuffò pulitamente per il naso (era un *nasone spropositato, che pareva fatto apposta per essere acchiappato dai carabinieri), e lo riconsegnò nelle proprie mani di Geppetto; il quale, . . ., voleva dargli subito una buona tiratina d'orecchi. Ma figuratevi come rimase quando, nel cercargli gli orecchi, non gli riuscì di poterli trovare: e sapete perché? perché, nella furia di scolpirlo, si era dimenticato di farglieli.*

'The carabiniere, without moving, neatly grabbed him by the nose (it was a huge nose, which seemed to be made precisely for the purpose of being grabbed by the carabinieri), and handed him back to Geppetto who, . . . wanted to tweak his ears right there. Imagine, then, how he felt when, looking for his ears, he couldn't find them; and do you know why? Because having carved him in such a haste, he had forgotten to make them for him.'

Notes

1 A fourth fairly small class includes invariable adjectives, primarily adjectives denoting colors (*viola* 'purple,' *rosa* 'pink').
2 When the preposition *di* merges with definite articles, [i] changes into [e]; this phonological process (known as vowel lowering, since the high front vowel becomes close-mid) is the outcome of diachronic change.
3 A third form from older stages of Italian, which survives in some regional varieties, is *codesto* 'near the addressee.'
4 Unaccusative verbs are a subclass of intransitive verbs characterized by a non-agentive subject, that is, a subject that is not the initiator of the event denoted by the verb (*cadere* 'fall,' *morire* 'die'). Unaccusative verbs contrast with unergative verbs, another subclass of intransitive verbs which have agentive subjects instead (*lavorare* 'work', *parlare* 'speak').

Bibliography

Aronoff, M., & Mark, L. (2014). Productivity, blocking, and lexicalization. In R. Lieber & P. Štekauer (Eds.), *The Oxford handbook of derivational morphology* (pp. 67–75). Oxford University Press.

Baker, M. C. (2003). *Lexical categories: Verbs, nouns, and adjectives*. Cambridge University Press.

Bauer, L. (2001). *Morphological productivity*. Cambridge University Press.

Bauer, L. (2016). Classical morphemics: Assumptions, extensions, and alternatives. In A. Hippisley & G. Stump (Eds.), *The Cambridge handbook of morphology* (pp. 331–355). Cambridge University Press.

Bauer, L. (2019). *Rethinking morphology*. Edinburgh University Press.

Bauer, L., Lieber, R., & Plag, I. (2013). *The Oxford reference guide to English morphology*. Oxford University Press.

Blevins, J. (2014). Infixation. In R. Lieber & P. Štekauer (Eds.), *The Oxford handbook of derivational morphology* (pp. 136–153). Oxford University Press.

Booij, G. (2000). Inflection and derivation. In G. Booij, C. Lehmann & J. Mugdan (Eds.), *Morphologie ein internationals Handbuch zur Flexion und Wortbildung, 1. Halbband/Morphology: An international handbook on inflection and word-formation* (Vol. 1) (pp. 360–369). Walter De Gruyter.

Booij, G. (2004). *Grammar of words: An introduction to linguistic morphology*. Oxford University Press.

Bybee, J. L. (1985). *Morphology: A study of the relation between meaning and form*. John Benjamins.

Carstairs-McCarthy, A. (1999). *The origins of complex language: An inquiry into the evolutionary origins of sentences, syllables, and truth*. Oxford University Press.

Collodi, C. (1983). *Le avventure di Pinocchio. Storia di un burattino*. Fondazione Nazionale Carlo Collodi.

D'Achille, P. (2010). *L'italiano contemporaneo* (3rd ed.). Il Mulino.

Dressler, W. U. (1989). Prototypical differences between inflection and derivation. *Zeitschrift für Phonetik, Sprachwissenschaft und Kommunikationsforschung, 42*, 3–10.

Evans, N. (2000). Word classes in the world's languages. In G. Booij, C. Lehmann, & J. Mugdan (Eds.), *Morphologie ein internationals Handbuch zur Flexion und Wortbildung, 1. Halbband/morphology: An international handbook on inflection and word-formation* (Vol. 1, pp. 708–732). Walter De Gruyter.

Fábregas, A., & Scalise, S. (2012). *Morphology: From data to theories*. Edinburgh University Press.

Greenberg, J. H. (1963). Some universals of grammar with particular reference to the order of meaningful elements. In J. H. Greenberg (Ed.), *Universals of language* (pp. 73–113). MIT Press.

Haspelmath, M. (1996). Category-changing inflection. *Yearbook of Morphology, 1995*, 54–66.

Haspelmath, M. (2002). *Understanding morphology*. Oxford University Press.

Hippisley, A., & Stump, G. (Eds.). (2016). *The Cambridge handbook of morphology*. Cambridge University Press.

Iacobini, C., & Thornton, A. (2016). Morphologia e formazione delle parole. In S. Lubello (Ed.), *Manuale di linguistica italiana* (pp. 190–221). de Gruyter.

Jensen, J. T. (1990). *Morphology*. John Benjamins.

Langacker, R. W. (1987). *Foundations of cognitive grammar. Vol. 1: Theoretical prerequisites*. Stanford University Press.

Lorenzetti, L. (2002). *L'italiano contemporaneo*. Carocci.

Matthews, P. H. (1991). *Morphology* (2nd ed.). Cambridge University Press.

McCarthy, J. J., & Prince, A. (1993). Generalized alignment. *Yearbook of Morphology, 12*. https://scholarworks.umass.edu/linguist_faculty_pubs/12

Mel'čuk, I. (2000). Morphological processes. In G. Booij, C. Lehmann, & J. Mugdan (Eds.), *Morphologie ein internationals Handbuch zur Flexion und Wortbildung, 1. Halbband/morphology: An international handbook on inflection and word-formation* (Vol. 1, pp. 523–535). Walter De Gruyter.

Palermo, M. (2020). *Linguistica italiana* (2nd ed.). Il Mulino.

Russi, C. (2006). A "usage-based" analysis of the allomorphy of the Italian masculine definite article. *Studies in Language, 30*(3), 575–598.

Scalise, S. (1984). *Generative morphology*. Foris.

Scalise, S. (1988). Inflection and derivation. *Linguistics, 26*, 561–581.

Scalise, S. (1994). *Morfologia*. Il Mulino.

Thornton, A. M. (2005). *Morfologia*. Carocci.

van Marle, J. (1996). The unity of morphology: On the interwovenness of the derivational and inflectional dimension of the word. *Yearbook of Morphology, 1995*, 67–82.

4

THE LEXICON

This chapter examines the Italian lexicon, that is, the body of 'words' available to Italian speakers. After providing a brief characterization of the notion of lexicon and introducing some related terminology, the basic structure of the Italian lexicon is sketched, focusing on its major components, lexical items inherited from Latin and lexical items borrowed from other languages. Next, the two main processes through which new words are formed are examined: derivation, which combines a free morpheme with one (or more) bound morpheme, and compounding, through which free morphemes join together to form a single (complex) word. Finally, some additional processes through which new words may be coined are briefly surveyed, namely, conversion, backformation, reduction, and blending.

4.1 Lexicon and related terms

In its technical (linguistic) meaning, the term **lexicon** denotes the complete set of words (more accurately, meaningful units) of a language; more broadly, however, it also refers to subparts of the set, such as the lexicon of a field of studies or a domain of activity (the lexicon of linguistics, chemistry, etc.), or even that of individuals (e.g., Dante Alighieri's lexicon). To some extent, *lexicon* is synonymous with **vocabulary**, though by 'vocabulary of a language' we typically mean a subset of its lexicon, mostly referring to technical, specialized languages, so that a vocabulary usually comprises terms whose meaning is highly specific and restricted. Moreover, *vocabulary* is synonymous with **dictionary**, which is basically a compilation (either in paper or electronic format) of words typically listed in alphabetical order and each accompanied by a description of their meanings, and possibly (depending on the dictionaries' size and scope) by some information about pronunciation, etymology, synonyms, and examples illustrating their various uses. Dictionaries, then, are practical guides which provide helpful references about the lexicon to language users. Dictionaries differ crucially from the lexicon because they will never cover the entire lexicon not only because of practical user-friendliness limitations but also (and more importantly) because the lexicon is in a constant state of change and expansion.

DOI: 10.4324/9781003057536-4

The scientific study of the lexicon in terms of its structure, the structural and semantic distinctive properties of its members, and the relationships holding among them both from a synchronic and diachronic perspective, is the domain of **lexicology**. **Lexicography**, on the other hand, deals with the collection and classification of the items of a given lexicon, by providing their formal, functional, and especially semantic characterization; consequently, compiling dictionaries also falls in the scope of lexicography.

The basic unit for the analysis of the lexicon is the **lexeme**, which is an abstraction of the notion of 'word,' a sort of common denominator to which all the actual forms of a given word can be related. A lexeme can be narrower than a word because it can encompass many formally different words, for instance, all the conjugated forms of a verb. But it can also be broader since it can comprise units that consist of more than one word (*fireplace, letter opener, forget-me-not*). These composite (or complex) lexemes are called **compound words** (or simply **compounds**) and are discussed later. The counterpart of lexeme in lexicography, that is, the form of a lexeme conventionally used to refer to it in dictionaries (and possibly in grammars) is the **citation form** (or **entry**; It. *lemma*). Citation forms are language-specific; for example, in Italian (and in Romance languages in general), the citation form for verbs is the infinitive (*amare* 'to love'), while in Latin, verb entries consist of five items: first- and second-person singular present indicative, first-person singular perfect indicative, supine, and present infinitive, as shown in (1).[1]

(1) ĂMO, ĂMAS, AMAVI, AMATUM, ĂMĀRE
    'I love', 'you love', 'I loved', 'loved', 'to love'

The choice of citation forms, then, is not fully arbitrary; rather, it tends to correspond to a form (or set of forms) of a lexeme that can occur in isolation.

An important distinctive feature of the lexicon is that, overall, it is an open category since new items are (constantly) added in the form of either words taken from foreign languages or new lexical items obtained by means of word-formation mechanisms. More precisely, the lexicon comprises two basic classes of items, content words and grammatical (or functional) words; the former is the one that is actually open, while the latter is essentially closed. The lexicon is the most external layer of language in the sense that it is the layer most exposed to contact and interaction with other languages. Moreover, lexical change is more immediately detectable than grammatical change because it is typically faster. Words become obsolete and may eventually disappear (i.e., they become archaisms), while new words (neologisms) appear. The lexicon is also the layer more opened to extralinguistic reality since, notwithstanding the fundamentally arbitrary relationship between words (signs) and referents, word meaning relates more or less directly to reality.

The lexicon is related to grammar both at the synchronic and diachronic level. At the **synchronic** level, the lexicon is organized into word classes on the basis of grammatical function, and a close link is obtained between grammar and lexicon in word-formation. At the **diachronic** level, grammar and lexicon are related by **grammaticalization**, a pervasive phenomenon across languages, which denotes a number of processes of language change that involve the development of grammatical words (e.g., prepositions, conjunctions, auxiliary verbs) and affixes from lexical items.[2]

4.2 The Italian lexicon

Typically, the lexicon of a language includes three distinct core categories: the **hereditary** lexicon, which in our case comprises words Italian inherited directly from Latin; **neologisms**, which are native words created by means of word-formation processes;[3] and **borrowings** (or **loanwords**), which are words of foreign origin.[4]

The Italian lexicon is considerably more conservative than the lexicons of the other Romance languages in that it is closest to Latin. Since Italian is also highly conservative at the phonological level, it is fairly easy to analyze both words that entered the language directly from Latin and words that were recovered from Latin at later stages, sometimes even through other languages. The drawback of this tight closeness to Latin, though, is that it may be hard (and at times, indeed, impossible) to distinguish between indigenous Italian words (i.e., words which are the outcome of word-formation processes) and words inherited directly from Latin. For instance, should nouns like *domatore* 'tamer' and *aratore* 'plowman' be considered direct continuations of Latin DOMATOR, –ORIS and ARATOR, –ORIS, or nouns derived from the verbs *domare* 'tame' and *arare* 'plow' by adding the nominalizing suffix –*tore*? Both accounts are actually suitable: from a diachronic perspective, these words unquestionably attest to inheritance, yet from a synchronic perspective (i.e., the perspective of 'normal' speakers who are unaware of etymology and language change in general), they are the outcome of a word-formation process, as we will see later in the chapter.

The size of the lexicon is measured in terms of lexemes rather than word forms, hence by referring to dictionaries. As noted in the preceding text, dictionaries are collections of lexemes which provide a (more or less) comprehensive summary of language users' lexical proficiency. A typical one-volume dictionary lists between 100,000 and 150,000 lexemes, which belong to different fields (i.e., technical languages), language varieties (e.g., regional and dialectal, youth language), and registers (e.g., formal, colloquial) and are characterized by different usage frequency rates. A review of the most important dictionaries of Italian is outside the scope of this section; nonetheless, two works deserve mention because they stand out for comprehensiveness and innovativeness: *Grande dizionario della lingua italiana* (*GDLI*) and *Grande dizionario italiano dell'uso* (*GRADIT*).

GDLI (also known as 'Battaglia,' after the name of its founder, Salvatore Battaglia) is the largest, most inclusive, and most systematic historical dictionary of the Italian language. Started in 1961, this monumental work was completed in 2002 under the direction of Giorgio Barberi Squarotti and comprises 21 volumes for a total of 22,700 pages. Two supplemental volumes were later published (2004 and 2009), and in 2019, an online version became available through the *Accademia della Crusca* (www.gdli.it/).[5] All senses of each entry are listed in their chronological order usage and painstakingly illustrated by numerous citations from a variety of authors and texts from the thirteenth century to the present. Its size and quality

> make it a reference point for any student of Italian language and literature. Its role is even more important when GDLI is considered not only as an exceptional tool of reference and study, but also as a way of reaching a better understanding of the culture rooted in the past, from the earliest century of the birth and development of Italian as a language.
>
> *(Beltrami & Fornara, 2004, p. 369)*

Grande dizionario italiano dell'uso (*GRADIT*), created and directed by Tullio De Mauro, is another foremost Italian dictionary; its first edition (1999–2000) comprises six volumes, and a second revised and updated eight-volume edition was published in 2007. With a total of about 260,000 entries, *GRADIT* is perhaps the most comprehensive non-historical Italian dictionary. One of its distinctive features is that it systematically details valuable information about usage by means of 11 specific usage tags (*marche d'uso*). (De Mauro, 1999–2000, pp. xx–xxi). Three main layers of the lexicon are first distinguished: basic (core), common, and extended. The **basic (core) lexicon** comprises the set of words that are central to ordinary, everyday communicative situations; they amount to about 7,000 items which are divided into three subgroups based on usage frequency. The first is the **fundamental** lexicon, which is made of 2,049 lexemes and includes both functional and lexical items referring to the essential life dynamics, which are known by all speakers (*pane* 'bread,' *dormire* 'to sleep,' *felice* 'happy,' *facilmente* 'easily,' *per* 'for; to; by'). The second subgroup is labelled **high-usage** and comprises 2,576 lexemes frequently used both in spoken and written language and known to all speakers with a medium-high level of education (*cucchiaio* 'spoon,' *nuotare* 'to swim,' *scuro* 'dark,' *velocemente* 'quickly,' *sebbene* 'although'). The third subset is the **high-availability** lexicon, consisting of 1,897 lexemes that are quite rare in both written and spoken language but are known by all speakers because they refer to entities and situations extremely relevant to daily life (*forchetta* 'fork,' *sciare* 'to ski,' *laborioso* 'difficult; industrious').

Eight additional usage labels are then provided, as illustrated in (2).

(2) a. **Common**: used and understood independently of our profession, trade, or geographical domain and generally known by anyone with a mid-high level of education (*cautela* 'caution,' *danzare* 'to dance,' *taciturno* 'quiet,' *pacatamente* 'calmly,' *seppure* 'even if').

b. **Technical-specialized**: predominantly or exclusively pertaining to technical or scientific fields, known mainly in relation to specific activities, technologies, sciences, additionally tagged for the specific field (*faringe* 'pharynx' is tagged as *anat(omia)* 'anatomy,' and *algoritmo* 'algorithm' as *mat(ematica)* 'mathematics').

c. **Literary only**: used in texts from the literary canon from the fourteenth to the early twentieth century (*aere* 'air'; *spème* 'hope').

d. **Regional**: partly (though not necessarily) of dialectal origin, used primarily in regional varieties of Italian (e.g., *anguria* 'watermelon,' northern; *bagnarola* 'tub,' southern).

e. **Dialectal**: recognized as dialectal and used as such in Italian contexts (Sic. *dammuso* 'stone house typical of Pantelleria').

f. **Exoticism**: recognized as foreign, displaying no phonological or morphological adaptation (*abat-jour* 'bedside lamp,' *movida* 'night life,' *up to date*).[6]

g. **Low-usage**: rarely occurring but found with relative frequency in twentieth-century texts and speech (*nitore* 'clearness,' *mescidare* 'to mix,' *edibile* 'edible,' *lorché* 'when').

h. **Obsolete**: archaic but still listed in popular dictionaries (*aio* 'tutor,' *fugare* 'chase away V,' *abbenché* 'although').

(De Mauro, 1999–2000, pp. xx–xxi)

Furthermore, though it is not a historical dictionary, *GRADIT* also provides the etymology and date of first attestation for most entries.[7]

4.2.1 The hereditary lexicon

As already noted, the Italian hereditary lexicon consists of words that came from Latin via uninterrupted transmission, though of course undergoing the expected phonological, morphological, and perhaps also semantic changes. It comprises about 4,500 items, which amounts to more of the basic lexicon, and represents the skeleton of the Italian lexicon since it includes the grammatical words, verbs, nouns, and adjectives with the highest frequency of use, as well as core items from the basic lexicon, such as numbers, and words referring to body parts, family relations, and nature.

Latin words also entered Italian indirectly through borrowing at different times in history, starting from the thirteenth century: these are known as **Latinisms**. Latinisms have an interrupted history; they stopped living at some point, to be resuscitated by learned people. They are (easily) identifiable because they entered Italian directly from written Latin and therefore do not display regular phonological changes, only phonological and morphological adaptation. For example, the adjective *orale* 'oral' derives from the Latin noun ōs, ORIS 'mouth,' which Italian replaced with *bocca* (< Latin BŬCCA(M) 'cheek'). Another example is the adjective *equino* 'equine,' from Latin EQUUS 'horse,' substituted by *cavallo* (< Latin CABALLU(M) 'work/castrated horse').

Latinisms may form pairs with hereditary words; in Italian, the words related by this type of relationship are traditionally called ***allotropi*** 'allotropes.' In short, allotropes are words with the same etymology but with different phonological and morphological shape, and generally also different meaning. *GRADIT* lists about 30,000 allotropes; some of the most common are given in Table 4.1.

Several non-adapted Latinisms still survive in the present-day language, though their usage is restricted to technical languages; some examples are *conditio sine qua non* 'necessary condition,' *par condicio* 'equal treatment,' *editio princeps* 'first printed edition,' *a priori/posteriori*, *curriculum vitae*.

4.2.2 Borrowings

There is widespread consensus that linguistic borrowing is not limited to lexical items and morphological material, and even syntactic constructions can also be borrowed; however,

TABLE 4.1 Common allotropes

Latin etymon	Hereditary item	Latinism
AREA 'open space; clearing'	*aia* 'farmyard'	*area* 'area'
CAUSA 'cause, reason'	*cosa* 'thing'	*causa* 'cause, reason'
CIRCULUS 'circle, circumference'	*cerchio* 'hoop; circle'	*circolo* 'circle; club'
DISCUS 'disk; plate'	*desco* 'table'	*disco* 'disk'
FRIGIDUS 'cold; lazy, indifferent'	*freddo* 'cold'	*frigido* 'frigid'
MACHINA 'war machine; device; mechanism'	*macina* 'millstone'	*macchina* 'machine; car'
VITIUM 'vice; defect'	*vezzo* 'habit'	*vizio* 'vice; defect'

lexical borrowing is the most common type cross-linguistically, and it is the only type addressed here. Different kinds of lexical borrowing (loanwords) can be distinguished according to a variety of parameters.[8] In terms of motivation, we distinguish between necessity and luxury loanwords. **Necessity** loanwords are adopted to name referents of foreign origin; thus, they bring with them the entity, situation, or concept they denote. Some common examples are *zucchero* 'sugar' (< Arabic *sukkar*), *cravatta* 'necktie' (< French *cravate* < Croatian *hrvat* 'Croat'), *tennis* (< English *tennis*). Conversely, **luxury** loanwords result from socio-cultural trends, typically related to the high-prestige status of the 'donor' language, as for example the English loanwords *leader* (vs. It. *capo*), *babysitter* (vs. It. *bambinaia*), *gay* (vs. It. *omosessuale*). However, a clear discrimination between necessity and luxury loanwords is difficult to achieve since new entities, situations, and concepts tend to enter foreign languages because they are trendy. Moreover, although technically it is always possible to coin native neologisms through various word-formation strategies, it may be difficult to find an equally efficient, incisive Italian equivalent.

Loanwords are also classified according to their degree of adaptation to the 'recipient' language (target). **Adapted** loanwords display partial or total assimilation to the phonological and/or morphological features of the target language, with phonological assimilation possibly reflected partly or completely in the spelling. *Burro* 'butter' (< Old French *burre*), *carciofo* 'artichoke' (< Arabic *xaršūf*) exemplify complete morphological, phonological, and orthographic assimilation, while *chattare* [tʃatˈtare] 'to chat online' illustrates a morphologically adapted loanword (the verb is conjugated like a regular first conjugation verb), with phonological adaptation unmatched in the spelling (recall that <ch> cannot occur before /a/, /o/, /u/, and the palatal [tʃ] is conveyed orthographically by <ci>). **Non-adapted** loanwords keep their original morphological and phonological features, but their pronunciation adjusts to the phonetics of the target language; some very frequent examples are *abat-jour* 'bedside lamp' from French, *würstel* 'frankfurter' from German, and *movida* 'lively nighttime life' from Spanish. Phonological and orthographical adaptation was basically the norm until the nineteenth century, but it has increasingly relaxed since then.

Calques are a specific subtype of lexical borrowing which consist in using native material to reproduce a foreign structure. Traditionally, two types of calques are distinguished. **Semantic** calques entail transfer (or extension) of 'foreign' meanings to indigenous words; they can result from formal similarity of the items involved (e.g., *realizzare* 'carry out; achieve' has acquired the meaning 'understand,' from Eng. *realize*) or from similarity of meaning (e.g., *stella* 'star' 'borrowed' the meaning 'celebrity' from Engl. *Star*, becoming a synonym of *divo/a*). **Structural** calques are a sort of 'loan translation'; they typically involve compound words (*grattacielo* 'lit. scrape-sky' < *skyscraper*) or phrases (*luna di miele* 'lit. moon of honey' < *honeymoon*).

Linguistic borrowing is driven by language contact (broadly understood to include also cultural contact) and governed by the prestige of the donor language in general or in specific fields (arts, fashion, music, gastronomy, technology, etc.). Presently, loanwords are spread primarily through mass media and social networks; in the past, they came via wars and invasions, trade, geographical discoveries, and pilgrimages. Three main kinds of influence between donor and recipient languages are commonly identified according to the social, cultural, and political relationships holding between them. **Substratum** influence refers to the impact of a nondominant language on a dominant one (e.g., Latin borrowing from languages of the conquered Italic populations); typically, substratum influence has a minor impact on the lexicon of the recipient language, usually limited to place-names (toponyms) and 'foreign' items or notions. **Superstratum** influence, in contrast, refers to the impact of a dominant language on another (nondominant) language (e.g., borrowing from Germanic languages during the barbaric invasions of the Italian peninsula). Finally, **adstratum** influence applies to cases where neither the donor nor the recipient language is clearly dominant (e.g., contemporary Italian borrowing from the United States).

Through its history, Italian borrowed lexical items from several languages, the most significant being old Germanic languages, French and Provençal, Spanish, Arabic, and English. French emerges as the strongest and most consistent source of loanwords (Gallicisms) from the thirteenth to the twentieth century, reaching exceptional peaks in the eighteenth century. Borrowing from Germanic languages was particularly intense during the early Middle Ages, though some Germanisms entered in Latin already before the fourth century and have been inherited by Italian.

The impact of Spanish, on the other hand, starts in the fifteenth century and peaks in the 1500s, when Spain ruled over a large part of Italy. A new wave of Hispanicisms arrived in the twentieth century, especially from American Spanish bringing many terms from Amerindian, and Asian languages found their way into Italian via Spanish (*patata* 'potato,' *cacao* 'cocoa,' *cioccolata* 'chocolate,' *condor, iguana*) and, to a lesser extent, Portuguese (*ananas* 'pineapple,' *banana, cocco* 'coconut,' *marmellata* 'jam,' *bambù* 'bamboo,' *bonzo* 'Buddhist monk').

Arabic was a significant donor during the Middle Ages due to intense commercial exchanges and the high cultural prestige it held at that time, as well as the Arab domination of Sicily.

English loanwords (Anglicisms) are irrelevant until the seventeenth century; later, their frequency increases considerably and has become massive since the last decades of the twentieth century, especially in scientific and technologic fields.[9]

Lastly, it should be noted that the Italian lexicon comprises about 8,000 words of Greek origin, forming the largest component after that of Latin origin; many of them entered the language via Latin due to the early contact between the two languages. Some examples of early loanwords denoting core vocabulary items are *braccio* 'arm,' *gamba* 'leg,' *spalla* 'shoulder,' *mandorlo* 'almond tree,' *olivo* 'olive tree,' *balena* 'whale,' *tonno* 'tuna,' *filosofia* 'philosophy,' *geometria* 'geometry,' *angelo* 'angel,' *basilica, battesimo* 'baptism,' *monaco* 'monk,' *vescovo* 'bishop.' Loanwords from the Middle Ages include *anguria* 'watermelon,' *molo* 'pier,' *ormeggiare* 'moor V,' while later ones pertain primarily to scholarly and scientific fields, especially from the second half of the seventeenth century. Many of these technical terms (e.g., *cardiopatia* 'cardiopathy,' *tassonomia* 'taxonomy') are obtained through the word-formation strategy known as Neoclassical composition (see following text).

Examples of 'early' loanwords (from the thirteenth to the sixteenth century) pertaining to the core lexicon are given in (3); they are fully assimilated to Italian, their foreign origins remaining obscure to 'normal' speakers.

(3) a. Gallicisms: *burro* 'butter,' *bugia* 'lie,' *cavaliere* 'knight,' *coraggio* 'courage,' *corsetto* 'corset,' *cugino* 'cousin,' *gioia* 'joy,' *gioiello* 'jewel,' *lignaggio* 'lineage,' *pensiero* 'thought,' *roccia* 'rock,' *speranza* 'hope,' *viaggio* 'journey,' *mangiare* 'eat,' *parlare* 'speak'; *giallo* 'yellow,' *vermiglio* 'vermillion.'

   b. Germanism: *anca* 'hip,' *bosco* 'wood,' *brindisi* 'toast,' *elmo* 'helmet,' *fiasco* 'bottle,' *giardino* 'garden,' *guancia* 'cheek,' *guerra* 'war,' *milza* 'spleen,' *orgoglio* 'pride,' *roba* 'things; stuff,' *sapone* 'soap,' *schiena* 'back,' *stalla* 'stable,' *stinco* 'shin,' *zolla* 'clod,' *guadagnare* 'earn,' *guardare* 'to look at,' *guarnire* 'to garnish,' *recare* 'carry,' *rubare* 'steal,' *scherzare* 'to joke,' *spiare* 'to spy,' *trottare* 'to trot,' *bianco* 'white,' *bruno* 'dark(-haired),' *grigio* 'gray,' *ricco* 'rich,' *schietto* 'frank.'

    c. Arabisms: *arancia* 'orange,' *assassino* 'assassin,' *cifra* 'figure; sum,' *cotone* 'cotton,' *dogana* 'customs,' *facchino* 'porter,' *limone* 'lemon,' *magazzino* 'warehouse,' *melanzana* 'eggplant,' *ragazzo* 'boy,' *tariffa* 'tarif,' *sœicco* 'sheik,' *zero* 'zero,' *zucchero* 'sugar,' *azzurro* 'blue.'

    d. Hispanicisms: *appartamento* 'apartment,' *baciamano* 'hand kissing,' *risacca* 'backwash,' *regalo* 'gift,' *uragano* 'hurricane,' *ammutinare* 'to mutiny.'

A quite-modest sample of more recent loanwords (from eighteenth century onward) is given in (4).[10]

(4) a. French: *besciamella* 'béchamel sauce,' *bigiù* 'beautiful thing,' *boutique* 'boutique,' *bignè* 'cream puff,' *burocrazia* 'bureaucracy,' *collant* 'pantyhose,' *caserma* 'barraks,' *consolle* 'console,' *croissant* 'croissant,' *foulard* 'headscarf,' *fuseaux* 'leggings,' *gilè* 'waistcoat,' *maionese* 'mayonnaise,' *moda* 'fashion,' *paltò* 'overcoat,' *ragù* 'meat sauce,' *soubrette* 'showgirl,' *soufflé/sufflè* 'soufflé,' *ammobiliare* 'to furnish,' *attivare* 'to activate,' *autorizzare* 'to authorize,' *beige* 'beige,' *plissé* 'pleated,' *sovversivo* 'subversive.'

    b. English: *bistecca* 'beefsteak,' *brandy*, *comitato* 'committee; board,' *computer*, *conformista* 'conformist,' *costituzione* 'constitution,' *cover girl*, *cowboy*, *dandy*, *detective*, *film*, *hippy*, *leader*, *popcorn*, *premier*, *fan* 'admirer,' *fashion*, *football*, *jet*, *jazz*, *playboy*, *self-service*, *sport*, *stilografica* 'fountain pen,' *suspense*, *vamp*, *vegetariano* 'vegetarian.'

    c. German: *strudel*, *goulash*, *valzer* 'waltz,' *würstel* 'frankfurter,' *lager*.

    d. Spanish: *compleanno* 'birthday,' *embargo*, *falange* 'Falange,' *fandango*, *miliziano* 'militiaman,' *siesta*, *sigaro* 'cigar'; *barocco* 'baroque,' *puntiglioso* 'punctilious'; via Latin America: *campesino* 'peasant,' *desaparecido* 'missing,' *golpe* 'coup,' *rumba*, *sandinista* 'Sandinista,' *tango*.

Non-European loanwords are more marginal, often coming via other major European languages. To name just a few, early (pre-twentieth century) Japanese loanwords include *geisha*, *cachi* 'persimmons,' *chimono* 'kimono'; among the twentieth-century loanwords are *azuki* 'Adzuki beans,' *bonsai*, *ikebana*, *karate*, *karaoke*, *katana*, *jujutsu*, *judo*, *samurai*, *sashimi*, *sumo*, *sushi*, *tatami*, *tsunami* (Nagami & Nannini, 2006). Some early Chinese loanwords (again, pre-twentieth century) are *cincin* 'cheers!' *ginseng*, *tè* 'tea,' while modern ones include *feng shui*, *kung fu*, *shantung* 'type of silk fabric,' *tai chi* (Masini, 2006).[11]

Loanwords were deeply ostracized by the Fascist regime's linguistic policy, whose main goal – in full conformity with its strong autarchic views – was to control the entire linguistic repertoire by promoting the diffusion of a standard unitary language while fiercely opposing the use of dialects and minority languages. The use of loanwords on commercial signs was taxed in 1923 (ultimately banned in 1938) and prohibited in newspapers in 1934, and in 1939, christening Italian newborns with foreign names was forbidden. The regime's strictest, most authoritarian measure in promoting linguistic purism (and prescriptivism) was taken in 1940, with a decree/law that banned the use of foreign words in industrial and commercial signs and professional activities and in advertising in general. Between 1941 and 1943, a special committee of the Royal Academy of Italy (*Commissione per l'italianità della lingua* 'Committee for the language Italianization') was formed to provide native alternatives for about

2,000 loanwords (most non-adapted) (Raffaelli, 2010), by means of phonological and/or morphological adaptation (*confettura* ~ French *confiture* 'jam,' *manichino* ~ *mannequin*) or 'translations' (*assegno* ~ *check/cheque*). Many of the proposed replacements were indeed successful (e.g., *antipasto* ~ French *hors-d'oeuvre*, *merenda* 'afternoon snack' ~ French *goûter* 'have an afternoon snack,' *pubblicità* ~ French *réclame* 'advertising,' *trucco* ~ French *maquillage*), though some loanwords resurfaced with different degrees of strength. Among the most notable failures are *arlecchino* ~ English *cocktail*, *uovo* **scottato** ~ French *à la coque* 'soft-boiled' (vs. the successful *uovo* **in camicia** ~ French *poché* 'poached' and *uovo* **strapazzato** ~ French *brouillé* 'scrambled'). Some loanwords were also embraced (e.g., *bar, camion, film, sport*), probably because they were viewed as fully integrated into the language (Raffaelli, 2010, p. 58).

4.2.3 Dialectal and regional lexicon

The Italian lexicon also includes items from dialects or regional varieties, which represent a sort of 'internal borrowing.' These display different degrees of geographical distribution outside their area of origin, and their diffusion may be spurred by the absence of Italian equivalents or their higher expressivity. Also, they are typically confined to everyday-life domains, especially food (Lombard *bresaola*, Sicilian *cannoli*, Neapolitan *mozzarella*, Milanese *panettone*), or local socio-cultural entities (Neapolitan *camorra*, Venetian *gondola*, Sicilian *mafia*).

Geo-synonyms and geo-homonyms constitute two specific instances of regionalisms. **Geo-synonyms** are different terms which designate the same referent across different geographical areas; their circulation usually remains confined to their area of origin, although some may spread to other areas and even become pan-Italian. Among the best-known examples are *anguria* 'watermelon' ~ central *cocomero* ~ southern *mellone (d'acqua)*; Sicilia *picciotto* 'boy,' central *ragazzino*, northern *toso*; southern *zito* 'fiancé,' northern *moroso*. **Geo-homonyms** are identical words with different meaning across different geographical areas and can be distinguished into two types: (a) words with the same etymology which underwent different semantic evolution, such as the adjective *fregno* (< dialectal *fregna* 'vulva'), which means 'cool' in Abruzzo but 'fool' in Lazio, and (b) words with distinct etymologies, such as Piedmontese *lea* 'boulevard' (< French *allée* 'boulevard') and Veneto *lea* 'mud' (< Latin LAETAMEN 'manure') (Telmon, 1993, p. 137).

4.3 Word-formation processes

Word-formation concerns the strategies languages employ to create new lexemes, or neologisms. It examines the internal structure of complex lexemes, identifying and categorizing their individual components, aiming to uncover patterns and regularities underlying the formation of lexemes using elements already available in a given language.[12] Word-formation is highly important for Italian since neologisms have always constituted a sizeable portion of the lexicon. The primary word-formation mechanisms of Italian are derivation (i.e., prefixation and suffixation) and compounding.

4.3.1 Derivation

Derivation consists in combining a free morpheme (the base) with one or more bound morphemes by means of affixation (suffixation, prefixation, or infixation), or even both (para-synthesis). Suffixation is far more extensive in scope and more productive than pre-fixation, while infixation is quite rare and restricted to evaluative derivation (see following). Derivation is subject to a number of constraints, that is, affixes show complex restrictions as for the bases they can modify. This phenomenon, known as **blocking**, can be phonologically motivated; for instance, the negative prefix *s-* (*comodo* 'comfortable'→ *s-comodo* 'uncomfort-able') cannot apply to bases beginning with <s> (*sincero* 'sincere' → ⋆*s-sincero* 'insincere') or vowel (*accettabile* 'acceptable' ⋆*s-accettabile* 'unacceptable'). Blocking can also be due to seman-tic factors, as in the case of the suffix *-iera*, which can only apply to nouns denoting concrete entities (*sale* 'salt' → *saliera* 'saltcellar'), or to pre-existing words: the existence of *inaugura-**zione*** 'inauguration' (← *inaugurare* 'inaugurate'), for example, may explain ⋆*inaugura-**mento***. Finally, blocking can affect only some senses of the base (*pienezza della salute* 'lit. fullness of health' vs. ⋆*pienezza di un bicchiere* 'fullness of a glass').

Two main paradigmatic models of derivation can be distinguished. In the first, one base takes an array of suffixes, resulting in a series of derivations; for example, the verbal base *adula-* (← *adulare* 'flatter') gives *adulatore* 'flatterer,' *adulazione* 'flattery,' *adulatorio* 'flattering,' *adulabile* 'flatterable'); in Italian linguistics, this pattern is known as *derivazione a ventaglio* 'fan-shaped derivation.' In the second, *derivazione a cumulo* 'recursive (lit. heap-shaped) derivation,' the output of a derivation process becomes, in turn, the base of another one; for instance, *permeare* 'permeate' gives the base for *permeabile* 'permeable,' which is the base for *im-permeabile* 'waterproof,' from which we derive *impermeabil-ità* 'waterproofness.' The two paradigm often combine, as illustrated in (5).

(5) Interaction of derivation paradigms

		nazionalizzazione	
	nazionalizzare →		
nazione → *nazionale* →		*nazionalizzabile*	
	nazionalismo →	*nazionalista* →	*nazionalistico*

Referring to their base, derived forms (derivatives) are classified as denominal (the base is a noun), deverbal (the base is a verb), and deadjectival (the base is an adjective), whereas suf-fixes are categorized as nominal (derivatives are nouns), adjectival (derivatives are adjectives), and verbal (derivatives are verbs). The same classification extends to suffixes with reference to derivatives (i.e., derivation outputs), so nominal suffixes derive nouns, adjectival suffixes derive adjectives, and verbal suffixes derive verbs.

(6) a. Denominal

  i.   Nominal: *art**ista*** 'artist' (← *arte* 'art')
  ii. Verbal: *baci**are*** 'kiss' (← *bacio* 'kiss')
  iii. Adjectival: *atom**ico*** 'atomic' (← *atomo* 'atom')

  b. Deverbal

  i.   Nominal: *lavor**atore*** 'worker' (← *lavorare* 'work')
  ii. Verbal: *scoprire* 'to uncover' (← *coprire* 'cover'); *rivedere* 'see again' (← *vedere* 'see')
  iii. Adjectival: *mangia**bile*** 'edible' (← *mangiare* 'to eat'); *in**felice*** 'unhappy' (← *felice* 'happy)

c. Deadjectival

    i.   Nominal: *bellezza* 'beauty' (← *bello* 'beautiful').
    ii.   Verbal: *calmare* 'calm' (← *calmo* 'calm').[13]

4.3.1.1 Suffixation

Suffixation generally leads to change of the base word class, though change of word class is not categorical (see (5) earlier). It is a highly dynamic derivational process since nouns, adjectives, and verbs can all serve as bases for and be the output of suffixation. Most commonly, suffixation involves only one suffix, though there is a rather-large body of (fairly frequent) words with two suffixes (*credi-bil-ità* 'credibility'). Words with three or more suffixes (*real-izza-bil-ità* 'realizability') are rarer, have lower frequency rate, and tend to be restricted to technical languages and/or formal registers.

Italian displays a quite vast array of derivational suffixes (see Grossmann & Rainer, 2004 for a truly comprehensive treatment), and several suffixes can select bases from different word classes. Here we can only offer a succinct survey of the most common and (synchronically) most productive ones.

4.3.1.1.1 Nominal suffixes

The suffix *-ista* is the most productive suffix in the derivation of nouns denoting professions (or occupations in general) (7a); experts in specialized (academic) fields and followers of a religion, ideology, and (political) movement (7b); and attitudes or behaviors (7c).

(7) a.   *autista* 'driver,' *dentista* 'dentist,' *giornalista* 'journalist,' *opinionista* '(political) column-ist,' *pianista* 'pianist,' *softwarista* 'software specialist.'

    b.   *anglista* 'anglicist,' *economista* 'economist,' *nutrizionista* 'nutritionist,' *buddista* 'Bud-dhist,' *ambientalista* 'environmentalist,' *animalista* 'animalist,' *comunista* 'communist,' *fascista* 'fascist,' *pacifista* 'pacifist.'

    c.   *allarmista* 'alarmist,' *consumista* 'consumerist,' *egoista* 'selfish person,' *ottimista* 'opti-mist,' *opportunista* 'opportunist.'

The suffixes *-aio* and its geographical (central) variant *-aro* (both < Latin -ARIUS) also derive nouns referring to less-prestigious occupations, particularly crafts, but are less productive than *-ista*. Among the most common bases that select *-aio* are nouns denoting animals, plants, substances, food, and objects (8a); for a number of nouns in *-aio*, only the feminine form is available since they denote occupations traditionally carried out by women only (8b). Its productivity, however, is declining considerably because its derivatives relate to occupations that overall have become obsolete; furthermore, it can carry pejorative value (8c). As for *-aro*, it is overall unproductive, though several twentieth-century neologisms, no longer perceived as geographically marked, are worth noting because of their socio-cultural import (8d).

(8) a.   *benzinaio* 'gas pump attendant,' *calzolaio* 'shoemaker,' *fornaio* 'baker,' *pecoraio* 'shep-erd,' *macellaio* 'butcher,' *orologiaio* 'watchmaker,' *sellaio* 'saddle maker.'

    b.   *asolaia* 'buttonhole seamstress,' *bambinaia* 'nursemaid,' *lavandaia* 'washerwoman,' *massaia* 'housewife.'

    c.   *pantofolaio* 'homebody' (vs. original 'slippers maker'), *parolaio* 'windback.'

    d.   *metallaro* 'heavy metal music fan,' *palazzinaro* 'unscrupulous developer,' *panchinaro* 'bench player.'

The suffixes *-aiolo/-arolo* (Latin -ARIUS plus diminutive -OLUS) are essentially equivalent to *-aio/-aro*; their distribution, though, is more restricted, the derivatives being often obsolete forms (9a); like *-aio*, *-aiolo* can carry a negative, pejorative connotation (9b).

(9)   a.   *barcaiolo* 'boatman,' *boscaiolo* 'lumberjack,' *pizzaiolo* 'pizza chef,' *pollaiolo* 'poultry-man,' *vignaiolo* 'vineyard owner/worker.'

    b.   *borsaiolo* 'pickpocket' (vs. *borsaio* 'purse maker'); *donnaiolo* 'womanizer.'

As for *-ario*, it is found primarily in Latinisms *bibliotecario* 'librarian,' *falsario* 'forger,' *legionario* 'legionary,' *mercenario* 'mercenary,' *segretario* secretary.'

The suffix *-aio/-aia* also derives nouns denoting places where the referent of the base lives (*colombaia* 'pigeon coop,' *formicaio* 'anthill,' *pollaio* 'henhouse,' *vespaio* 'wasps' nest') or gathers (*acquaio* 'kitchen sink,' *giacciaio* 'glacier,' *ghiacciaia* 'icebox,' *grondaia* 'gutter,' *legnaia* 'woodshed,' *pagliaio* 'haystack,' *risaia* 'paddy field').

Two other suffixes used to derive nouns denoting occupations are *-ino* (10a) and *-iere* (10b), which is also used, though less frequently, to form nouns denoting objects (10c).

(10)   a.   *bagnino* 'lifeguard,' *ciabattino* 'cobbler,' *vetturino* 'coach driver.'

    b.   *barbiere* 'barber,' *cameriere* 'waiter,' *contrabbandiere* 'smuggler,' *ferroviere* 'railroad man,' *ragioniere* 'accountant.'

    c.   *braciere* 'brazier,' *candeliere* 'candlestick.'

Highly productive in the derivation of nouns denoting a large variety of objects, particularly everyday life instruments (11a) and containers (11b), is the suffix *-iera* (the feminine variant of *-iere*).

(11)   a.   *bistecchiera* 'gridiron,' *caffettiera* 'coffeemaker,' *yogurtiera* 'yoghurt maker'

    b.   *acquasantiera* 'holy water font,' *biscottiera* 'cookie jar,' *cappelliera* 'hat box,' *formaggiera* 'cheese bowl,' *oliera* 'oil and vinegar cruet,' *saliera* 'saltcellar,' *scarpiera* 'shoe rack,' *zuppiera* 'tureen.'

Another very productive suffix is *-eria*. It is the most common suffix to derive nouns denoting places where certain products are sold and/or manufactured (12a) and, possibly, the craft in general. Moreover, it can form collective nouns (12b), with the different meanings overlapping in some cases (12c)

(12)   a.   *acciaieria* 'steel factory,' *birreria* 'bierkeller; brewery,' *libreria* 'bookstore,' *panetteria* 'bakery,' *pescheria* 'fish shop,' *salumeria* 'delicatessen,' *vetreria* 'glassworks.'

    b.   *argenteria* 'silverware,' *tifoseria* 'fans,' *rubinetteria* 'bathroom fixtures' (← *rubinetto* 'faucet').

    c.   *erboristeria* 'herbalism; herbalist's shop,' *gioielleria* 'jewel's shop; jewelry,' *cristalleria* 'crystalware; crystal glassworks/shop,' *pasticceria* 'pastry; cake shop.'

One of the most productive suffixes used to derive abstract nouns is *-ismo*, which can also attach to adjectives (*abusivismo* 'building without permits,' *ambientalismo* 'environmentalism') and sporadically to verbs (*illuminismo* 'Enlightenment,' *trasformismo* 'transformism'). It covers a wide range of meanings, the core ones being political, philosophical, scientific, religious, artistic, etc. thought (13a); behaviors and dispositions (13b); social phenomena, including sports and recreational activities (13c); medicine (13d); and language-related terminology, though primarily with adjectival bases (*arabismo* 'Arabism,' *esotismo* 'non-adapted loanword') (13e). Proper names are quite common as its base (13f) and are strictly connected to nouns in *-ista* (13g).

(13) a. *capitalismo* 'capitalism,' *zarismo* 'tzarism,' *atomismo* 'atomism,' *espressionismo* 'expressionism,' *totemismo* 'totemism'.[14]

      b. *eroismo* 'heroism,' *patriottismo* 'patriotism.'

      c. *analfabetismo* 'illiteracy,' *brigatismo* 'the phenomenon of the Red Brigades',[15] *gallismo* 'machismo' (← *gallo* 'rooster'), *mammismo* 'excessive attachment to own's mother,' *nomadismo* 'nomadism,' *yuppismo* 'yuppie behavior'; *automobilismo* 'motoring; motor racing,' *(moto)ciclismo* '(motor)cycling,' *paracadutismo* 'parachuting.'

      d. *alcolismo* 'alcoholism,' *nanismo* 'dwarfism,' *tabagismo* 'nicotine/smoking addiction.'

      e. *consonantismo* 'consonant system,' *dialettismo / dialettalismo* 'dialectal word/ expression.'

      f. *berlusconismo* 'Berlusconi's politics/ideologies,' *calvinismo* 'Calvinism,' *daltonismo* 'color blindness' (← Eng. *Daltonism*), *platonismo* 'Platonism.'

      g. *italianista* 'scholar of Italian,' *positivista* 'exponent/supporter of positivism.'

Some overall unproductive nominal suffixes found in fairly common words are illustrated in (14).

(14) a. *-aglia* derives mass/collective nouns: *ferraglia* 'scrap iron,' *sterpaglia* 'brushwood'; often with pejorative connotations: *brodaglia* 'dishwater,' *gentaglia* 'ill-mannered people.'

      b. *-ata* forms nouns denoting:

          i. Content: *forchettata* 'forkful,' *manciata* '(← *mano* 'hand') 'handful,' *palata* 'shovelful.'

          ii. Instrument used to hit: *coltellata* (← *coltello* 'knife') 'stab,' *fucilata* 'rifle shot,' *manata* (← *mano* 'hand') 'slap,' *sassata* 'stone blow.'

          iii. Act: *gomitata* 'elbow blow,' *occhiata* 'glance,' *risata* 'laugh.'

          iv. Collective meaning: *balconata* 'balcony,' *scalinata* 'stairs'; *grigliata* 'mixed grill/ barbeque,' *peperonata* 'pepper-based dish.'

          v. Time: *annata* 'year,' *giornata* 'day,' *mattinata* 'morning,' *serata* 'evening,' *nottata* 'night.'

          vi. With human nouns and proper names, the meaning 'typical of': *vigliaccata* 'cowardly action,' *berlusconata* 'action/behavior typical of Berlusconi.'

          vii. In (lower-register) informal/familiar speech, attachment to a range of more or less negatively connoted bases to derive 'stupid thing': *cavolata* (← *cavolo* 'cabbage'), *cazzata* (← *cazzo* 'penis, vulg.').

      c. *-ato* forms nouns designating position or office: *dottorato* 'doctorate,' *consolato* 'consulate,' *papato* 'papacy.'

      d. *-eto/-eta* applies primarily to bases denoting trees: *aranceto* 'orange grove,' *roseto* 'rose garden,' *carpineta* 'hornbeam forest,' *pineta* 'pine forest.'

      e. *-ile* derives noun indicating locations where the referent of the base is: *campanile* 'belfry,' *canile* 'kennel,' *porcile* 'pigsty' (especially figuratively).

Moving to deadjectival nominal suffixes, the most productive are *-ità* and its allomorphs *-età* (primarily with nouns ending in *-io*: *varietà* 'variety' ← *vario* 'various') and *-tà*, with very restricted, unsystematic distribution (15a); *-ezza* and *-izia*, which are allotropes from Latin -ITIA and may display meanings and uses (15b); and *-ìa* (15c), which selects a small group of high-frequency words and is highly productive in technical/scientific vocabulary involving formative element of Greek origins, such as *-cromo* 'color,' *-fobo* 'fear,' *-gino* 'woman' (15d).

(15) a. *creatività* 'creativity,' *diversità* 'diversity'; *caparbietà* 'stubbornness,' *notorietà* 'fame'; *fedeltà* 'loyalty; fidelity,' *vanità* 'vanity.'

   b. *giustezza* 'accuracy,' *giustizia* 'justice'; *stoltezza* 'foolishness' ~ archaic/literary *stoltizia*.

   c. *allegria* 'cheerfulness,' *pulizia* 'cleanliness.'

   d. *monocromo* 'monochrome' → *monocromia* 'monochromy,' *omofobo* 'homophobe' → *omofobia* 'homophobia,' *misogino* 'misogynous' *misoginia* 'misogyny.'

Two other productive suffixes are *-aggine* (16a) and *-erìa* (16b), which carry negative/pejorative value and select nominal bases denoting typical negative human traits (16c).

(16) a. *pignoleria* 'fastidiousness,' *spilorceria* 'stinginess,' *vigliaccheria* 'cowardice; cowardly action.'

   b. *balordaggine* 'foolishness,' *goffaggine* 'clumsiness,' *testardaggine* 'stubborness',

   c. *civetteria* 'flirtatiousness' (← *civetta* 'owl'), *ocaggine* 'silliness' (← *oca* 'goose').

The suffix *-zione* is by far the most productive suffix to derive action nouns from verbs, also due to its strict relation with verbs ending in *-izzare* and *-ificare* (see following) (17a). Its allomorph *-sione* is restricted to verbs of the second and third conjugation (*decidere* 'decide,' *aggredire* 'assault') and takes as a base the past participle or learned forms directly related to Latin rather than the infinitive (17b). Nouns ending in *-zione* are feminine and may also denote the object or result of the action, or even the location where it takes place.

(17) a. *demolizione* 'demolition,' *liberazione* 'release,' *promozione* 'promotion,' *traduzione* 'translation.'

   b. *astensione* 'abstension,' *discussione* 'discussion,' *invasione* 'invasion,' *scansione* 'scansion; scanning.'

Three other prominent deverbal nominal suffixes that derive action nouns are *-mento* (which is very common with verbs ending in *-eggiare*; see following text) (18a), *-tura* (18b), and *-aggio* (18c). The last two are particularly common with nouns pertaining to technical/specialized domains; *-mento* and *-aggio* select the theme as their base, while *-tura* attaches to the past participle.

(18) a. *differenziamento* 'differentiation,' *insegnamento* 'teaching,' *provvedimento* 'measure; step.'

   b. *cucitura* 'stitching; seam,' *battitura* 'typing; threshing,' *filatura* 'spinning (mill),' *spremitura* 'squeezing; pressing,' *tiratura* 'circulation; printing.'

   c. *lavaggio* 'washing,' *montaggio* 'assembly; editing (film),' *riciclaggio* 'recycling,' *tatuaggio* 'tattoo.'

Cases of multiple derivatives from the same base are available, which may differ in meanings or uses.

(19) a. *anda**tura*** 'gait, walk; pace' ~ *anda**mento*** 'course; trend; progress; *nutri**zione*** 'nutrition' ~ *nutri**mento*** 'nourishment; food.'
      b. *trivella**zione*** 'drilling' ~ less common *trivella**mento*** ~ *trivella**tura*** 'debris from drilling.'

As for deverbal nouns denoting agents and instruments, the most productive suffix is *-tore* (mas.)/*-trice* (fem.). The semantic domain this suffix covers is indeed quite vast and can be summarized as 'someone who does the action specified by the verb, habitually or occasionally,' which makes it a close equivalent of English *-er* (*writer, walker*) (20a). Grammatical gender matches biological gender for human referents, while non-human ones can be either masculine or feminine, though feminine ones are predominant (20b). For several nouns, both masculine and feminine forms are available either as synonyms or with some semantic differences (20c).

(20) a. *idea**tore**/**trice*** 'inventor,' *diret**tore**/**trice*** 'director,' *trucca**tore**/**trice*** 'makeup artist,' *bevi**tore**/**trice*** 'drinker,' *cammina**tore**/**trice*** 'walker.'
      b. *estin**tore*** 'fire extinguisher,' *frulla**tore*** 'blender'; *asciuga**trice*** 'dryer,' *fotocopia**trice*** 'photocopy machine,' *friggi**trice*** 'fryer.'
      c. *calcola**tore**/calcola**trice*** 'calculator'; *impasta**trice*** 'mixing machine' vs. *impasta**tore*** 'professional qualification' (i.e., someone who prepares ingredients and supervises the mixing process'); *trebbia**tore*** 'thresher' vs. *trebbia**trice*** 'threshing machine'; *scola**trice*** 'drainer' vs. *scola**tore*** 'drinker (humorous)' (i.e., 'someone who drains bottles').

The suffix *-ino* is a close semantic equivalent of *-tore/-trice* and is also quite common, though it tends to denote humbler and/or outdated occupations and attitudes charged with negative nuances.

(21) a. *imbianc**hino*** 'housepainter,' *spazz**ino*** 'streetsweeper,' *mond**ina*** 'paddy field worker'; *lecc**hino*** 'lickspittle,' *traffic**hino*** 'schemer; hustler,' *vagheg**gino*** 'fop.'
      b. *cancell**ino*** 'blackboard eraser,' *frull**ino*** 'whisk,' *macin**ino*** 'grinder,' *pass**ino*** 'strainer.'

Although nouns with human referents can be either feminine or masculine (i.e., grammatical gender can match biological gender), in some cases gender is actually fixed, being assigned on the basis of the job the noun denotes. Forms like *imbianchina* and *mondino* are practically non-existent because traditionally house painting was a men's job, and working in paddy fields a women's one. Also, some nouns have been replaced by newer, more socio-culturally neutral neologisms (e.g., *operatore/trice ecologico/a* 'lit. ecological operator' for *spazzino*). Nouns with non-human referents, on the other hand, are always masculine.

The last deverbal nominal suffix to note is *-io*, which carries iterative-intensifying (i.e., aspectual) value and predominantly selects verbs related to sounds. Although derivatives in *-io* are overall few, they are quite common (*borbott**io*** 'muttering,' *cinguett**io*** 'twittering,' *luccic**hio*** 'sparkling,' *mormor**io*** 'murmur(ing); rustling').

4.3.1.1.2 Adjectival suffixes

The most productive denominal adjectival suffixes are illustrated in (22).

(22) a. *-ale* is possibly the most productive and unrestricted, with its allomorph *-are* in bases with [l] in the last (or even previous) syllable: *caricaturale* 'ridiculous' (← *caricatura* 'caricature'), *facciale* 'facial,' *grammaticale* 'grammatical,' *invernale* 'of winter,' *promozionale* 'promotional'; *clientelare* 'crony,' *lunare* 'lunar,' *familiare* 'familial; familiar,' *tubolare* 'tubular.'

    b. *-ario*: *abitudinario* 'habitual,' *monetario* 'monetary,' *sanitario* 'pertaining to health; sanitary.'

    c. *-ile*: *giovanile* 'youthful,' *maschile* 'masculine,' *minorile* 'juvenile,' *primaverile* 'of spring.'

    d. *-ico* is predominant in technical/specialized vocabulary; nouns in *ia* are consistent bases: *astrologico* 'astrological,' *etnico* 'ethnic,' *filmico* 'filmic,' *scenico* 'scenic.'

    e. *-ivo*: *abusivo* 'illegal,' *festivo* 'festive,' *oggettivo* 'objective,' *sportivo* 'pertaining to sports'; it also takes verbal bases: *creativo* 'creative,' *corrosivo* 'corrosive,' *incisivo* 'incisive,' *protettivo* 'protective.'

A few other common denominal adjectival suffixes are illustrated in (23).

(23) a. *-ato*, *-uto* (which carries emphatic value): typically derive adjectives referring to physical features or qualities: *alato* 'winged,' *fortunato* 'lucky,' *palestrato* 'buff; iron.' (← *palestra* 'gym'); *baffuto* 'with a (big) moustache,' *forzuto* 'very strong; hum.,' *occhialuto* 'bespectacled; hum.,' *puntuto* 'pointy.'

    b. *-oso*: *angoscioso* 'distressing,' *facoltoso* 'wealthy,' *odoroso* 'sweet-smelling,' *muscoloso* 'muscular,' *noioso* 'boring,' *spiritoso* 'witty.'

    c. *-esco*: *camerateresco* 'inspiring comradeship' (← *camerata* 'dormitory'), *gigantesco* huge,' *pittoresco* 'picturesque'; it may bear a negative connotation: *animalesco* 'animal-like,' *manesco* 'ready with one's hands,' *pappagallesco* 'parrot-like'; and often take proper names as base: *modiglianesco* 'relative to A. Modigliani or his work.'

    d. *-ese* derives ethnic adjectives: *congolese* 'Congolese,' *finlandese* 'Finnish'; since the 1970s, it has been used to derive nouns denoting jargons and sector-based languages, often with a negative, pejorative connotation: *giornalese* 'journalist language' (← *giornale* 'newspaper'), *sinistrese* 'leftist language' (← *sinistra* 'left').

    e. *-ano/-iano* also derives ethnic adjectives: *americano* 'American,' *colombiano* 'Colombian'; it also forms adjectives referring to planets: *mercuriano* 'Mercurial,' *saturniano* 'Saturnian'; it is also quite productive with proper nouns as base: *luterano* 'Lutheran,' *fantozziano* 'slapstick; preposterous' (← *Fantozzi*, the name of a popular movie character), *trumpiano* 'pertaining to D. Trump.'

The most productive deverbal adjectival suffix is *-bile* (24a), while *-evole* is very common but no longer productive (24b). Several pairs of derivatives are available (24c) where the form in *-bile* commonly conveys the notion of possibility.

(24) a. *databile* 'datable,' *mangiabile* 'eatable,' *sopportabile* 'bearable, *vendibile* 'sellable.'

    b. *amichevole* 'friendly,' *incantevole* 'enchanting,' *meritevole* 'worthy of,' *vomitevole* 'nauseating.'

    c. *ingannabile* 'that can be deceived' ~ *ingannevole* 'deceiving,' *maneggiabile* 'that can be handled' ~ *maneggevole* 'easy to handle,' *mutabile* 'that can be changed' ~ *mutevole* 'that changes.'

Present and past participles can function as adjectives and, as most adjectives, may be nominalized (*un ragazzo drogato* 'a drugged boy,' *è un drogato* 'he is a drug addict' ← *drogare* 'drug'). This process is also referred to as conversion (see following).

4.3.1.1.3 Verbal suffixes

The derivation of verbs from nouns and adjectives via the infinitival suffixes *-are* and (more marginally) *-ire* is a core, extremely productive word-formation strategy in Italian, with nouns ending in *-zione* being a very common base.

(25) a. Denominal: *arpionare* 'harpoon,' *camminare* 'walk,' *cestinare* 'throw away,' *faxare* 'fax,' *testare* 'test,' *stazionare* 'be parked,' *surfare* 'surf (the internet),' *zappare* 'hoe,' *zuccherare* 'sugar'; *fiorire* 'flower,' *gestire* 'manage (a business, etc.),' *tornire* 'turn on a lathe.'

      b. Deadjectival: *basare* 'base,' *curiosare* 'look around; poke one's nose,' *seccare* 'dry'; *brunire* 'burnish,' *scurire* 'darken,' *snellire* 'make slim (also fig.).'

Three other important suffixes are *-izz-*, *-eggi-/-aggi-*, and *-ific-*, all followed by *-are*; *-izz-* carries primarily the meanings 'make/transform into' and 'do by means of something' (i.e., it carries factitive value).[16]

(26) a. Denominal: *anestetizzare* 'anesthetize,' *computerizzare* 'computerize,' *gambizzare* 'shoot someone in the legs,' *lottizzare* 'divide into lots,' *motorizzare* 'motorize,' *scannerizzare* 'scan,' *teorizzare* 'theorize.'

      b. Deadjectival: *americanizzare* 'Americanize,' *commercializzare* 'commercialize,' *modernizzare* 'modernize,' *formalizzare* 'formalize,' *pedonalizzare* 'pedestrianize,' *pubblicizzare* 'advertise,' *urbanizzare* 'urbanize.'

The suffix *-eggi-/-aggi-* typically conveys the meanings 'do/obtain something,' 'be/put in a state,' and 'imitate.'

(27) a. Denominal: *boccheggiare* 'gasp,' *cazzeggiare* 'fool around,' *corteggiare* 'woo,' *festeggiare* 'celebrate,' *lampeggiare* 'flash,' *messaggiare* 'text, message,' *ombreggiare* 'shade,' *patteggiare* 'negotiate,' *sorseggiare* 'sip,' *troneggiare* 'tower over.'

      b. Deadjectival: *amareggiare* 'embitter,' *biancheggiare* 'look white,' *frivoleggiare* 'act frivolously,' *rotondeggiare* 'be/become roundish,' *scarseggiare* 'be scarce/lacking.'

As for, *-ific-*, it carries factitive value and is strongly linked to nouns ending in *-zione* and *-tore/-trice*; it is less productive but is found in many common words.

(28) a. Denominal: *classificare* 'classify,' *cornificare* 'cheat on; colloq.' (← *fare le* **corna**; lit. 'make the horns'), *mummificare* 'mummify,' *personificare* 'personify,' *tonificare* 'invigorate.'

      b. Deadjectival: *diversificare* 'diversify,' *falsificare* 'falsify,' *solidificare* 'solidify,' *vanificare* 'nullify,' *umidificare* 'humidify.'

Once again, sets of two or even three derivatives with the same base are possible, which can be (quasi-)synonyms (*versificare* ~ *verseggiare* 'compose/put in verses' ← *verso* 'verse'), contrast in transitivity (*italianizzare* 'Italianize; transitive' ~ *italianeggiare* 'imitate Italians; intransitive'), or bear different meanings corresponding to different meanings of the base (*fiscalizzare* 'exempt from taxes' ← *fiscale* 'pertaining to taxes' ~ *fiscaleggiare* 'be uncompromising' ← *fiscale* 'uncompromising').

4.3.1.1.4 Evaluative suffixes

Evaluative suffixes hold a key place in the Italian lexicon due to their high productivity and frequency of use and the wide variety of subtle semantic and discourse pragmatic values they carry. They can be examined referring to two basic semantic domains: size and dis/approbation. Simply put, they express speakers' subjective evaluations concerning physical dimensions (small/big, young/old) or qualities in general (positive/negative). This is why they are often classified as diminutive, augmentative, and pejorative. However, evaluative suffixes also convey affective, emotive connotations subtly related to socio-cultural phenomena and conventions and regulated by the communicative setting, which is why they are much frequent in the context of family communication and prevail in the expression of humor with attenuating function but are not allowed in serious and official contexts.

The use of evaluative suffixes is also very irregular and overall unpredictable. It is not always clear whether or not a given evaluative suffix can apply to a certain base. Usually, blocking is triggered by lexicalized homonyms, that is, items originally modified by an evaluative suffix which developed a specific meaning and are no longer analyzable as including an evaluative suffix. Thus, *corpetto* 'bodice' (← *corpo* 'body' + -*etto*) has lost its connection to 'body' and no longer denotes 'a small body'; in order to convey such notion, the suffix -*ino* is used. Yet again, lexicalized homonyms may not block evaluative suffixation, as shown by *pancetta* (← *pancia* 'belly' + -*etta*), which has both the lexicalized meaning 'bacon' and the evaluative meaning 'round belly.' Phonological restrictions may also apply; for instance, words ending in /tV/ and /lV/ tend to refuse, respectively, -*etto* and -*ello*, while words ending in /inV/ tend to reject -*ino*. But these are just broad tendencies, and there are numerous exceptions.

Matching individual suffixes to one of the basic semantic domains is generally feasible, yet highly productive ones actually carry multiple (even opposite) connotations and pragmatic functions. Thus, augmentative -*one* normally conveys also pejorative value, while diminutive -*ino* is typically associated to positive value but can also convey negative connotations (indeed, it is also a 'proper' derivational affix, as seen earlier). Arbitrary, puzzling cases are not uncommon, one of the classic examples being *maschietto* 'little boy' (← *maschio* 'male' + -*etto*) and *femminuccia* 'little girl' (← *femmina* 'female' + -*uccia*) vs. *maschiuccio* and *femminetta*.

All word classes accept evaluative suffixation, though it is most productive with nouns (including compounds and proper names), followed by adjectives, then verbs. Evaluative suffixes attach to stem (*naso* 'nose' *nas-ino* 'cute little nose') and do not change the grammatical category of the base so that semantic features like 'abstract'/'concrete,' 'mass'/'count,' 'animate'/'inanimate' remain the same. They can change the inflectional class of the base, though (class 4 *poeta* ← class 1 *poetino*), and occasionally its gender (*sapone* 'soap.M' → *saponetta* 'soap bar.F'). Masculine/feminine pairs exist, in which case gender difference can correspond to semantic difference and the masculine member tends to be more lexicalized (*finestra* 'window.F' *finestrina* 'small window.F' vs. *finestrino* 'vehicle window.M').

The most common and most productive evaluative suffixes in Italian are briefly introduced in (29). If simple English glosses are unavailable for the derivative, only the primary semantic/pragmatic values of the diminutives are noted. We must keep in mind, though, that the semantic/pragmatic range of most evaluative suffixes is wide and complex, and that the proper interpretation of their semantic/pragmatic contribution is contingent upon the discourse setting.

(29) a. *-ino/a* is the most productive and has the widest semantic and pragmatic range, including diminutive (*scatolina* 'small box,' *verdino* 'light green'), attenuating/de-emphasizing (*regalino* 'little gift'), intensifying/emphasizing, often accompanied by irony (*difficilino* 'quite difficult,' *tardino* 'rather late').

   b. *-etto/a* is also widely productive; in addition to diminutive value (*casetta* 'small house'), it can connote mediocre or inferior quality (*attricetta* 'B-movie/mediocre actress,' *romanzetto* 'second-rate novel'), carry attenuating/de-emphasizing function (*bere una birretta/un goccetto* 'drink a beer/drop' to set a friendly, relaxed tone or offset negative links to alcohol drinking), and approbation/endearment value (*uomo* 'man' → *ometto* referring to a boy to express praise and affection). With verbs, it has mainly attenuative function (*picchiettare* 'tap' ← *picchiare* 'hit,' *scoppiettare* 'crackle' ← *scoppiare* 'burst').

   c. *-ello/a* is also very productive but more common in southern Italy; it carries irony and mild negative value (*viziatello* ← *viziato* 'spoiled') and shows a propensity toward lexicalization (*campana* 'bell' → *campanella* 'small bell; school bell, F' and *campanello* 'door/bicycle bell, M,' *forno* 'oven' → *fornello* 'stove,' *riga* 'line.F' → *righello* 'ruler.M').

   d. *-uccio/a* and its variant, *-uzzo/a*, more common in the south, carry both affective/attenuating value (*boccuccia* 'cute/little mouth,' *cosuccia* 'little thing; trifle,' *peccatuccio* 'minor sin') and depreciative/pejorative connotation (*botteguccia* 'second-rate shop,' *deboluccio* 'weakish').

   e. *-one* is widely productive and, basically, the augmentative counterpart of *-ino*; like *-ino*, it can have positive and negative value, though the meaning of big remains constant (*nasone* 'big nose,' *verdone* 'dark green,' *filmone* 'great movie'), and it more typically carries pejorative connotations with masculine nouns. With feminine nouns, it can trigger gender change (*donnone*.M and *donnona*.F 'big woman,' *gambone*.M and *gambona*.F 'big leg'). It productively derives nouns denoting people characterized by a given feature or quality that is perceived as negative: *guardone* 'peeping Tom' (← *guardare* 'to watch'), *spaccone* 'braggart' (← *spaccare* 'unpack'), *straccione* 'ragamuffin' (← *straccio* 'rag'), *ubriacone* 'drunkard' (← *ubriaco* 'drunk'). Two socio-culturally relevant, highly derogative nouns whose emergence is linked to the economic boom of the 1950s/1960s and the related massive immigration from the poor rural South to the wealthier industrial North are *polentone* 'northerner' (← *polenta*, which was the staple food in northern Italy) and *terrone* 'southerner' (← *terra* 'earth').

   f. *-accio/a* (and the regional (both northern and southern) variant *-azzo/a*) essentially carries pejorative value (*cappellaccio* 'ugly hat,' *donnaccia* 'bad woman; slut,' *fattaccio* 'foul deed').

The most common evaluative suffixes restricted to verbal bases are illustrated in (30). They derive *-are* verbs, and in addition to evaluation, they may also convey aspectual information, mainly frequentative aspect (i.e., repetition).

(30) a. *-acchi-/-icchi-*: *canticchiare* 'hum,' *dormicchiare* 'doze,' *lavoricchiare* 'work a little (lazily),' *ridacchiare* 'giggle,' *sputacchiare* 'spit.'

b. *-(er/ar)ell-*: *bucherell*are 'puncture,' *giocherell*are 'fiddle with,' *saltell*are 'hop, skip,' *trotterell*are 'trod along.'

c. *-ucchi-* and *-uzz-* carry pejorative connotation: *leggiucchi*are 'read listlessly,' *mangiucchi*are 'nibble,' *tagliu**zz**are* 'chop; shred.'

Multiple suffixes are possible in several combinations: *caffettino* 'coffee,' *ricciolettino* 'little ringlet.'

As already mentioned, nouns modified by evaluative suffixes often lose their semantic relationship to their bases. Some examples of common everyday items are *barella* 'stretcher' (← *bara* 'coffin'), *bocchetta* 'mouthpiece; nozzle,' *bocchino* 'cigarette holder,' *boccone* 'mouthful' (← *bocca* 'mouth'), *bugiardino* 'patient information leaflet' (← *bugiardo* 'liar'), *camicetta* 'blouse' (← *camicia* 'shirt'), *cappuccino* 'Capuchin' (← *cappuccio* 'hood' ← *cappa* 'cape'), *cartina* 'map, cigarette paper' (← *carta* 'paper'), *fantino* 'jockey' (← *fante* 'infantryman'), *figurina* 'figurine; picture card,' *figurino* 'fashion sketch' (← *figura* 'figure'), *forchetta* 'fork' (← *forca* 'pitchfork'), *lampadina* 'light bulb' (← *lampada* 'lamp'), *mattonella* 'tile' (← *mattone* 'brick'), *spaghetti* (← *spago* 'string'), *scappatella* 'fling' (← *scappata* 'short visit'), *spazzolino* 'toothbrush,' *spazzolone* 'scrubbing brush' (← *spazzola* 'brush'), *telefonino* 'cellphone' (← *telefono* 'telephone'), *uncinetto* 'crochet hook' (← *uncino* 'hook').

4.3.1.2 Prefixation

In Italian, prefixation is the second most productive word-formation process after suffixation and is widespread in the core vocabulary. Generally, prefixes are less restricted than suffixes in terms of the types of base they can select so that many prefixes productively select bases from all word classes. Moreover, unlike suffixation, prefixation does not result in change of word class, though there are exceptions, as for instance the prefix *anti* 'against,' which derives adjectives from nouns (*antiruggine* 'anti-rust').

Most commonly, prefixes develop from prepositions and adverbs whose (core) semantic values they retain; thus, they can be grouped into different classes according to their meaning. One of the main semantic domains covered by prefixes is space and time relations. The array of prefixes which convey locative and temporal meanings is rather large and includes prefixes which are no longer or are minimally productive but appear in common, high-frequency items. We can only examine a small selection, focusing on highly productive prefixes.

(31) a. 'In front; before'

i. *Anti-/Ante-*: it is hardly productive with both spatial and temporal value but is found in some common, everyday-life terms: *anticamera* 'hall; anteroom,' *anteguerra* 'prewar period' and 'prewar; inv. A,' *antipasto* 'appetizer' (← *pasto* 'meal'), *anteprima* 'show preview.'

ii. *Pre-*: with locative value, it is productive almost exclusively in technical/specialistic domains: *prefrontale* 'prefrontal,' *prenominale* 'prenominal position'; with temporal value, it is found in several common neologisms: *precotto* 'precooked,' *prelavaggio* 'prewash,' *prepensionamento* 'early retirement.' It also select verbs (*preconfezionare* 'prepackage,' *prepagare* 'prepay,' *prevedere* 'foresee') and adjectives (*prebellico* 'prewar,' *prematrimoniale* 'premarital').

   b. 'Back; after'

       i.   ***Post*-**: overall, it is restricted to technical/specialistic terminology, both with locative (***post***occipitale 'post occipital,' ***post***verbale 'postverbal') and temporal value (***post***operatorio 'post surgery,' ***post***parto 'postnatal').

       ii. ***Retro*-**: ***retro***bottega 'back shop,' ***retro***formazione 'backformation,' ***retro***marcia 'reverse (gear),' ***retro***attivo 'retroactive,' ***retro***datare 'backdate.'

   c. 'Outside': ***extra*-** (***extra***comunitario 'non-EU (national),' ***extra***coniugale 'extramarital,' ***extra***parlamentare 'extra-parliamentary,' ***extra***terrestre 'extraterrestrial').

   d. 'Above; over': ***sopra*-/*sovra*-** (***sopra***bito 'overcoat,' ***sopra***cciglia (above.lashes) 'highbrows'; ***sopra***nnaturale 'supernatural,' ***sopra***elevare 'elevate'; ***sovra***mano 'superhuman'; ***sovra***stare 'dominate; hang over').

   e. 'Below; under': ***sotto*-** (***sotto***bicchiere 'coaster,' ***sotto***cutaneo 'subcutaneous,' ***sotto***marino 'submarine,' ***sotto***passaggio 'underpass,' ***sotto***veste 'slip').

Another important semantic domain covered by prefixes is that of evaluative relations pertaining to both quantity and quality, as well as to role hierarches. Evaluative relations can be viewed as metaphorical extensions of spatial relations, given the strong conceptual link between 'more/better' and 'above' (positive), and 'less/worse' and 'below' (negative) (Lakoff & Johnson, 1980). A brief overview of the current most prominent Italian evaluative prefixes is offered in (32) and (33). Note that these prefixes usually carry emphatic value and thrive in the languages of advertising and media.

(32) 'More; better'

   a. ***Extra*-**: ***extra***fine 'high/higher-quality (food product),' ***extra***rapido 'very fast,' ***extra***vergine 'extra virgin (oil).'

   b. ***Iper*-**: ***iper***calorico 'high-calorie,' ***iper***critico 'hypercritical,' ***iper***sensibile 'hypersensitive'; ***iper***mercato 'hypermarket,' ***iper***dosaggio 'hyper-dosage.'

   c. ***Maxi*-**: ***maxi***cappotto 'ankle-long overcoat,' ***maxi***nchiesta 'gloss,' ***maxi*-***ingorgo 'huge traffic jam,' ***maxi***processo 'trial involving many defendants,' ***maxi***schermo 'giant screen,' ***maxi***multa 'maxi-fine.'

   d. ***Mega*-**: ***mega*-***appalto 'big (important) contract,' ***mega***concerto 'mega-concert,' ***mega***promozione 'big advertising campaign,' ***mega***vincita 'huge win,' ***mega***galattico 'gigantic; massive.'

   e. ***Stra*-** carries the connotation 'excessive': ***stra***colmo 'overflowing,' ***stra***fatto 'totally drunk/stoned; coll.,' ***stra***ricco 'extremely rich,' ***stra***vecchio 'very old.'

   f. ***Super*-**: ***super***alcolico 'hard liquor,' ***super***carcere 'maximum security prison,' ***super***latitante 'super-fugitive,' ***super***mercato 'supermarket,' ***super***petroliera 'supertanker,' ***super***procuratore 'special prosecutor,' ***super***testimone 'star witness,' ***super***accessoriato 'fully accessorized,' ***super***dissetante 'very thirst-quenching,' ***super***idratante 'super-moisturizing.'

   g. ***Ultra*-**. ***ultra***destra/sinistra 'extreme right/left (politics),' ***ultra***rapido 'high-speed,' ***ultra***moderno 'ultramodern,' ***ultra***piatto 'ultra-thin,' ***ultra***sensibile 'ultrasensitive.'

(33) 'Less; worse'

   a. ***Mini*-** is highly productive: ***mini***abito 'mini-dress,' ***mini***appartamento 'studio apartment,' ***mini***confezione 'minipack,' ***mini***criminale 'underage criminal,' ***mini***serie 'limited TV series.'

b. **Sotto-:** *sottocommissione* 'sub-committee,' *sottogruppo* 'sub-group,' *sottomarca* 'generic brand,' *sottopagato* 'underpaid,' *sottosegretario* 'undersecretary,' *sottotenente* 'second lieutenant,' *sottovalutato* 'underrated.'

c. **Vice-:** *viceparroco* 'vice parish priest,' *vicepreside* 'vice-principal,' *vicequestore* 'assistant/deputy commissioner,' *viceré* 'viceroy,' *vicesegretario* 'vice-secretary,' *vicesindaco* 'vice-major.'

A third core semantic domain often expressed by prefixes is 'negation,' which encompasses the following values: adversative (against, opposing), privative (absence, scarcity), reversative (reverse, undo), and pejorative.

(34) a. **a-:** *asociale* 'antisocial; unsociable,' *asessuale* 'asexual,' *asettico* 'aseptic,' *asimmetria* 'asymmetry,' *atipico* 'atypical.'

b. **anti-:** *antieroe* 'antihero,' *antiterrorismo* 'antiterrorism'; recent formations include many invariable denominal adjectives: *antimacchia* 'stain proof,' *anticellulite* 'anticellulite,' *antismagliature* 'anti-stretchmark.'

c. **contro-:** *controbilanciare* 'counterbalance,' *controinterrogare* 'cross-examine,' *controfigura* 'double,' *contrordine* 'counter-order,' *contromarca* 'pass-out ticket.'

d. **dis-:** *disabile* 'disable,' *disaccordo* 'disagreement,' *disagio* 'discomfort,' *disalberare* 'dismast,' *disconnetere* 'disconnect,' *discontinuità* 'discontinuity,' *disfare* 'undo,' *disonesto* 'dishonest,' *disonorare* 'dishonor,' *disordine* 'untidiness; disorder,' *disseppellire* 'unearth,' *disunire* 'separate.'

e. **in-** is very productive but restricted to adjectives: *inesperto* 'inexperienced,' *indesiderato* 'unwanted,' *impotente* 'impotent,' *illegale* 'illegal,' *irriconoscente* 'ungrateful'.[17]

f. **s-** is no longer productive with adversative value but conveys this meaning in a score of frequent adjectives (*scomodo* 'uncomfortable,' *scortese* 'impolite,' *sleale* 'disloyal; unfair'). With verbs, it is quite productive with privative and reversative value (*smacchiare* 'remove stains,' *sradicare* 'uproot,' *stappare* 'uncork; uncap,' *struccare* 'remove make-up'; *scongelare* 'defrost,' *smagnetizzare* 'demagnetize') and often carries negative, pejorative connotation (*sfortuna* 'misfortune,' *sparlare* 'bad-mouth,' *sragionare* 'to rave'). It is extremely productive in parasynthesis (see following text).

One last prefix worth attention is *ri-*, which carries iterative (repetition), reversative, and intensifying value and is highly productive with verbs: *riacquistare* 'regain,' *ricucire* 'stich/sew again/up; mend,' *rifare* 'do again,' *ripulire* 'clean up/again,' *rivedere* 'see again.'

4.3.1.3 Parasynthesis

Parasynthesis involves simultaneous application of prefixation and suffixation. It is very productive in Italian (and Romance languages in general), especially in the derivation of denominal and deadjectival verbs, and it produces many common, high-frequency verbs. The distinctive feature of parasynthetic derivatives is that neither the un-prefixed derivative nor the un-prefixed nominal/adjectival base are actually attested; for example, *sbalordire* 'stun, amaze' is derived from the adjective *balordo* 'stupid, silly' via prefixation of *s-* and suffixation of *-ire*, but neither does the verb ★*balordire* nor the adjective ★*sbalordo* exist. Parasynthetic verbs typically belong to the first conjugation (in *-are*) and more marginally to the third conjugation (*-ire*), though actually parasynthesis is what keeps the third conjugation productive.

The prefixes most commonly involved in parasynthesis are *ad-*, *de-*, *dis*, *in-*, and *s-*. Parasynthetic verbs in *ad-* and *–in-* carry primarily causative/factitive and ingressive/inchoative value (i.e., 'make/become (like)'), as well as locative (i.e., 'put in/on') and instrumental (i.e., 'do by means of').

(35) a. **ad-**[18]

    i. Denominal: **ab**bindolare 'trick,' abbracciare 'hug,' accerchiare 'surround,' addentare 'bit into,' addolorare 'sadden,' affettare 'slice,' affollare 'crowd.'

    ii. Deadjectival: **ab**bellire 'embellish,' addolcire 'sweeten,' arricchire 'make wealthy; enrich,' arrossire 'blush.'

  b. **in-**

    i. Denominal: **in**cartare 'wrap,' incipriare 'powder,' infornare 'put in the oven,' impallinare 'riddle with shots,' insabbiare 'bury in sand; fig.,' invigorire 'strengthen.'

    ii. Deadjectival: **im**biancare 'whiten,' imbruttire 'make/become ugly,' infradiciare 'soak,' ingiallire 'become yellow,' ingrassare 'gain weight,' intubare 'intubate.'

Verbs in *de-*, *dis,-* and *s-* carry privative (i.e., 'remove') and reversative (i.e., 'undo' do the opposite') value (36), and can also have intensifying function (37).

(36) a. **de-/di-**

    i. Denominal: **de**caffeinare 'decaffeinate,' derattizzare 'rat exterminate,' dirottare 'hijack.'

    ii. Deadjectival: **di**margire 'lose wight,' denudare 'strip',

  b. **dis-**

    i. Denominal: **dis**boscare 'deforest,' discolpare 'clear someone (of blame),' diserbare 'weed,' disossare 'debone,' dissanguare 'bleed dry.'

    ii. Deadjectival: **dis**acerbare 'soothe,' disambiguare 'disambiguate.'

  c. **s-**

    i. Denominal: **s**bottonare 'unbutton,' sbucciare 'peel,' scartare 'unwrap,' sfamare 'feed,' sfornare 'take out of the oven,' snodare 'untie.'

    ii. Deadjectival: **s**foltire 'thin out.'

(37) a. Denominal: **s**bandierare 'wave a flag; show off,' sbocciare 'bloom,' sbriciolare 'crumble,' sferragliare 'rattle.'

  b. Deadjectival: **s**biancare 'whiten; grow white,' scaldare 'warm up,' spianare 'level,' sprofondare 'sink.'

Most parasynthetic verbs can occur with *si*, which can have pronominal reflexive/reciprocal function (*imbottirsi* 'stuff oneself,' *abbracciarsi* 'hug each other'), have ingressive/inchoative or intensifying function (*invecchiarsi* 'become old'), or be lexicalized (*arrabbiarsi* 'get angry' vs. *⋆arrabbiare* 'make angry'). Parasynthesis has produced several rather-expressive verbs commonly used in informal/colloquial registers (*imputtanarsi* 'disgrace oneself,' *sputtanare/ sputtanarsi* 'discredit someone/oneself in a resounding way' ← *puttana* 'whore'; *scornarsi* 'be disappointed/humiliated/laughed at' ← *corna* 'horns') or typical of youth language (*impasticcarsi* 'use drugs' ← *pasticca* 'pill'; *infrattarsi* 'hide (to be intimate with someone)' ← *fratta* 'bush'; *intripparsi* 'be passionate about something' ← Engl. *trip*).

4.3.2 Compounding

Compounding (or **composition**) consists in joining two (possibly/rarely more) words from the same or different word categories to derive a composite word, or **compound** (*ladyfinger* (NN), *pickpocket* (VN), *skyscraper* (NV), *overcoat* (PrN), *undermine* (PrV). Compounds can be written as one word (*dishwasher, sunflower*), as hyphenated (*check-in, long-term*), or as separate words (*barbed wire, peanut butter*). Generally, older compounds, particularly those whose meanings are no longer compositional, tend to be written as one word (*ladybug, redneck*), and guidelines are provided in manuals and grammars; however, these are only spelling conventions since compounds always constitute single lexical items both semantically and (morpho) syntactically. In Italian, compounding has been increasing considerably since the last decades of the nineteenth century and continues to expand steadily especially in technical/specialized lexicons. Before reviewing the main compound types found in Italian, some key classificatory terminology must be introduced.

One important distinction is that between endocentric and exocentric compounds. In **endocentric** compounds, one constituent, the **head**, is more prominent than the other, the **modifier** – that is, the head determines the grammatical category of the compound, while the modifier determines its semantics. Thus, endocentric compounds denote 'a type of X,' where X stands for the head; for instance, *greenhouse* and *ferryboat* are endocentric compounds since they denote, respectively, a specific type of house/building and a specific a kind of boat. The position of the head varies across languages. Italian endocentric compounds are primarily left-headed (**nave** *traghetto* vs. *ferry***boat**). Right-headed compounds are either Latinisms (*terremoto* 'earthquake') or modelled on loanwords (*guerra lampo* ← German *Blitzkrieg*, *baby gang* 'a gang whose members are very young'). In contrast, the constituents of **exocentric** compounds do not stand in a head–modifier relationship; rather, the head is unexpressed, or 'external,' and the compound does not denote 'a type of X': a *blackhead* is not a type of head, a *redneck* a type of neck, and *belladonna* (← *bella* 'beautiful' + *donna* 'woman') is not a beautiful lady.

Another important distinction is between **subordinate** compounds, where one constituent functions as a sort of complement of the other (*tosaerba* (mow.lawn) 'lawnmower' is a machine that cuts the grass), and **coordinative** compounds, where both constituents are on the same level syntactically and semantically (*divano letto* 'sofabed' is a piece of furniture that functions both as a couch and a bed).

Essentially, Italian has only compound nouns and adjectives; compound verbs are quite marginal and typically involve repetition (*fuggi fuggi* (flee.flee) 'stampede') or a combination of two verbs with opposite meaning (*bagnasciuga* (wet.dry) 'water's edge,' *saliscendi* (climb. descend) 'latch,' *toccasana* (touch.heal) 'miracle cure').

The most productive pattern for compound nouns is by far NN, which derives primarily endocentric compounds.

(38) a. Subordinate: *capostazione* (head.station) 'station master,' *carro bestiame* (wagon. livestock) 'animal wagon,' *fondovalle* (bottom.valley) 'valley bottom,' *posto auto* (place. car) 'parking space,' *treno merci* (train.freight) 'freight train,' *sala parto* (hall.delivery) 'delivery room.'

   b. Coordinate: *bambino prodigio* 'child prodigy,' *cassapanca* (box.bench) 'settle,' *cane poliziotto* (dog.policeman) 'police dog,' *quartiere dormitorio* (neighborhood.dormitory) 'commuter area,' *ristorante-pizzeria* 'restaurant-pizzeria,' *vetroresina* (glass.resin) 'fiberglass.'

The head assigns gender to the compound (*il* 'the.M' *carro bestiame, la* 'the.F' *sala parto*), though with human referents, gender may match biological sex (*il/la capostazione*). Only the head is pluralized (*capistazione/*capistazioni, ristoranti-pizzeria/*ristorante-pizzerie*), though the modifier can be in plural to begin with (*sala giochi* 'amusement arcade').

Another prominent pattern is VN, a typical Romance pattern which is highly productive to derive endocentric subordinate compounds denoting machines, instruments, and containers/receptacles (39a) and, more infrequently, nouns denoting occupations or dispositions (39b).[19]

(39) a. *apriscatole* 'can opener,' *asciugacapelli* 'hair dryer,' *bloccasterzo* 'steering lock,' *lavastoviglie* 'dishwashing machine,' *passaverdura* 'vegetable mill,' *portaombrelli* 'umbrella stand,' *puntaspilli* 'pincushion,' *salvagente* 'life buoy,' *spazzaneve* 'snowplow,' *tergicristallo* 'windshield wiper,' *tritaprezzemolo* 'parsley chopper.'

   b. *guardaboschi* (watch.forests) 'forester,' *guardaspalle* (watch.shoulders) 'body guard,' *lavapiatti* 'dishwasher,' *portabandiera* 'standard bearer,' *portaborse* (carry.bags) 'lackey, pejor.,' *rubacuori* (steal.heart) 'charmer,' *strizzacervelli* 'headshrinker' (loanword from Eng.).

Compounds of this type are masculine (with the usual proviso about human referents) and invariable in number (*nuovo* 'new.M.SG' *passaverdura* ~ *nuovi* 'new.M.PL' *passaverdura*). The status of the verbal constituent remains controversial, and it has been viewed as the second singular imperative form, the third singular present indicative, and the verb theme.

The pattern AN is also productive and typically derives nouns displaying features expressed by the adjective, though fully lexicalized compounds (i.e., compounds whose meaning is no longer derivable by the constituents' meaning) are not uncommon. As the VN pattern, it forms primarily endocentric compounds.

(40) *altoparlante* '(laud)speaker,' *alta/bassa marea* 'high/low tide,' *alto/bassorilievo* 'high/bas-relief,' *buonuscita* (good.exit) 'golden handshake,' *biancospino* (white.thorn) 'hawthorn,' *galantuomo* and *gentiluomo* 'gentleman,' *grancassa* (big.box) 'bass drum.'

Gender is assigned by the nominal constituent, which also receives number marking (*biancospini, grancasse*).

The pattern NA displays low productivity; it derives both endocentric (41a) and exocentric compounds (41b), many of which are calques from English.

(41) a. *acqua santa* 'holy water,' *chiave inglese* (key.English) 'monkey wrench,' *cassaforte* (box.strong) 'safe,' *filospinato* 'barbed wire,' *scala mobile* 'escalator,' *sciopero bianco* (strike.white) 'slowdown,' *tavola calda* (table.warm) 'snack bar.'

   b. *colletto bianco* 'white-collar worker,' *casco blu* (helmet.blue) 'UN military member,' *casco rosso* (helmet.red) 'firefighter,' *pellerossa* (skin.red) 'Native American Indian,' *piedipiatti* (feet.flat) 'cop,' *viso pallido* (face.pale) 'white person.'

Two patterns are available for compound adjectives: AA (42a) and VN (42b).

(42) a. *agrodolce* 'sweet-and-sour,' *dolceamaro* 'bittersweet.'

   b. *mozzafiato* 'breathtaking,' *strappalacrime* 'tear-jerker.'

AA is highly productive, particularly for deriving ethnic adjectives (*anglo-normannno* 'Anglo-Norman,' *cecoslovacco* 'Czechoslovakian') and adjectives referring to soccer teams by the colors of their uniforms (*giallorosso* (yellow.red) 'of AS Roma').

4.3.2.1 Neoclassic compounds

Neoclassical compounding is the word-formation process that involves formative elements of Latin and Greek origin, commonly referred to as **affixoid**. Like affixes, affixoids are bound morphemes, which can be either in word-initial (**prefixoids**, *poli*ambulatorio 'health center' ← Gr. *polús-* 'many' + *ambulatorio* 'doctor's office') or word-final position (**suffix-oids**, *video*teca 'video store' ← Latin -THECA 'collection'), and many can occur in both positions (*filo*americano 'pro-American' ← Gr. *phílo* 'friend,' americano*filo* 'pro-American'). Unlike affixes, though, affixoids carry lexical meaning and can also combine with each other (*encefalo-grafia* 'encephalography' ← Gr. *egképhalos* 'which is inside the head' + *graphía* 'writing'), even in combination of more than two (*elettro*encefalografia 'electroencephalography' ← Latin ELĔCTRU(M) 'amber'). Finally, neoclassical compounds differ from 'normal' compounds in being more commonly right-headed, following the compounding pattern of Greek and Latin

Although neoclassical compounding is especially productive in technical/specialized languages, it also accounts for an important part of the common contemporary lexicon, and those involving prefixoids appear to be expanding. Small illustrative samples are given in (43) and (44), focusing on more recent and socio-culturally relevant neologisms.

(43) a. **auto-** 'self': **auto**pilota 'autopilot,' **auto**ritratto 'self-portrait,' **auto**scatto 'self-timer,' **auto**stima 'self-esteem.'

 b. **auto-** 'car-related' (← **auto**mobile 'car'): **auto**accessori 'car accessories,' **auto**blindata 'armored car,' **auto**scontro 'bumper cars,' **auto**scuola 'driving school,' **auto**stop 'hitch-hiking,' **auto**strada 'highway.'

 c. **bio-** (Gr. -bíos 'life'): **bio**agricoltura 'organic farming,' **bio**carburante 'biofuel,' **bio**pulitura 'cleaning by means of bacteria' and **bio** restauro 'restoration using *biopulitura*',[20] **bio**testamento 'living will.'

 d. **eco-** (←ecologia 'ecology'): **eco**catastrofe 'environmental disaster,' **eco-**edilizia 'eco-construction,' **eco-**hotel, **eco**mafia 'mafia involved in environmental crimes,' **eco**mostro 'ugly and environmentally damaging building,' **eco**pacifista 'eco-pacifist,' **eco**strage 'environmental massacre,' **eco**tassa 'green tax,' **eco**terrorismo 'ecoterrorism,' **eco**turismo 'ecotourism.'

 e. **foto-** (← fotografia 'photography'): **foto**composizione 'filmsetting,' **foto**modella 'fashion model,' **foto**montaggio 'photomontage,' **foto**romanzo 'photoromance.'

 f. **tele-** (← Gr. tēle- 'far-off'): **tele**comando 'remote control,' **tele**fax 'fax,' **tele**obiettivo 'telephoto lens,' **tele**pass 'electronic pass,' **tele**visione 'television.'

 g. **tele-** (← televisione 'television'): **tele**film 'TV movie,' **tele**quiz 'TV game show,' **tele**vendita 'teleshopping.'

 h. **termo-** (← Gr. thermós 'warm'): **termo**arredo (termo.furnishings) 'towel warmer,' **termo**coperta 'electric blanket,' **termo**ventilatore 'hot-air fan,' **termo**visiera (termo.visor) 'detached defroster.'

(44) a. **-manìa** (← Gr. manía 'madness'): cioccolato**mania** 'chocolate-mania,' rambo**mania** 'Rambo-mania.'

 b. **-metro** (← Gr. métron 'measure'): applauso**metro** 'applause meter,' parchi**metro** 'parking meter,' pedo**metro** 'pedometer,' reddito**metro** 'system for assessing income,' tachi**metro** 'speedometer,' tassa**metro** 'taximeter.'

The formative -*poli* (← Gr. *polís* 'city') instantiates an interesting case of socio-culturally driven semantic change. Due to the success of the neologism *tangento**poli*** 'protection money. poli' coined by the press to refer to the massive scandal that arose in the early 1990s exposing the deeply corrupted Italian political and economic situation, -*poli* acquired the connotation of 'scandalous; illegal,' as attested by neologisms like *baracco**poli*** (← *baracca* 'shack') and *tendo**poli*** (← *tenda* 'tent'), which denote (unauthorized) provisional conglomerations of non-permanent dwellings established after a natural disaster or related to immigration and often related to corruption, and *calcio**poli*** (← *calcio* 'soccer'), which denotes the notorious match-fixing soccer scandal from 2006.

4.3.2.2 Syntagmatic constructions

Syntagmatic constructions are lexical units typically comprising more than two words; they can belong to all word classes, though nominal and verbal are by far more common.[21] One of their distinctive features is that they tend to carry idiomatic meaning (*lupo di mare* (wolf.of.sea) 'sea dog,' *numero verde* (number.green) 'toll-free number'), though many of them are semantically transparent (*macchina da cucire* (machine.for.sew) 'sewing machine'). With two-word items, determining whether they are syntagmatic constructions or compounds may be rather challenging. Semantic transparency is typically taken as a key distinguishing parameter, with low transparency linked to syntagmatic constructions, though borderline cases are not rare; for instance, *effetto serra* (effect.greenhouse) 'greenhouse effect' is alternately considered a syntagmatic construction (Dardano, 2009, p. 227; Voghera, 2004, p. 63) and a compound (Palermo, 2020, p. 135).

The main patterns for nominal syntagmatic constructions are NA (45a), AN (45b), and NPrN (45c), which possibly is the most productive.

(45) a. *anima gemella* (soul.twin) 'soulmate,' *capitale sociale* (capital.social) 'capital stock,' *casa editrice* 'publishing house,' *musica leggera* (music.light) 'pop/mainstream music,' *ora legale* (hour.legal) 'daylight saving time,' *scheda bianca* (card.white) 'unmarked ballot paper,' *voce bianca* (voice.white) 'treble.'

   b. *alte sfere* 'upper echelons,' *bella/brutta copia* (beautiful/ugly.copy) 'final/rough draft,' *terzo mondo* 'third world,' *ultima spiaggia* (last.shore) 'last resort.'

   c. *avviso di sfratto* (warning.of.eviction) 'eviction order,' *bagaglio a mano* (luggage. on.hand) 'carry-on luggage,' *benzina senza piombo* (gas.without.lead) 'unleaded gas,' *borsa di studio* (bag.of.study) 'scholarship,' *carta di credito* (card.of.credit) 'credit card,' *cibo per cani* (food.for.dog) 'dog food,' *ferro da stiro* (iron.for.ironing) 'iron,' *ferro di cavallo* (iron.of.horse) 'horseshoe,' *permesso di soggiorno* (permit.of.stay) 'residence permit,' *punto di vista* 'viewpoint,' *mulino ad acqua/a vento* 'water/wind mill,' *vigile del fuoco* (vigilant.of.the.fire) 'fire fighter.'

The NN pattern is also available, but many members of this class are controversial in that they are variably viewed as compounds or syntagmatic expressions.

(46) *busta paga* (envelop.pay) 'pay slip,' *campo profughi* 'refugee camp,' *conferenza stampa* 'press conference,' *fine settimana* 'weekend,' *piano terra* 'ground floor,' *punto vendita* 'retail outlet,' *rimborso spese* (reimbursement.expenses) 'reimbursement.'

Two interesting syntagmatic constructions involving verbal components are (scratch.and. win) *gratta e vinci* 'scratch-card (lottery)' and *usa e getta* (use.and.throw away) 'disposable.'

Verbal syntagmatic constructions are also common and display a variety of structures and varying degrees of semantic complexity and expressivity, as shown in (47).

(47) *andare via* 'go away; disappear,' *avere le mani bucate* (have.hands.with.holes) 'spend money like water,' *buttare giù* 'take down; depress; swallow; write quickly,' *dare buca* (give.hole) 'flake on someone,' *dare i numeri* (give.the.numbers) 'talk nonsense,' *essere alla frutta* (be.at.the.fruit) 'be exhausted/done,' *piantare in asso* (leave.in.ace) 'leave somebody in the lurch,' *prendere con le pinze* (take.with the.tongs) 'handle cautiously/ with a grain of salt,' *prendere di petto* (take.from.breast) 'face head on,' *smaltire la scimmia* (get over.the.monkey) 'sober up,' *tirare le cuoia* (pull.the.hide) 'die,' *tirare su* 'lift up; inspire; comfort; raise.'

One important subclass of syntagmatic verbs is represented by *verbi procomplementari* (De Mauro, 1999–2000, p. xxxiv). These are high-frequency verbs that incorporate one or more atonic pronouns and tend to be highly idiomatic and/or expressive.

(48) a. *entrarci* (enter.here) 'be related to/involved into something,' *starci* (stay.here) 'agree'; *darla* (give.it.F) 'have sex easily, of women,' *farla* (do.it.F) 'deceive; prevail upon some-one cunningly; defecate'; *darle* (give.them.F) 'beat; defeat,' *prenderle* (take.them.F) 'be beaten; be defeated.'
   b. *andarsene* (go.*si.ne*) 'leave; go away,' *farcela* (do.*ci*.it.F) 'manage,' *prendersela* (take.*si*.it.F) 'take offence, be upset.'

Some common syntagmatic adjectives are *acqua e sapone* (water.and.soap) 'who does not use makeup,' *alla mano* (at.the.hand) 'easygoing,' *al verde* (at.the.green) 'penniless,' *andata e ritorno* (and.return) 'roundtrip,' *pasta **in bianco*** (in.white) 'pasta dressed with butter/oil only,' and two peculiar interjections are *buonanotte ai suonatori/al secchio* (goodnight.to.the.musi-cians/to.the.pail) 'and that's that!' *in bocca al lupo* (in.mouth.of.the.wolf) 'break a leg.'

4.3.3 Other strategies

4.3.3.1 Conversion

Conversion is a derivational process that derives lexemes belonging to a different word class than their base with no affix marking the change. Overall, conversion is fairly marginal in Italian, where it concerns primarily the derivation of deadjectival nouns (49a), which includes past and present participles (49b), followed by deverbal nouns (49c).

(49) a. *accademico/a* 'university/college member' (← *accademico* 'academic'), *anziano/a* 'elderly person,' *pubblico* 'audience' (← *pubblico* 'public'), *quotidiano* 'daily paper' (← *quotidiano* 'daily').
   b. *stretta* 'grip,' *vista* 'sight,' *taglio* 'cut'; *credente* 'believer,' *dirigente* 'executive' (← *dirigere* 'manage'), *mutante* 'mutant' (← *mutare* 'change'), *passante* 'passer-by,' *stampante* 'printer.'

   c. *arrivo* 'arrival,' *assaggio* 'taste,' *balzo* 'leap,' *coccola* 'caress' (← *coccolare* 'cuddle'), *consegna* 'delivery,' *indirizzo* 'address,' *ritorno* 'return,' *scherzo* 'joke,' *sveglia* 'alarm clock' (← *svegliare* 'wake up'), *traccia* 'mark; trace.'

Among nominalized present participles, the neologism *badante* 'caregiver' (← *badare* 'look after; take care of') is worth noting for its current socio-cultural import since it has come to denote a specific kind of caregiver, namely, a usually non-professional female immigrant, primarily from Eastern Europe or South America, who takes care of the elderly.

The nominalization of infinitives and gerunds may also be considered as conversion, though it is quite marginal. In the case of infinitives, it is basically limited to *dovere/i* 'duty/ies' (← *dovere* 'have to'), *piacere/i* 'pleasure/s' (← *piacere* 'like'), *potere/i* 'power/s' (← *potere* 'be able'), *volere/i* 'wish/es' (← *volere* 'want'). Nominalized gerunds are typically restricted to technical/specialized vocabulary, mostly directly inherited from Latin: *addendo* 'addend' (← Latin ADDĔRE 'to add'), *laureando* 'senior (student)' (← *laureare* 'confer a degree').

Some linguists include, under conversion, the derivation of verbs from nouns (*visionare* 'examine; screen' ← *visione* 'vision; view') and adjectives (*chiarire* 'clarify; clear up' ← *chiaro* 'clear'), even though addition of the infinitival suffix is involved in this case.

4.3.3.2 Backformation

Backformation is a word-formation strategy which derives neologisms through deletion of affixes (mainly suffixes) or elements interpreted as such. Simply put, backformation implies 'incorrect' etymologies and is driven by analogy: words which display a morphological structure conforming to productive derivational patterns are analyzed as derivatives of non-existing bases, which are then created by removing the material interpreted as affix. One common case of backformation in Italian is the creation of verbs from non-derived nouns in *-zione* by reverting the productive process that derives noun in *-zione* from verbs; two examples are *perquisire* 'search (in an official investigation)' back-formed from *perquisizione* 'search' (< Latin PERQUISITIONE(M) 'thorough investigation'), *correlare* 'correlate' derived from *correlazione* 'correlation.' Though backformation is most productive for deriving verbs, it can also target nouns; for instance, *postfazione* 'postface' is derived from *prefazione* 'preface' by reanalysis of *fazione* as a nominal base to which the prefix *post-* is attached, and *canotta* 'undershirt; sleeveless top' comes from *canottiera* (← *canottiere* 'rower'), with the same meaning.

4.3.3.3 Shortening

Shortening is a cover term for several word-abbreviation strategies; technically, then, it is not an actual word-formation process, as it derives reduced variants of existing lexical items. Two main types of shortening are observed in Italian clipping and acronyms.

  Clipping involves deleting material from the beginning, end (or even both) of a word ((*tele*)**phone**, **info**(*rmation*), (*in*)**flu**(*enza*)). For Italian, the term *truncation* might be preferable since only word-final material is removed. A sample of frequent examples is given in (50).

(50) a. *auto* (← *automobile*) 'car,' *bici* (← *bicicletta*) 'bicycle,' *chilo* (← *chilogrammo*) 'kilogram,' *cinema/cine* (← *cinematografo*) 'movie theatre,' *etto* (← *ettogrammo*) 'hectogram,' *flebo*

(← *fleboclisi*) 'drip,' *foto* (← *fotografia*) 'photo,' *frigo* (← *frigorifero*) 'refrigerator,' *tele* (← *televisore*) 'television set,' *meteo* (← *meteorologico*) 'meteorologic,' *moto* (← *motocicletta*) 'motorcycle,' *polio* (← *poliomielite*) 'poliomyelitis,' *porno* (← *pornografico/pornografia*) 'pornographic/pornography,' *radio* (← *radiofonia*).

b. *sub* (← *subacqueo*) 'skin-diver,' *etero, trans* (← *etero/transessuale*) 'hetero/trans-sexual.'

Reduced forms can correspond to morphemes, precisely prefixoids or prefixes (*bici, tele; sub, trans*) or not (*cine, frigo*), and can also be the first part of a compound (***tossico**(dipendente)*) 'drug addict). They are invariable in number but retain the gender of the full form with inanimate referents (feminine *la foto*, masculine *il cinema* vs. *un/a tossico/a* 'a drug addict'). The reduced variants usually differ from the full equivalents in terms of register and communicative context, typically being informal/colloquial, though geographical variation may apply; for instance, *auto* means 'car' for northern speakers, but 'bus' (← Fr. *autobus*) for central/southern ones. Reduced words are very common in youth language; well-known examples are *prof*, which is considered an extension of the written abbreviation *Prof.* to the spoken language, and *tossico*. Some increasingly common English loanwords are *demo, info*, and *promo*.

4.3.3.4 Acronyms

Acronyms are words formed by the initial segments and/or syllables of a phrase; precisely, they are proper names modified by the definite article. Their spelling ranges from all capitals (*AVIS* → *Associazione volontari italiani del sangue* 'Association of voluntary Italian blood-donors'), capitalization of the first-word initial letter only (*Fiat* ← *Fabbrica italiana automobili* 'Italian automobile factory'), or all low-case (*pm* = ***p**ubblico **m**inistero* 'state prosecutor'), and so does their pronunciation: they can be pronounced letter by letter based on the sound of the initial letter of the components (*pm* [pi'ɛmme]), *DNA* [diɛnne'a]) or as a word (*Fiat* ['fiat], *ONU* ['onu] *Organizzazione delle Nazioni Unite* 'United Nation Organization'). Gender and number agreement is governed by the head of the phrase (***la** Fiat* from feminine head *fabbrica*).

Acronyms are frequent in certain domains. For instance, they often designate names of institution and organizations (as shown by the earlier examples) and political parties (*DC* [ditʃ'tʃi] *Democrazia Cristiana* a former political party of the center) and names of provinces and countries in official, administrative contexts (*TO* for *Torino* 'Turin'). Also, they are prominent in scientific lexicons. Many are actually borrowings (*NATO* [nato], *AIDS* [eidz]/[aidz]). Some relevant acronyms are listed and divided chronologically in older acronyms (51a) and more current ones (51b).

(51) a. *ACI* (***A**utomobile **C**lub d'**I**talia*) 'Italian automobile association,' *TIR* (***T**rasporti internazionali stradali*) 'International road transport,' *ECG* (*elettrocardiogramma*) 'electrocardiogram,' *ISTAT* (***I**stituto **c**entrale di **stat**istica*) 'Central institute of statistics.'

b. *co-co-co* ((*contratti di*) ***co**llaborazione **co**ordinata e **co**ntinuativa*) 'type of job contract,' *colf* (***col**laboratrore/trice **f**amiliare*) 'home help,' *dad* (***d**idattica **a** **d**istanza*) 'remote instruction' (from the Covid-19 pandemic), *doc* and *dogc* (***d**enominazione di **o**rigine **g**arantita e **c**ontrollata*) 'with a guarantee of quality and origin,' *gip* (***g**iudice per le **i**ndagini **p**reliminari*) 'magistrate in charge of preliminary investigations,' *onlus* (***o**rganizzazione **n**on **lucra**tiva di utilità **s**ociale*) 'non-profit organization for community work.'

4.3.3.5 Blends

Prototypical lexical **blends** result from the merging of two words, specifically taking the initial part of the first word and the last part of the second (*brunch* ← *breakfast-lunch, guestimate* ← *guess-estimate, smog* ← *smoke-fog*), that is, they are combinations of word segments which are not morphemes, so that they stand in between compounding and acronyms.[22] This type of blends is quite uncommon in Italian since most typically the second word remains whole (52a); it is most common for names of corporations, organizations, and associations (52b).

(52) a. *apericena* (**aperi**tivo 'aperitif'-*cena* 'dinner'), *discobar, discopub* (**disco**teca 'disco'- *bar/ pub*), *cattocomunista, catto-laico* (**catto**lico 'catholic'-*comunista* 'communist'/*laico* 'secular'); *metalmezzadro* 'metal worker who works as farmer in their free time' (**metal**lurgico 'metallurgical'-*mezzadro* 'sharecropper').

   b. **Conf**commercio (*Confederazione generale italiana del **commercio**, turismo e servizi* 'General confederation of Italian commerce, tourism and services'); *Confindustria* (**Confeder**azione generale dell'**industria** italiana 'General confederation of Italian industry'); *Fininvest* (**Fin**anziaria d'**invest**imento, name of a holding company controlled and managed by the Berlusconi's family).

Two examples of Italian 'true' blends are the fruit name *mapo* (← **ma**ndarino 'mandarin'-*pompelmo* 'grapefruit'; cf. Eng. *tangelo* ← **tang**erine-*pumelo*), and the animal names *tigone* (← **tig**re 'male tiger'-le**one** 'female lion') and *ligre* (← **l**eone (male)-ti**gre** (female)).

4.4 Exercises

1. Give concise but complete answers to the following questions, providing illustrative examples.

   a. Briefly define the notions of lexeme and lexicon.
   b. What are the domains of lexicology and lexicography?
   c. What are the main components of the Italian lexicon?
   d. What are the primary motivations for borrowing? How many types of borrowings can be found in Italian?
   e. Identify the main strategies Italian employs to create neologisms.
   f. What is an allotrope?
   g. What is the difference between compound and neoclassic compound?

2. Identify and classify the affixes found in the following words (ex. *fornaio* 'baker': root *forn-* (← *forno* 'oven') + denominal suffix *-aio*):

   a. *autolesionismo*
   b. *cappelliera*
   c. *impossibilità*
   d. *macchinista*
   e. *parrucchiere*
   f. *professionalizzazione*
   g. *sbaciucchiare*
   h. *televisione*

3. Match each of the following words to the word-formation process they exemplify. Note that some words may illustrate more than one process.

> abbottonare, aeroporto, agrodolce, alfabeta, apericena, apribottiglie, arrivo, autocritica, batticuore, bastonare, bibliotecario, bistecca, capoufficio, colf, copridivano, dad, decaffeinare, dentista, disboscare, ecostrage, extracomunitario, Fiat, flebo, gestire, gip, grammaticale, imbottigliare, incatenare, indirizzo, insano, libreria, ligre, ludoteca, mapo, moto, patata, parcheggio, pescespada, postino, prevedere, primaverile, quattroruote, radio, realizzare, ristampare, slavofilo, smacchiare, sveglia, tango, termocoperta, telelavoratore, tossico, traccia, travasare, zuccherare.

4. Provide **five** examples for each of the following word-formation processes. Try to find original examples rather than drawing from the textbook.

   a. Acronym
   b. Backformation
   c. Blending
   d. Clipping
   e. Compound
   f. Conversion
   g. Neoclassical compound
   h. Parasynthesis
   i Prefixation
   j. Suffixation
   k. Syntagmatic construction

5. True or false? Explain your choices.

   a. *Portacenere* is a classical compound.
   b. Prefixation is by far the most productive word-formation process in Italian.
   c. *Cliccare* is an example of adapted borrowing.
   d. 'Conversion' is the word-formation process that derives lexemes belonging to a different word class than their base with no affix marking the change.
   e. *Rubacuori* is an example of 'noun-verb' compound.
   f. 'Blending' is the word-formation process that derives neologisms by merging two words.
   g. *Ombretto* is an example of evaluative suffixation.
   h. –aio is the most productive denominal suffix to derive nouns denoting professions.
   i. *Filologia* is a classical compound.
   j. *Sbriciolare* is a parasynthetic verb.
   k. –ale (and its allomorph –are) is the most productive Italian denominal adjective.
   l. *Medio* and *mezzo* are allotropes.

6. Which of the following are instances of evaluative suffixation and which are lexicalized forms? Justify your answers.

   > bambina, budino, carrozzina, cestino, farfallino, finestrino, forchettina, orecchino bacetto, bocchetta, calcetto, dolcetto, fioretto, pancetta, saponetta
   > alberello, barella, cartello, cestello, nasello, pagnottella, gazzella
   > boccone, ombrellone, manona, minestrone, portone, polverone, straccione

Notes

1 The supine is a non-finite verbal form used only in the accusative and ablative cases primarily to express purpose or the beginning of an action.

2 Two model examples of grammaticalization are the development of the future tense auxiliaries or markers from verbs denoting motion (e.g., Eng. *I go to work by bus* vs. *I'm going to/gonna go home*) and the development of indefinite articles from the numeral 'one' (It. *un* 'a.mas'/*una* 'a.fem' < Latin UNU(M) 'one').

3 A distinction must be made between lexical neologisms (i.e., actual new words obtained through word-formation processes) and semantic neologisms, which are existing words that have acquired a new meaning; they are particularly common in technical languages (e.g., *finestra* 'window', *icona* 'icon', *sito* 'site', *scaricare* 'to download' in computer science). Semantic extension is a highly operative process across time (and languages), the analysis of which fall more properly within the domain of diachronic semantics.

4 The Italian lexicon, like any language's lexicon, includes also common nouns derived from proper nouns, onomatopoeic words, and invented original words common in advertising, literature, arts, etc. These won't be addressed here.

5 The *Accademia della Crusca* was established in Florence between 1582 and 1583 by a group of intellectuals who used to meet to discuss on current cultural topics, including language, which eventually became their main focus. Its name comes from *cruscate*, from *crusca* 'bran,' which was how they jokingly called their meetings and was intended to convey its primary objective: to 'sieve' the language (the flour) from 'impurities' (the bran), with the objective of achieving a proper (written) standard. Its main work is the *Vocabolario*, whose first edition appeared in 1612, and the last (fifth) in 1863–1923. Presently, the *Crusca* is the most important academic center for the study and promotion of Italian in Italy and abroad (https://accademiadellacrusca.it/).

6 *Esotismo* is a more technical synonym of *prestito* 'borrowing, loanword'; it specifically refers to phonologically/morphologically non-adapted loanwords. Other terms used to refer to borrowings are *barbarismo* 'barbarism,' which carries a negative connotation and is now obsolete, *forestierismo* 'foreign item' (from *forestiero* 'foreign; foreigner'), and *xenismo* 'foreign item,' which is quite rare.

7 *Il Nuovo De Mauro* 'The new De Mauro' is an online dictionary based on *GRADIT* (https://dizionario.internazionale.it/avvertenze).

8 Cf., for instance, "as far as the strictly linguistic possibilities go, *any linguistic feature* can be transferred from *any language to any other language*" (Thomason & Kaufman, 1988, p. 14); "given enough time and intensive contact, virtually anything can (ultimately) be borrowed" (Campbell, 1993, pp. 103–104).

9 Since the last 1980s, Italian linguists and language scholars in general have been concerned about the surge of Anglicism ("*morbus anglicus*" Castellani, 1987; "*tsunami anglicus*" De Mauro, 2016) that has been hitting Italian. For a recent examination of this issue, see Marazzini and Petralli (2015).

10 More detailed discussions are offered by the contributions in Serianni (2002); cf. also De Mauro and Mancini (2003). For early borrowing, see also Castellani (2000).

11 About borrowing from 'exotic' languages, see Banfi and Iannàccaro (2006).

12 Technically, word-formation is distinguished from word-creation, which does not resort to native elements of the language to produce new words. The most typical outcome of word-creation is perhaps brand names.

13 Within suffixation, deadjectival adjective and deverbal verbs are derived by means of evaluative suffixes only (e.g., *bello* → 'beautiful' *bellino* 'cute'; *cantare* 'sing' *canticchiare* 'hum').

14 The allomorph *-ésimo* is productive only with adjectives (*anglicanesimo, cristianesimo, luteranesimo, paganesimo*).

15 The *Brigate rosse* 'Red brigades' were a terrorist group active from 1970 to 1988.

16 Since they occur between the verb root and the infinitive suffixes (*-are, -ere, -ire*), *-izz-, -eggi-,* and *-ific-* might be viewed as infixes, though infixes typically occur inside the root (e.g., *-n-* in Latin FRANGĔRE 'break' < the root frag-).

17 Note that [n] assimilates to word-initial [l] and [r] and bilabial stops.

18 Note that [d] and [n] assimilate to the verb-initial consonant.

19 From now on, compound nouns will be broken down only if their meaning is not compositional (e.g., *guardaboschi* (watch.forests) 'forester', *tavola calda* (table.warm)).

20 From *Repubblica* (www.repubblica.it/); retrieved June 9, 2021.
21 Syntagmatic constructions are also known as *unità polirematiche* 'multiword units,' a term introduced in *GRADIT*.
22 In Italian, blends are commonly called *parole macedonia* 'fruit salad words,' a term coined by Migliorini (1949, p. 89).

Bibliography

Adamo, G., & Della Valle, V. (2008). *Le parole del lessico italiano*. Carocci.

Agnello, G. (2006). *Made in Italy: Il purismo di ieri, le paure di oggi, gli auspici futuri*. L'autore libri.

Banfi, E., & Iannàcaro, G. (2006). *Lo spazio linguistico italiano e le "lingue esotiche": Rapporti e reciproci influssi*. Bulzoni.

Baroni, M., Guevara, E., & Emiliano, V. (2007). N-N compounds in Italian: Modelling category induction and analogical extension. *Lingue e Linguaggio, 6*, 263–290.

Battaglia, S. (1961). *Grande dizionario della lingua italiana*. UTET.

Beltrami, P. G., & Fornara, S. (2004). Italian historical dictionaries: From the accademia della crusca to the WEB. *International Journal of Lexicography, 17*(4), 358–384.

Campbell, L. (1993). On proposed universals of grammatical borrowing. In H. Aertsen & R. J. Jeffers (Eds.), *Historical linguistics 1989* (pp. 91–109). John Benjamins.

Casadei, F. (2003). *Lessico e semantica*. Carocci.

Castellani, A. (1987). Morbus anglicus. *Studi Linguistici Italiani, 13*, 137–153.

Castellani, A. (2000). *Grammatica storica italiana*. Il Mulino.

D'Achille, P. (2005). Le retroformazioni in italiano. In C. Giovanardi (Ed.), *Lessico e formazione delle parole: Studi offerti a Maurizio Dardano per il suo 70° compleanno* (pp. 75–102). Cesati.

Dardano, M. (2009). *Costruire parole: La morfologia derivativa dell'italiano*. Il Mulino.

De Mauro, T. (1999–2000). *Grande dizionario italiano dell'uso*. UTET.

De Mauro, T. (2005). *La fabbrica delle parole*. UTET.

De Mauro, T. (2016). *È irresistibile l'ascesa degli anglismi?* Retrieved March 2021, from www.internazionale.it/opinione/tullio-de-mauro/2016/07/14/irresistibile-l-ascesa-degli-anglismi

De Mauro, T., & Mancini, M. (2003). *Parole straniere nella lingua italiana*. Garzanti.

Dressler, W. U., & Merlini Barbaresi, L. (1993). Italian diminutives as non-prototypical word formation. In L. Tonelli & W. U. Dressler (Eds.), *Natural morphology: Perspectives for the nineties* (pp. 21–30). Unipress.

Dressler, W. U., & Merlini Barbaresi, L. (1994). *Morphopragmatics: Diminutives and intensifiers in Italian, German, and other languages*. Mouton de Gruyter.

Dressler, W. U., & Merlini Barbaresi, L. (2001). Morphopragmatics of diminutives and augmentatives: On the priority of pragmatics over semantics. In F. Kiefer, I. Kenesei, & R. M. Harnish (Eds.), *Perspectives on semantics, pragmatics, and discourse: A Festschrift for Ferenc Kiefer* (pp. 43–58). John Benjamins.

Foresti, F. (Ed.). (2003). *Credere, obbedire, combattere: Il regime linguistico nel Ventennio*. Pendragon.

Fradin, B. (2005). Problemi semantici in morfologia derivazionale. In M. Grossmann & A. M. Thornton (Eds.), *La formazione delle parole: Atti del XXXVII congresso della SLI* (pp. 163–192). Bulzoni.

Golino, E. (1994). *Parola di Duce: Il linguaggio totalitario del fascismo*. Rizzoli.

Grandi, N. (1998). Sui suffissi diminutivi. *Lingua e Stile, 33*, 627–653.

Grossmann, M., & Rainer, F. (Eds.). (2004). *La formazione delle parole in italiano*. Niemeyer.

Grossmann, M., & Rainer, F. (2009). Italian adjective-adjective compounds: Between morphology and syntax. *Rivista di Linguistica, 21*, 71–96.

Iacobini, C. (2004a). Prefissazione. In M. Grossmann & F. Rainer (Eds.), *La formazione delle parole in italiano* (pp. 97–163). Niemeyer.

Iacobini, C. (2004b). Parasintesi. In M. Grossmann & F. Rainer (Eds.), *La formazione delle parole in italiano* (pp. 165–188). Niemeyer.

Jurafsky, D. (1996). Universal tendencies in the semantics of the diminutive. *Language, 72*, 533–578.

Klein, G. (1986). *La politica linguistica del fascismo*. Il Mulino.

Lakoff, G., & Johnson, M. (1980). *Metaphors we live by*. University of Chicago Press.

Marazzini, C., & Petralli, A. (Eds.). (2015). *La lingua italiana e le lingue romanze di fronte agli anglicismi*. goWare.

Masini, F. (2006). Rapporti fra spazio linguistico italiano e ambiente cinese. In E. Banfi & G. Iannàcaro (Eds.), *Lo spazio linguistico italiano e le "lingue esotiche": Rapporti e reciproci influssi* (pp. 7–25). Bulzoni.

Merlini Barbaresi, L. (2004). Alterazione. In M. Grossmann & F. Rainer (Eds.), *La formazione delle parole in italiano* (pp. 264–292). Niemeyer.

Merlini Barbaresi, L. (2015). Evaluative morphology and pragmatics. In N. Grandi & L. Körtvélyessy (Eds.), *The Edinburgh handbook of evaluative morphology* (pp. 32–42). Edinburgh University Press.

Micheli, S. M. (2020). *La formazione delle parole*. Carocci.

Migliorini, B. (1949). Uso ed abuso delle sigle. In B. Migliorini (Ed.), *Conversazioni sulla lingua italiana* (pp. 86–90). Le Monnier.

Monelli, P. (1933). *Barbaro dominio: Cinquecento esotismi esaminati, combattuti e banditi dalla lingua con antichi e nuovi argomenti*. Hoepli.

Montermini, F. (2008). *Il lato sinistro della morfologia: La "prefissazione" in italiano e nelle alter lingue del mondo*. Angeli.

Nagami, S., & Nannini, A. (2006). Italianismi in giapponese, nipponismi in italiano. In E. Banfi & G. Iannàcaro (Eds.), *Lo spazio linguistico italiano e le "lingue esotiche": Rapporti e reciproci influssi* (pp. 117–156). Bulzoni.

Palermo, M. (2020). *Linguistica italiana* (2nd ed.). Il Mulino.

Peša Matracki, I. (2006). Linee di tendenza nella formazione delle parole nell'italiano contemporaneo. *Studia Romanica et Anglica Zagrabiensia*, *51*, 103–146.

Raffaelli, A. (2010). *Le parole straniere sostituite dall'Accademia d'Italia (1941–1943)*. Aracne.

Raffaelli, S. (1983). *Le parole proibite: Purismo di stato e regolamentazione della pubblicità in Italia (1812–1945)*. Il Mulino.

Ricci, L. (2005). *La lingua dell'Impero*. Carocci.

Russi, C. (2011). Clitics of Italian *verbi procomplementari*: What are they? In M. Maiden, J. C. Smith, M. Goldbach, & M.-O. Hinzelin (Eds.), *Morphological autonomy: Perspectives from Romance inflectional morphology* (pp. 382–400). Oxford University Press.

Scalise, S., & Bisetto, A. (2008). *La struttura delle parole*. Il Mulino.

Serianni, L. (Ed.). (2002). *La lingua nella storia d'Italia*. Società Dante Alighieri.

Telmon, T. (1993). Varietà regionali. In A. A. Sobrero (Ed.), *Introduzione all'italiano contemporaneo* (Vol. 2, pp. 93–149). Laterza.

Thomason, S. G., & Kaufman, T. (1988). *Language contact, creolization, and genetic linguistics*. University of California Press.

Thornton, A. M. (2004a). Reduction. In M. Grossmann & F. Rainer (Eds.), *La formazione delle parole in italiano* (pp. 569–571). Niemeyer.

Thornton, A. M. (2004b). Parole macedonia. In M. Grossmann & F. Rainer (Eds.), *La formazione delle parole in italiano* (pp. 557–566). Niemeyer.

Voghera, M. (2004). Polirematiche. In M. Grossmann & F. Rainer (Eds.), *La formazione delle parole in italiano* (pp. 56–95). Niemeyer.

Zolli, P. (1976). *Le parole straniere*. Zanichelli.

5

STRUCTURES

This chapter deals with **syntax**, the branch of linguistics that studies the configuration of language structures above the word level, that is, how words come together to form larger speech units which native speakers consider well-formed. Thus, syntax examines the individual components of acceptable word sequences (or constituents) and categorizes constituents into classes according to their distinctive structural features. Moreover, syntax studies the strategies through which words and constituents connect to and depend upon one another to form even larger structures. Briefly put, then, syntax analyzes both the internal configuration of basic units of language structure above the word level and the principles and relations which produce such units. The chapter starts with introducing and classifying three essential types of multiword utterances – phrases, clauses, and sentences – in terms of their individual components and the structural and semantic relations that hold among them. Next, the chapter addresses some aspects of the interface between syntax and discourse pragmatics (or **information structure**, that is, how sentences are used in different communicative settings) by reviewing the communicative functions carried by different word-order patterns.

5.1 Phrases, clauses, and sentences

Language is structured in a hierarchical fashion: single sounds come together to form words, which then combine in various ways to craft three basic hierarchically ordered language units: phrases, clauses, and sentences. The primary goal of syntax is to identify and describe word sequences that (native) speakers of a given language consider grammatical or well-formed, then uncover the principles which account for their well-formedness. Speakers' intuitions about whether or not a certain chain of words is possible in their native language are quite strong, just like their intuitions about which sound combinations are (in)valid. And syntax aims at discovering the rules that govern the formation of well-formed utterances in a given language. (Un)grammaticality, though, is not the same as (un)acceptability, since the former pertains solely to structure, whereas the latter relates to factors such as meaning, speech/writing styles, communicative/contextual appropriateness. Thus, the legendary sentence *colorless green idea sleep furiously* (Chomsky, 1957) is totally grammatical yet unacceptable in terms

DOI: 10.4324/9781003057536-5

of meaning; similarly, *give me a hand* is perfectly fine in terms of syntax but unacceptable if addressed to someone the speaker doesn't know well (i.e., in a formal context).

The rules syntax seeks are different from the rules presented in grammar books. The word **grammar** has two primary meanings. In linguistics, *grammar* designates the whole system of sounds, words, structures, and meaning shared by all speakers of a given language, which, crucially, also includes the rules governing that system. For linguists, then, the grammar of a language amounts to the speakers' implicit, instinctive knowledge of their language. In ordinary, non-technical language, however, grammar denotes a reference book which collects the rules speakers are assumed to follow in order to speak and write 'correctly,' according to the 'standard' language. But language is utterly complex and involves different types and degrees of variation, linked to geographical and socio-cultural factors, among others, as well as to diachronic change. Thus, grammar books cannot provide a fully comprehensive description of any given language; they can only offer approximations. This means that they may include inaccurate or even incorrect rules, that is, rules that do not conform to the native speakers' rule-system, which is the only one that matters. Language varieties displaying syntactic variation (actually, variation at any level of language) from the 'standard' model are deemed (and labeled) 'sub-standard,' that is, second-rate and inadequate. When it comes to language, though, standard status is a mere fabrication rooted in sociological, cultural, and most of all, political power; any language variety sanctioned by speakers (and attested in usage) is first-rate and adequate. To conclude, the rules found in grammar books are prescriptive, while the rules uncovered by syntax are descriptive, because prescriptivism does not pertain to linguistics by definition.

Like descriptions pertaining to any other level of language, syntactic descriptions are usually couched into theoretical frameworks, which are meant to provide the 'machinery' to adequately formulate and systematize them. Different theoretical approaches have been adopted in syntax; some are laden with overly technical and highly theory-specific assumptions and terminology, and the accounts they propose are often controversial. On the whole, this chapter adopts an atheoretical approach, though it may occasionally be inspired by so-called 'functional' frameworks. These are discourse-based frameworks which study language structures in relation to their actual use in speech, their core premise being that language is shaped and governed by general cognition principles and communicative functions. They differ crucially from so-called 'formalist' frameworks, which, in contrast, rely primarily on abstract categories, structures, and principles in their analyses, while rejecting the idea that cognitive and communicative forces play a role in molding language and, consequently, drastically minimizing (if not wholly discarding) actual speech.

The next sections survey the individual modules that constitute sentences examining their internal structure and the functions they can fulfill.

5.1.1 Phrases

Speakers constantly produce novel word combinations, and as noted earlier, they are strongly aware of which arrangements are well-formed (and in which communicative setting) and which are not. So what does it take to be a well-formed arrangement of words? Consider the utterance in (1).

(1) *Quel ragazzo legge una rivista.*
    'That boy reads/is reading a magazine.'

How many acceptable, coherent units does (1) contain? We will most likely agree that two are identifiable straightforwardly: *quel ragazzo* and *legge una rivista*. Both are adequate, articulate units; for example, they can successfully be used to answer questions: *chi legge una rivista?* 'who reads/is reading a magazine?' – *quel ragazzo*; *che fa quel ragazzo?* 'what is that boy doing?' – *legge una rivista*. Indeed, a closer look reveals that *legge* and *una rivista* may also be constituents since they work perfectly well as answers to a question: *che fa quel ragazzo?* – *legge*; *che legge quel ragazzo?* 'what is that boy reading?' – *una rivista*. On the other hand, *quel* and *una* seem to be simply fragments which cannot be used meaningfully in isolation. Well-formed, coherent language units are called **constituents**; syntactic constituents are more precisely named **phrases** and are traditionally enclosed in brackets ([*quel ragazzo*]).

Establishing whether or not a given unit is actually a phrase (i.e., it holds constituent status) is not always clear-cut. Several tests have been devised to assess constituency, whose validity and applicability may vary across languages. It must be kept in mind, of course, that constituency tests may fail for independent reasons. Therefore, a unit can be assumed to lack constituent status only if no test can provide positive evidence for constituency. Three established tests that apply to Italian are reported in (2).

(2) a. **Pronominalization**. Phrases can be replaced felicitously by a pronoun.
    b. **Movement**. Phrases move as cohesive units; hence, the fact that a given word sequence can occupy a different spot within the sentence evinces constituency.
    c. **Coordination**. Phrases of the same type can be conjoined by coordinating conjunctions.

Applying these tests to our sentence confirms that the units we identified are indeed phrases. As seen in (3), both [*quel ragazzo*] and [*una rivista*] can be pronominalized, respectively, by *lui* 'he' and *la* 'it.F.SG.' The unstressed pronoun *la* does not occupy the same position as *una rivista*, but this is due to a distinctive property of Italian unstressed pronouns, namely, that they occur before the verb when it is in a finite form (but they follow the verb attaching to it orthographically if it is in a non-finite form: *voglio legger***la** 'I want to read it'). The phrase [*legge una rivista*], in contrast, cannot be pronominalized because Italian lacks a pronoun for this type of phrases.

(3) **Lui** *la* **legge**.

Our phrases pass also the movement test since they can occupy different positions within the sentence (4a) as long as their components keep together (4b).

(4) a. [*Legge una rivista*], [*quel ragazzo*]./[*Una rivista*] [*legge*], [*quel ragazzo*]./[*Legge*], [*quel ragazzo*], [*una rivista*].
    b. **Legge una quel ragazzo rivista./*Una legge quel rivista ragazzo./*Quel legge ragazzo una rivista.*

And they also meet the coordination test: both [*quel ragazzo*] and [*una rivista*] can be coordinated to units of the same sort, in this case, 'demonstrative + noun' (5a); [*legge una rivista*] can be conjoined to units of the type 'verb + article + noun' (5b), and [*legge*] can be coordinated to another verb (5c).

(5) a. [*Quel ragazzo*] *e* [*quella ragazza*] *leggono* [*una rivista*] *e* [*un giornale*].
    'That boy and that girl are reading a magazine and a newspaper.'

   b.   *Quel ragazzo* [*legge una rivista*] *e* [*ascolta la musica*].
'That boy is reading a magazine and listening to music.'
   c.   *Quel ragazzo* [*legge*] *e* [*sbadiglia*].
'That boy is reading and yawning.'

Phrases have a precise internal organization. The order of the individual components within the phrase is constrained; more precisely, while some orders are simply unacceptable, others carry specific meanings or communicative functions (see next section). Also, in multiword phrases, one word, the **head**, plays a leading role in the phrase; it is the predominant element both semantically, because it gives content to the phrase and labels it, and syntactically, because it determines its syntactic category, as we will see in more detail shortly. The nouns *ragazzo* and *rivista*, respectively, head [*quel ragazzo*] and [*una rivista*] because they give the phrases content and structure, that is, they bestow semantic and syntactic properties to the phrases, as evinced, for instance, by pronominalization: only the masculine singular personal pronoun *lui* can replace [*quel ragazzo*] because *ragazzo* is masculine singular, and only the feminine singular pronoun *la* can replace [*una rivista*] because *rivista* is feminine singular (see (3) earlier). So [*quel ragazzo*] and [*una rivista*] are **noun phrases** (NPs).[1] The phrases [*legge una rivista*] and [*ascolta la musica*], on the other hand, are headed by verbs, so they are **verb phrases** (VPs). As evinced by [*legge*], single-word phrases are possible, but the word must belong to a lexical word class, that is, the word has to refer to an entity, concept, or situation. Functional words, that is, words expressing relations rather than content – like, for instance, prepositions or demonstratives – cannot be autonomous heads.

Italian phrasal heads are listed in (6), accompanied by illustrative phrases.

(6)   a.   Noun: [**Francesco**]$_{NP}$, [*quel* **ragazzo**]$_{NP}$, [*quel* **ragazzo** *americano*]$_{NP}$ 'that American boy.'
   b.   Verb: [**legge**]$_{VP}$, [**legge** *una rivista*]$_{VP}$, [**legge** *una rivista di linguistica*]$_{VP}$ 'reads a magazine of linguistics.'
   c.   Adjective: [**preoccupati** *per la loro salute*]$_{AP}$ 'worried.M.PL for their health,' [*molto* **preoccupati**]$_{AP}$ 'very worried.'
   d.   Preposition: *andare* [**a** *scuola*]$_{PP}$ 'go to school,' *una rivista* [**di** *linguistica*]$_{PP}$ 'a linguistics magazine.'
   e.   Adverb: *ascoltare* [**distrattamente**]$_{ADVP}$ 'listen to absent-mindedly,' *parlare* [*troppo* **velocemente**]$_{ADVP}$ 'speak too fast.'

The elements that accompany the head to supply additional information about it are called **complements** or **modifiers**. In the phrase [*quel ragazzo americano*], the demonstrative *quel* and the adjective *americano* are both modifiers; in the phrase [*legge una rivista*], *una rivista* is the complement of *legge*, and in the phrase [*a scuola*], *scuola* is the complement of *a*.

The position the head occupies inside the phrase varies across languages. In Italian (and Romance languages in general) heads typically precede their modifiers, that is, Italian is a left-headed (or head-first) language. However, as the examples examined so far show, this is not a categorical rule, and in noun phrases, all determiners (articles, demonstratives, possessives, quantifiers) actually precede the head.

(7)   a.   [**Mia** *sorella*]/*[*Sorella* **mia**] *abita in Italia*.
'My sister lives in Italy.'

b. *Ho comprato [**alcuni** libri]/*[libri **alcuni**].*
'I have bought some books.'

c. *Ho mangiato [**due** mele]/*[mele **due**].*
'I have eaten two apples.'

Also, phrases of the same type are exchangeable (8), and as you will have gathered by now, phrases can contain other phrases (9).

(8)   a.   *[Claudia]*~NP~ */[Mia sorella]*~NP~ */[La mia sorella minore]*~NP~ *prepara [una torta]*~NP~ */[una torta al cioccolato]*~NP~ */[la torta per il compleanno di Francesco.]*~NP~
'Claudia/My sister/My younger sister is making a cake/a chocolate cake/a cake for Francesco's birthday.'

b.   *Viaggiano [in treno]*~PP~ */[di notte]*~PP~ */[con alcuni amici.]*~PP~
'They travel by train/at night/with some friends.'

(9)   a.   [legge [una rivista [di linguistica]~PP~]~NP~]~VP~
's/he reads a linguistics journal'

b.   [trovarsi [in [una situazione spiacevole]~NP~]~PP~]~VP~
'find oneself in an unpleasant situation'

So far, we have used brackets to represent phrases; a common alternative representation is the tree diagram shown in (10).

(10)   *[legge [una rivista]*~NP~ *[in [giardino]*~NP~*]*~PP~*]*~VP~
's/he reads a magazine in the garden'

Phrase labels indicate the syntactic category of each constituent and are called **nodes**. Each node, then, represents a constituent. In more technical terms, a word sequence forms a constituent if there is a node that dominates that sequence and nothing else, that is, if the node is above the sequence in the tree and only one direct line of branches links them. The different relations between nodes are traditionally expressed referring to the 'family' metaphor, so that

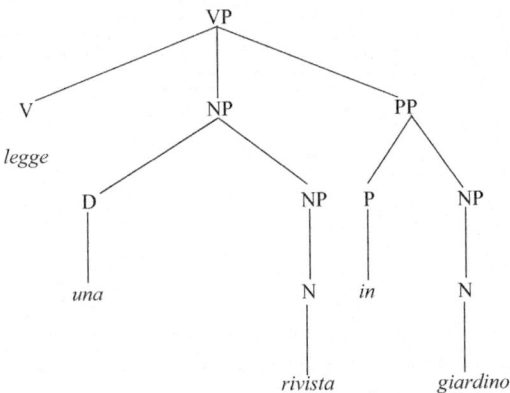

FIGURE 5.1   Phrase structure tree diagram for the phrase '*legge una rivista in giardino.*'

immediately dominating nodes are 'mothers' and nodes sharing the same mother are 'sisters.' In (10), VP is the mother of NP and PP, which are sisters.

Constituency is key to resolve sentence ambiguity, since differences in constituency result in different meanings, as shown by the different readings of (11a) and (11b): while the former means 'Francesco watches the man who has binoculars,' the latter means 'Francesco watches the man by using binoculars.'

(11) a. *Francesco guarda* [*l'uomo* [*con il binocolo.*]$_{PP}$]$_{NP}$
    b. *Francesco* [*guarda* [*l'uomo*]$_{NP}$ [*con il binocolo.*]$_{PP}$]$_{VP}$
      'Francesco watches the man with binoculars.'

The two different interpretations stem from [*l'uomo con il binocolo*] being a single constituent in (11a) but two separate constituents, [*l'uomo*] and [*con il binocolo*], in (11b).

In the next section, we will see that verbs (or VPs) are the essential component of clauses. A proper description of clauses, then, requires surveying the syntactic and semantic relations that link NPs and PPs to verbs.

5.1.1.1 Syntactic functions

Syntactic (or grammatical) functions are purely structural relations holding between verbs and phrases which provide the information needed to get a correct construal of the situation denoted by the verb (i.e., 'who does what to whom, when, where, why, etc.'). Depending on the type of relation they bear to verbs, a distinction is traditionally made between argument (or complement) and adjunct (or adverbial) phrases. **Argument** phrases are tied to verbs by an intrinsic relation which is governed by the verb's meaning, that is, they provide information necessary for achieving a proper representation and construal (i.e., conceptualization) of the event denoted by a given verb, particularly in terms of the participating entities; hence, they are obligatory. Conversely, **adjuncts** typically provide supplementary information about the circumstances in which the event denoted by the verb took place, most commonly information pertaining to time, place, manner, cause, purpose, etc. Adjuncts, then, are optional; they can be omitted while compromising neither the syntactic nor the semantic well-formedness of a clause.

One of the core syntactic functions NPs bear relative to a verb is **subject**. A distinguishing syntactic feature of Italian subjects is that they require the verb to agree in person and number when the verb is in a finite form. Thus, the present indicative form of the verb 'talk' is second-person singular in (12a), because the subject is the second-person singular pronoun *tu*, while it is third-person plural in (12b) because the subject is the third-person plural pronoun *loro*.

(12) a. *Tu parli/*parlano troppo.*
      'You talk too much.'
    b. *Loro parlano/*parla troppo.*
      'They talk too much.'

In Italian, then, verb agreement is the property that unequivocally detects subjects.

Two other distinctive structural properties of Italian subjects are that (a) they normally occur before the verb (although, as discussed later, they can follow the verb in specific contexts), and (b) they are not obligatory. Unlike English, Italian belongs to the group of so-called **null-subject** languages, which allow for unexpressed subjects. As shown in (13), subjects are identifiable through verbal endings rather than by pronouns.[2]

(13) *sorrido,*   *sorridi,*   *sorride,*   *sorridiamo,* *sorridete,*   *sorridono*
     smile.1SG smile.2SG smile.3SG   smile.1PL   smile.2PL   smile.3PL
      'I smile' **'you** smile' **'s/he** smiles' **'we** smile' **'you**.PL smile' **'they** smile'

Overt expression of the subject is governed by syntactic contexts, as addressed in more detail later, and communicative functions, such as, for example, to introduce a new referent in the discourse, or to express contrast/emphasis.

Verb agreement, on the other hand, is not a distinguishing property of Italian **object** arguments since it is restricted to few environments.[3] The most important structural properties of Italian objects is that they normally occur immediately after the verb, though they can occupy a different position within the clause to fulfill specific communicative functions, as we will see when we examine word order. Two types of objects are distinguished on the basis of their meaning or, more precisely, the event participant they refer to (we will go back to this issue shortly, when we survey clause types): **direct** objects, which designate entities affected by the action expressed by the verb and are expressed by NPs (14a), and **indirect** objects, which designate entities that receive something and are expressed by a PP headed by *a* 'to' (14b).[4]

(14) a. *Francesco mangia [**una mela**.]*$_{NP/DO}$
        'Francesco is eating an apple.'
    b. *Francesco ha prestato la macchina [**a sua sorella**.]*$_{PP/IO}$
        'Francesco lent the car to his sister.'

PPs arguments other than indirect object are known as **oblique** arguments.

(15) a. *Francesco è partito [**da Milano**]*$_{PP/OBL}$ *alle 19,00.*
        'Francesco left from Milan at 7pm.'
    b. *Francesco ha appeso la foto di Gaia [**in camera da letto**.]*$_{PP/OBL}$
        'Francesco hung Gaia's photo in the bedroom.'

The PPs *da Milano* 'from Milan' (15a) and *in camera da letto* 'in the bedroom' (15b) are arguments rather than adjuncts because they are required by the meaning of the verbs *partire* 'leave' and *appendere* 'hang': the event of 'leaving' entails a place of departure, just like the event of 'hanging' involves both an entity to be hung and a place where it is hung. The PP *alle 19,00* 'at 7pm,' on the other hand, is an adjunct because temporal specification (i.e., the time at which the event of leaving took place) is not entailed in the event itself.

Summarizing, arguments contrast crucially from adjuncts concerning the nature of their relationship with the verb. Arguments have an inherent, permanent relation with the verb which is determined by the verb's meaning; they are required for the complete and correct construal of the event expressed by the verb, particularly in terms of the participating entities. In contrast, adjuncts are just optional, and leaving them out has no consequence on the syntactic or the semantic well-formedness of a clause. Thus, optionality is the defining property of adverbials, and obligatoriness is that of subjects and objects. Note that in this context, obligatoriness does not mean obligatory overt expression. Like subjects, direct objects can be unexpressed in Italian; this issue is addressed in more detail in the context of the examination of clauses, but to give one anticipatory example, the fact that the object of the verb *mangiare* 'eat' can be unexpressed – *mangiamo* 'we eat' is totally well-formed – does not change the fact that the event of eating entails an eating entity (the subject) and an eaten one (the object).

5.1.1.2 Semantic roles

All the participants in a scene evoked by a verb play a conceptual role, which is assigned to them by the meaning of the verb. Thus, in characterizing clausal constituents (which express the event participants), syntactic functions (which, as we recall, designate structural relations) are complemented by **semantic roles** (also **thematic roles/relations**), which, as their name suggests, are meaning-based and fill in important details needed for the proper construal of the situation denoted by a verb, particularly in terms of the entities participating in it. The basic, most common semantic roles proposed in the literature are given in (16).

(16) a. **Agent**. An entity performing an action; more technically, the volitional initiator of an activity (hence, most typically human or animate): *Francesco ha rotto un bicchiere* 'Francesco broke a glass,' *il gatto ha mangiato il canarino* 'the cat ate the canary.'

   b. **Patient**. An entity undergoing a change of state due to a given event: *un bicchiere* and *il canarino* in the sentences in the preceding text.

   c. **Theme**. An entity undergoing motion or being positioned: *mettere i fiori in un vaso* 'put **the flowers** in a vase,' *chiudere la finestra* 'close **the window**.'

   d. **Recipient**. An entity getting a theme: *Francesco ha dato un libro a Gaia* 'Francesco gave a book **to Gaia**.'

   e. **Experiencer**. An entity experiencing a physical or emotional state (therefore, sentient): *Francesco ascolta la musica/guarda la televisione/sente freddo* 'Francesco listens to music/watches TV/feels cold.'

   f. **Benefactive** (or **beneficiary**). An entity profiting from an event: *ho comprato un regalo per mia madre* 'I bought a gift for my mother,' *combattere per la patria* 'fight for the homeland.'

   g. **Goal**. Respectively, the endpoint and starting point of a motion trajectory or of an action: *arrivare a Parigi* 'arrive to Paris,' *ambire al ruolo principale* 'aspire to the main role.'

   h. **Source**. The starting point of a motion trajectory: *partire da Roma* 'leave from Rome,' *il Rio Grande nasce in Colorado* 'the Rio Grande originates in Colorado.'

   i. **Locative** and **temporal**. Respectively, the place where and time when an event happens: *abitano in un appartamento* 'they live in an apartment,' *la lezione d'italiano dura un'ora* 'the Italian lesson lasts one hour.'

   j. **Instrument**. An entity (tool, device) by means of which an action is carried out or a natural force that causes an event to come about: *tagliare con le forbici* 'cut with the scissor,' *il vento ha spazzato via le foglie* 'the wind swept away the leaves.'

   k. **Stimulus** (also **percept**). An entity perceived or experienced: *mi fa male la schiena* 'my back hurts (lit. the back makes bad to me),' *avere paura del buio* 'be afraid (lit. have fear) of the dark.'

The importance of distinguishing between semantic roles and syntactic functions (then integrating them) becomes apparent when we take a closer look at subjects and objects.

Subjects often denote the performer of an action, and objects commonly refer to entities affected by an action, that is, the syntactic functions subject and object strongly correlate, respectively, to the semantic roles agent and patient/theme. However, this correlation may not hold in some context; for instance, in passive constructions, syntactic functions and semantic roles no longer match: in the active construction, *il gatto* is the subject/agent and *il canarino* is the direct object/patient (17a). Conversely, in the passive construction, *il canarino* is the subject/patient and the agent *il gatto* is expressed by a PP (17b).

(17) a. [*Il gatto*]$_{SUBJ/AGENT}$ *ha mangiato* [*il canarino.*]$_{DO/PATIENT}$
        'The cat ate the canary.'
     b. [*Il canarino*]$_{SUBJ/PATIENT}$ *è stato mangiato* [*dal gatto.*]$_{AGENT}$
        'The canary was eaten by the cat.'

Another example of misalignment between the syntactic functions of subject and object and the semantic roles of agent and patient/theme is given by verbs like *piacere* 'like'; in the sentence *a Francesco piace la cioccolata* 'Francesco likes chocolate,' the subject is *la cioccolata*, which is a theme (the 'liked' entity), and the indirect object *a Francesco* bears the semantic role of experiencer (the 'liker' entity).

To conclude, semantic roles and syntactic functions are related notions, which differ from each other in some important ways: (a) semantic roles are the realization of syntactic functions, while syntactic functions reflect the grammaticalization of semantic roles; (b) syntactic functions are language-specific, whereas semantic roles are universal; (c) syntactic functions are defined by their grammatical form and are limited in number, while semantic roles are not clearly identifiable and their number is not clearly determined; and (d) a one-to-one correlation between semantic roles and syntactic categories is extremely rare (if at all possible), and the same holds for semantic roles and syntactic functions. Syntactic functions and semantic roles, then, are equally important for achieving a correct characterization of verbs and, consequently, of clauses.

5.1.2 Clauses

As already noted, clauses are syntactic units above the phrase, and like phrases, they have internal structure. This section introduces the principal types of clauses found in Italian.

The necessary components of a clause are the verb and its argument(s), which form the **nucleus**; the nucleus can be completed by adjuncts, but as we recall, these are optional. Clause type, then, is contingent on verb type: the number and kinds of arguments a verb requires (i.e., the verb's argument structure) shape the structure of clauses. The term **valency** (or **valence**) is often used to refer specifically to the number of core arguments required by a verb, or its argument structure. Valency, then, refers to the set of semantic and syntactic requirements of a verb; it is the set of features that characterize the types of constituents linked to a verb by a dependency relation, or the number of participants in the scene evoked by the verb.[5]

The valency of Italian verbs ranges from zero to four. The class of **zero-argument** (or **avalent**) verbs is restricted to weather verbs, which involve no participant, only occur in the third-person singular, and don't require a dummy subject, because Italian is a null-subject language: *grandina* 'it's hailing,' *lampeggia* 'there is lightening,' *nevica* 'it's snowing,' *piove* 'it's raining,' *tuona* 'it's thundering.'

One-argument (or **monovalent**) verbs require a single argument, the subject.

(18) [*Francesco*]$_{SUBJ}$ *dorme/lavora/nuota/ride.*
'Francesco sleeps/works/swims/laughs.'

Two-argument (or **divalent**) verbs require two arguments: the subject and a second argument, which can be of different kinds, ranging from direct object patient/theme, as in (17a) earlier, to experiencer, locative, temporal, or goal.

(19) a. [*A Francesco*]$_{EXPERIENCER}$ *servirebbe* [*un caffè.*]$_{SUBJ}$
'Francesco would need a coffee.'
 b. [*Francesco*]$_{SUBJ}$ *abita* [*a Roma/in un appartamento.*]$_{LOCATIVE}$
'Francesco lives in Rome/in an apartment.'
 c. [*Lo spettacolo*]$_{SUBJ}$ *è durato* [*due ore.*]$_{TEMPORAL}$
'The show lasted two hours.'
 d. [*Francesco*]$_{SUBJ}$ *si è dedicato* [*alla collezione di francobolli.*]$_{GOAL}$
'Francesco has devoted himself to collecting stamps.'

Three-argument (or **trivalent**) verbs typically express either some type of exchange, in which case they call for a subject, a direct object theme, and an indirect object recipient (20a) or a source argument (20b), or a directed motion event, thus requiring a subject, a goal, and source argument (20c).

(20) a. *dare/dire/promettere/spedire/vendere* [*qualcosa*]$_{DO}$ [*a qualcuno*]$_{IO}$
'give/say/promise/send/sell/ something to someone'
 b. *ottenere/raccogliere/ricevere* [*qualcosa*]$_{DO}$ [*da qualcuno/qualche luogo*]$_{SOURCE}$
'obtain/pick up/receive something from someone/somewhere'
 c. *andare/arrivare/venire* [*a scuola*]$_{GOAL}$ [*da casa*]$_{SOURCE}$
'go to/arrive at/come to/go school from home'

Four-argument (or **tetravalent**) verbs are not very frequent. They designate a transfer of location (concrete or metaphorical), so besides a subject agent, they involve a direct object theme, a source, and a goal (21), or commercial transactions, in which case the fourth argument is the entity denoting the expense, or payment exchanged (22).

(21) a. [*Adria*]$_{SUBJ/AGENT}$ *ha spostato* [*il vaso di gerani*]$_{DO/THEME}$ [*dalla veranda*]$_{SOURCE}$ [*alla cucina.*]$_{GOAL}$
'Adria moved the vase of geraniums from veranda the to the kitchen.'
 b. [*Adria*]$_{SUBJ/AGENT}$ *ha tradotto* [*molti racconti*]$_{DO/THEME}$ [*dall'italiano*]$_{SOURCE}$ [*all'inglese.*]$_{GOAL}$
'Adria translated many stories from Italian into English.'

(22) a. [*Francesco*]$_{SUBJ/AGENT}$ *ha comprato* [*un chilo di ciliegie*]$_{DO/THEME}$ [*da un contadino*]$_{SOURCE}$ [*per due euro.*]$_{EXCHANGE}$
'Francesco bought a kilo of cherries from a farmer for two euros.'
 b. [*Il contadino*]$_{SUBJ}$ *ha venduto* [*un chilo di ciliegie*]$_{DO}$ [*a Francesco*]$_{RECIPIENT}$ *per due euro.*]$_{EXCHANGE}$
'The farmer sold a kilo of cherries to Francesco for two euros.'

Verbs like 'buy' and 'sell' show that it may be useful to distinguish two types of semantic roles: (a) semantic roles 'which participate in the linguistic schematizing of acts, events, and states-of-affairs into very general patterns,' and (b) semantic roles which are 'frame-specific' in the sense that they are specified by the lexical meaning of a specific verb (Fillmore, 1985; Fillmore & Kay, 1995). Thus, in the case of *comprare* 'buy,' the frame-specific semantic roles of the subject and source argument can be labeled, respectively, 'buyer' and 'seller'; that of the entity being bought/sold is 'goods,' and that of the exchange is 'money.'

The notion of valency is correlated to the notion of transitivity since both have to do with the number of arguments selected by verbs. Nonetheless, the two notions differ in an important aspect: transitivity crucially relies on direct and indirect object arguments, whereas valency does not. In terms of transitivity, monovalent verbs that require neither a direct nor an indirect object are called **intransitive**; bivalent verbs that select a direct object only are called **transitive**, and trivalent verbs that call for both a direct and an indirect object are called **ditransitive**. However, the correlation between valency and transitivity is not direct. Transitivity is a complex notion; it is strongly connected to degree of subject's agentivity and direct object's patient status, and it is better accounted for by embracing a gradient, prototype approach (i.e., distinguishing between best/better vs. worst/worse transitive verbs). Proto-typical transitive verbs entail highly agentive subjects (i.e., human and volitional) and highly patient-like direct objects (i.e., highly affected by the action denoted by the verb); *uccidere* 'kill,' then, is a good example of prototypical transitive verb. On the other hand, verbs that take a direct object bearing the semantic role of theme (i.e., direct objects that are not significantly affected) and an experiencer subject, as for instance *credere* 'believe,' sit lower on the transitivity gradient (Givón, 1984; Hopper & Thompson, 1980; Langacker, 1987, 1991). The items in (23) illustrate the range of transitive verbs.

(23) a. [*Godzilla*]$_{SUBJ/AGENT}$ ***ha ucciso*** [*Bambi.*]$_{DO/PATIENT}$
'Godzilla killed Bambi.'[6]

b. [*Francesco*]$_{SUBJ/AGENT}$ ***ha spostato*** [*la foto di Gaia.*]$_{DO/THEME}$
'Francesco moved Gaia's photo.'

c. [*Francesco*]$_{SUBJ/EXPERIENCER}$ ***ha creduto*** [*alle bugie di Gaia.*]$_{OBLIQUE/STIMULUS}$
'Francesco believed Gaia's lies.'

d. [*L'incendio*]$_{SUBJ/INSTRUMENT}$ ***ha bruciato*** [*la casa.*]$_{DO/PATIENT}$
'The fire burned the house.'

e. [*Il tuono*]$_{SUBJ/STIMULUS}$ ***ha spaventato*** [*Ellie.*]$_{DO/EXPERIENCER}$
'The thunder scared Ellie.'

Also, as already noted, verbs may allow for their direct object to be unexpressed (*bere* 'drink,' *leggere* 'read,' *mangiare* 'eat,' *scrivere* 'write'). Regarding these verbs, traditional grammars speak of transitive vs. intransitive use of the verbs; following Fillmore's (1986) approach, we would say that these verbs allow for **null-object** instantiation. Null objects may have generic referents, for example, food in the case of *mangiare*, or any written material in the case of *leggere*; but they can also acquire very specific referents, as in the case of *bere*, where the referent of the null object is alcohol.

The picture is even more tangled when we look at intransitive verbs. Under the assumption that the distinctive feature of intransitive verbs is that they do not select a direct object, the verbs *ballare* 'dance,' *crescere* 'grow,' *migrare* 'migrate,' *sognare* 'dream' all qualify as intransitive. A closer scrutiny, however, reveals that intransitive verbs can be divided into two main classes, unergative and unaccusative, according to the subject's semantic role and various distinctive structural properties.

The **unergative** class includes verbs with agentive subjects (*lavorare* 'work,' *giocare* 'play,' *passeggiare* 'stroll') and verbs denoting natural, uncontrollable bodily functions or reactions, whose subjects are experiencers (*dormire* 'sleep,' *respirare* 'breathe,' *starnutire* 'sneeze'); this class is indeed intransitive and monovalent. The **unaccusative** class, on the other hand, comprises verbs denoting a state (*rimanere* 'remain'), a change of state (*crescere* 'grow,' *nascere* 'be born,' *invecchiare* 'grow old'), or a change of location resulting from directed motion (*partire* 'leave,' *uscire* 'exit') or a happening (*accadere* 'happen'). Subjects of unaccusative verbs resemble patients/themes because they undergo some change rather than actively engage into the event denoted by the verb. Unaccusatives include a number of so-called **pronominal verbs** (*verbi pronominali*), which are verbs that have incorporated the particle *si*, such as *arrabbiarsi* 'become angry' or *preoccuparsi* 'worry' (a more detailed account of *si* comes later in the chapter). Unaccusative verbs are certainly intransitive in that they cannot select a direct object argument but they are not necessarily monovalent; for instance, as seen earlier, so-called 'verbs of inherently directed motion,' like *arrivare* 'arrive'/*partire* 'leave,' *entrare* 'enter'/*uscire* 'exit,' are actually trivalent because, besides the subject, they require both a source and a goal argument, that is, the conceptualization of an event of 'arriving'/'entering' or 'departing'/'exiting' entails both a place where the subject gets to and the place from where the subject left.

In terms of structural properties, the two classes differ in the auxiliary they require in compound verb forms: unergatives select *avere* 'have' (24), while unaccusatives select *essere* 'be,' which triggers gender and number agreement between subject and past participle (25).

(24) a. *La rana*.FSG /*il rospo*.MSG **ha** *nuotato*.MSG.
        'The frog/the toad has swum.'
    b. *Le rane*.FPL /*i rospi*.MPL **hanno** *nuotato*.MSG.
        'The frogs/the toads have swum.'

(25) a. *La rana*.FSG *è morta*.FSG.   *Il rospo*.MSG *è morto*.MSG.
        'The frog has died.'   'The toad has died.'
    b. *le rane*.FPL *sono morte*.FPL.   *i rospi*.MPL *sono morti*.MPL.
        'The frogs have died.'   'The toads have died.'

A second important difference between unergative and unaccusative verbs pertains to **aspect**, the grammatical category that specifies how the state of affairs conveyed by a verb extends over time (for example, if it is habitual, punctual, ongoing, complete, etc.). Unaccusative verbs tend to be **telic** (from Greek τέλος 'goal; end'), that is, they portray events as complete or as having an endpoint or purpose, which makes them inherently incompatible with durative temporal adverbials and compatible with goal adverbials (26a). Unergatives, on the other hand, are typically **atelic**, that is, they depict events as incomplete or lacking an endpoint or purpose; thus, they reject punctual temporal adverbials and goal adverbials but allow locative adverbials (26b).

(26) a. *È arrivata **in un'ora**/****per un'ora**/**a casa***.
        'She arrived in one hour/*for one hour/at home.'
    b. *Ha passeggiato **per un'ora**/****in un'ora**/**nel parco**/****a casa***.
        'S/he strolled for one hour/*in one hour/in the park/*at home.'

Also, besides bearing the semantic role of patient/theme, unaccusative subjects display an important structural parallel with direct objects: their canonical position is after the verb and not before as unergative subjects (27), and they can be replaced by the pronoun *ne* when modified by a numeral or quantifier (28).

(27) a. [***Il gatto***]$_{\text{SUBJECT}}$ *ha mangiato* [*il canarino.*]$_{\text{DO}}$
'The cat ate the canary.'

     b. *È entrato* [***il gatto.***]$_{\text{SUBJECT}}$
'The cat came in.'

(28) a. *Il gatto ha mangiato* [***tre/molti*** *canarini.*]$_{\text{DO}}$ →   ***Ne*** *ha mangiati tre/molti.*
'The cat ate three/many canaries.'   '(The cat) ate three/many of them.'

     b. *Sono entrati* [***tre/molti*** *gatti.*]$_{\text{SUBJ}}$ →   ***Ne*** *sono entrati tre/molti.*
'Three/Many cats came in.' 'Three/Many of them came in.'

Unaccusative and unergative verbs hold a special place in Italian/Romance syntax (indeed, in syntax in general) and have been a very fertile research field since pioneering works such as Perlmutter (1978), Burzio (1986), Van Valin (1987, 1990), Levin and Rappaport Hovav (1995), to name only a few.

In conclusion, although transitivity and valency are related notions, they are certainly not equivalent; rather, they contribute in different ways to the proper characterization of verbs.

Now that we have reviewed clause types in relation to verb types (i.e., how verb semantics shapes clauses so as to reflect the proper conceptualization of the state of affairs portrayed by a given verb), we can examine clauses in relation to the functions they carry in speech. The primary communicative function clauses serve in discourse is to convey information about entities and/or events (**declarative** function), either in affirmative or negative mode. Declarative affirmative (active) clauses, as illustrated by the examples presented so far, are the most prototypical clauses cross-linguistically.

In standard Italian, sentential negation is expressed by means of a single negative marker, *non* 'not,' which always occurs before the main verb when it is in a simple form, either finite (29a) or non-finite (29b).

(29) a. *Francesco **non** mangia il pesce.*
'Francesco does not eat fish.'

     b. ***Non** mangiare la carne sta diventando sempre più comune.*
'Not eating meat is becoming more and more common.'

If the verb is in a compound form, the negative marker appears before the auxiliary (30a), and if an object clitic pronoun is present, the negative marker precedes the clitic (30b, c).

(30) a. *Francesco **non** ha finito di mangiare.*
'Francesco has not finished eating.'

     b. *Avevo cucinato <u>un ottimo branzino</u> ma Francesco **non** <u>lo</u> ha mangiato.*
'I had cooked an excellent branzino, but Francesco did not eat it.'

     c. *Ho cucinato un ottimo branzino <u>per Gaia</u> ma **non** <u>le</u> è piaciuto.*
'I cooked an excellent branzino for Gaia, but she didn't like it.'

Italian is a **negative concord** (or **double negation**) language, that is, it makes use of two negative elements (precisely, *non* and an indefinite negative pronoun, adjective, or adverb) in a sentence without them canceling each other to make the sentence affirmative.

(31) a. ***Non*** *ho visto* ***nessuno****,* ***non*** *ho detto* ***niente****.*
   'I haven't seen anybody (I saw nobody), I haven't said anything (I said nothing).'

   b. ***Non*** *hai visto* ***nessuno*** *studente?*
   'Have you seen any student?'

   c. ***Non*** *è* ***mai*** *stato in Africa.*
   'He has never been to Africa.'

Clauses can also serve to request information. **Interrogative** clauses come in two primary kinds. **Total** (or **polar**) **interrogatives** ask about the entire clause and are also known as **yes/no** questions because they can be answered simply by yes or no. They have the same structural configuration as declarative clauses, but a rising intonation contour (represented graphically by the question mark) rather than a falling one.

(32) a. *Francesco lavora in banca?* Interrogative [⟋]
   'Does Francesco work in a bank?'

   b. *Francesco lavora in banca.* Declarative [⟍]
   'Francesco works in a bank.'

Partial interrogative clauses ask about one clausal element only. They are introduced by a so-called 'operator,' which can be an adjective (33a), a pronoun (33b), or an adverb (33c). The canonic position of the subject is after the verb, while preverbal subjects are used for making their referents discourse prominent. They are also known as '*wh*-questions,' from the initials of the English operators (*who, what, which, when*).

(33) a. ***Che*** *libro sta leggendo Francesco?* 'What book is Francesco reading?'; ***Quale*** *gelato vuoi?* 'Which ice-cream do you want?'; ***Quanto*** *zucchero prende Francesco nel caffè?* 'How much sugar does Francesco take in his coffee?.'

   b. ***Chi*** *è quel ragazzo?* 'Who is that boy?'; ***Che cosa*** *sta facendo Francesco?* 'What is Francesco doing?';[7] ***Quanto*** *costa questa camicetta?* 'How much does this blouse cost?.'

   c. ***Come*** *stai?* 'How are you?'; ***Dove*** *sei?* 'Where are you?'; ***Quando*** *arrivi?* 'When do you arrive?'; ***Perché*** *stai piangendo?* 'Why are you crying?'

A third type are **disjunctive** interrogatives, which involve an option and are characterized by the conjunction *o/oppure* 'or': *guardiamo un film* ***o*** *facciamo una passeggiata?* 'shall we watch a movie or go for a walk?.'

Finally, we distinguish **imperative/exhortative** clauses, which impart commands (*Torna immediatamente a casa!* 'Come (you.SG) back home immediately!') and exhortations (*Andiamo a fare una passeggiata!* 'Let's go for a walk!').

5.1.3 Sentences

Let's now climb one step further above the clause level to examine sentences. *Sentence* can be defined as cohesive syntactic units, which include at least one clause. Clauses can be sentences on their own, yet it is not the case that any clause makes a sentence. Put differently, a clause is a portion of a sentence that may equal a sentence, as opposed to an utterance, which is any portion of discourse independent of length and, most of all, structure.

Sentences comprising a single clause are called **simple** (this is, when clause and sentence coincide). It is important to keep in mind that length is irrelevant in the categorization of sentences: both (34a) and (34b) are examples of simple sentences because they both consist of one clause (i.e., one verb) only.

(34) a. *Sono arrivati.*
'They arrived.'
   b. *Gli ospiti sono arrivati in albergo a notte fonda dopo uno spossante viaggio in treno di sei ore.*
'The guests arrived at the hotel in the middle of the night after an exhausting six-hour long train trip.'

Two (or more) clauses can combine to form **complex** sentences following two main strategies, namely, coordination and subordination. Before we examine each strategy in more detail, it should be noted that the term 'sentence' may be ambiguous, since it can be viewed from (at least) three different perspectives. From a syntactic (i.e., formal) perspective, we have main and subordinate clauses. From a semantic perspective, on the other hand, sentences are seen as expressing a judgment/statement (cf. Latin SENTENTIA 'judgment,' from which 'sentence' came via French *sentence* in the twelfth century); they are conceptual units bearing truth value. And from the perspective of discourse, sentences are acts of communication, and although a sentence has one single form and one single meaning, it can be employed for an infinite number of utterances. The concept of 'sentence,' then, is extremely abstract.

5.1.3.1 Coordination

Coordination (or **parataxis** from Gr. *παρά* 'beside' and *τάξις* 'position') combines simple sentences, putting them on the same level – that is, under coordination, individual one-clause sentences are conjoined at the same level of structure and linked to one another in a non-hierarchical relation by coordinating conjunctions. Each sentence, then, forms a single cohesive unit, which is fully meaningful by itself. Clauses which can alone form such a cohesive unit are called **main** (also **matrix** or **independent**) clauses/sentences.

Three core types of coordination are copulative, adversative, and disjunctive. **Copulative** (from the Latin verb CŌPŬLĀRE 'join; pair') coordination simply adds two sentences, most typically by means of the conjunctions *e* 'and' and *né* 'nor' in the context of negation.

(35) a. [*Francesco legge il giornale*]$_{S1}$ *e* [*sorseggia un tè freddo.*]$_{S2}$
'Francesco is reading the newspaper and sipping an iced tea.'
   b. [*Francesco non ha fatto i compiti*]$_{S1}$ *né* [*ha rassettato la sua stanza.*]$_{S2}$
'Francesco didn't do his homework nor did he tidy up his room.'

However, note that *e* can indeed acquire a range of meanings from the discourse context, that is, it can establish a relationship between clauses that resembles subordination (i.e., a hierarchical relation; see following). For instance, in (35a) *e* could establish a temporal link between the two clauses, leading to the interpretation 'Francesco is reading the newspaper

while sipping a hot tea,' or it could set up a causal relationship, as shown by *era stanco e ha fatto un pisolino* 'he was tired **therefore** he took a nap.'

Adversative coordination establishes a contrast (36a), while **disjunctive** coordination presents an alternative or an opposition (36b, c) (cf. disjunctive interrogative clause above). The most common adversative conjunctions are *ma/però* 'but,' and among the most frequent disjunctive conjunctions are *o/oppure* 'or' and *altrimenti* 'otherwise.'

(36) a. [*È una giornata stupenda*]_{S1} *ma/però* [*non ho voglia di uscire.*]_{S2}
      'It's a gorgeous day, but I don't want to go out.'
   b. [*Guardiamo un film*]_{S1} *o* [*giochiamo a carte.*]_{S2}
      'Let's watch a movie, or play cards.'
   c. [*Non fare tardi*]_{S1} *altrimenti* [*mi arrabbio.*]_{S2}
      'Don't be late, otherwise, I will get mad.'

Two other relevant types of sentential coordination are **declarative** coordination, which introduces an explanation (37a), and **conclusive** coordination, which establishes an inference relation (37b).

(37) a. [*Non si sente molto bene*]_{S1} *infatti/ovvero/cioè* [*ha la febbre.*]_{S2}
      'S/he doesn't feel very well, indeed, s/he has a fever.'
   b. [*È vegano*]_{S1} *dunque/sicché/pertanto/perciò/quindi* [*non mangia le uova.*]_{S2}
      'He is vegan, so he doesn't eat eggs.'

Summing up, under coordination, sentences form unified components which, however, are fully independent of each other because they can meaningfully stand on their own. This, on a par relation among sentences, is lost in subordination, which, conversely, combines clauses, arranging them in a hierarchical structure.

5.1.3.2 Subordination

As the term suggests, **subordination** (also **hypotaxis**, from Gr. ὑπό 'under' and τάξις 'position') sets up a relationship of dependency among clauses, setting apart main clauses from **subordinate** (also **embedded** or **dependent**) clauses. Subordinate clauses combine with main clauses through subordinating conjunctions, which signal the type of relationship holding between them. Three main classes of subordinate clauses are traditionally distinguished: argument (or complement), adverbial, and relative.

5.1.3.2.1 Argument clauses

Argument subordinate clauses function just like arguments of the verb, specifically, subject and direct object. **Subject** clauses occur primarily with impersonal verbs (38) and impersonal verbal periphrases comprising the verb *essere* 'be' and an adjective (39), or the verb *fare* 'make' and an adverb or noun (40).

(38) a. *Bisogna* [*avere pazienza nella vita.*]_{SUBJ}
      'One should/must have patience in life.'
   b. *Sembra* [*funzionare perfettamente.*]_{SUBJ}
      'It seems to work perfectly.'

(39) a. *È importante [fare attività fisica regolarmente.]*_{SUBJ}
         'It is important to exercise regularly.'

   b. *[Ringraziare l'ospite]*_{SUBJ} *è appropriato.*
       'Thanking one's host is appropriate.'

(40) a. *[Bere troppo]*_{SUBJ} *fa male.*
         'Drinking too much is unhealthy (lit. makes bad).'

   b. *Fa comodo [abitare vicino un supermercato e alla fermata dell'autobus a.]*_{SUBJ}
       'It's (lit. makes) convenient to live close to a supermarket and the bus stop.'

The verb of the subject clause is in the infinitive form since it does not entail a specific referent, that is, the entire sentence is impersonal.

   Another viable context for subject clauses are verbs of the *piacere* 'like' type, which, as we recall, select a subject/theme and an indirect object/experiencer. In this case, we no longer have an impersonal sentence; the infinitive verb of the subject clause does have a specific referent, which is the same referent as the experiencer.

(41) a. *A Francesco piace/manca [passeggiare sulla spiaggia.]*_{SUBJ}
         'Francesco likes/misses strolling on the beach.'

   b. *A Francesco rincresce **di** [essere arrivato in ritardo.]*_{SUBJ}
       'Francesco regrets having arrived late.'

As shown by the earlier examples, subject clauses can either precede or follow the main clause. The postverbal position is overall more common, yet whether the subject clause precedes or follows the main clause ultimately depends on the verb of the main clause and the communicative function of the sentence. Normally, no subordinating element (or **subordinator**) is involved, the two clauses being simply adjoined; in some cases, however, depending on the verb of the main clause, the subject clause is introduced by the preposition *di* 'of' (41b).

   Before continuing with our review of the second type of subordinate argument clauses (i.e., subordinate clauses which function as direct objects), an important structural distinction should be addressed: the difference between implicit and explicit subordinate clauses, which applies to both argument and adverbial clauses. Subordinate clauses with the verb in the infinitive form (or non-finite verb forms in general) are known as **implicit** and contrast with **explicit** subordinate clauses, which have a verb in the finite form and are introduced by the subordinator *che* 'that.'

(42) a. *Bisogna*   **che**   *[tu   abbia   pazienza   con   Francesco.]*_{SUBJ}
         must.3SG.PI   that   you   have.2SG.PS   patience   with   Francesco
         'You must be patient with Francesco.'

   b. *Sembra*   **che**   *[funzioni   perfettamente.]*_{SUBJ}
       seem.3SG.PI   that   work.3SG.PS   perfectly
       'It seems to work perfectly.'

   c. *È importante **che** [tu faccia attività fisica regolarmente.]*_{SUBJ}
       'It is important that you exercise regularly.'

   d. *Sarebbe opportuno **che** [li ringraziassimo per la loro ospitalità.]*_{SUBJ}
       'It would be appropriate that we thank them for their hospitality.'

The explicit construction allows the verb of the embedded clause to have its own subject, thus making the sentence non-impersonal. Also, this is the only option if the subordinate expresses an event that occurred before the event denoted by the main clause (43a) and in the context of the construction *essere molto/tanto* 'be much/very' with temporal value (and synonyms like *è una vita* 'it's been a lifetime,' *sono secoli* 'it's been centuries') (43b).

(43) a. *Sembra **che** [ieri funzionasse.]*_{SUBJ}
     a'. **Sembra ieri funzionare.*
       'It seems that it worked/was working yesterday.'
    b. *È tanto/una vita **che** [non ci vediamo.]*_{SUBJ}
     b'. **È tanto/una vita non ci vediamo.*
       'It's been a lifetime since we've seen each other.'

Finally, as noted earlier, the implicit construction requires that the referent of the subject of the subordinate clause and the referent of the indirect object/experiencer of the main clause be the same. In technical terms, implicit constructions entail **co-referentiality** of the subject of the main clause and the indirect object of the subordinate; consequently, the explicit construction is ruled out if the subject of the main clause and the indirect object of the embedded clause are co-referential.

(44) a. *Forse vi conviene non rispondere.*
     a'. **Forse **vi** conviene che **voi** non rispondiate.*
       'Maybe it's better if you.PL don't answer.'
    b. ***Mi** rincresce che **tu** non resti a cena.*
     b'. **Mi rincresce tu non restare a cena.*
       'I am sorry that you.SG cannot stay for dinner.'

Subordinate argument clauses also function as **direct object** of both transitive verbs (45) and pronominal verbs that select as their second argument PPs introduced by *di* (*interessarsi* 'to be interested in': *mi interesso **di politica*** 'I am interested in politics') (46).

(45) a. *Ammetto **che** [avevi ragione.]*_{DO}
       'I admit that you were right.'
    b. *Vedo **che** [hai mangiato tutti i cioccolatini.]*_{DO}
       'I see that you ate all the chocolates.'

(46) a. *Non si rende conto **di** [essere sgarbato.]*
       'He doesn't realize he is rude.'
    b. *Ci rifiutiamo **di** [ascoltare queste sciocchezze.]*_{DO}
       'We refuse to listen to this nonsense.'

The examples in (45) and (46) illustrate, respectively, explicit and implicit constructions. As in the case of subject clauses, the implicit construction is linked primarily to co-referentiality between the main and subordinate subject, as illustrated further in (47), which also shows that the presence, absence, or optionality of the subordinator *di* is governed by the main verb.[8]

(47) a. *Spero **di** [arrivare per le 17,00.]*_{DO}   a'. *Spero **che** [arrivino per le 17,00.]*_{DO}
       'I hope to arrive by 5pm.'   'I hope they arrive by 5pm.'

    b. *Voglio [andare a casa.]*$_{DO}$ b'. *Voglio **che** [andiate a casa.]*$_{DO}$
        'I want to go home.'   'I want that you.PL go home.'
    c. *Mi dispiace (**di**) [essere in ritardo.]*$_{DO}$ c'. *Mi dispiace **che** [siano in ritardo.]*$_{DO}$
        'I am sorry to be late.'   'I am sorry that they are late.'

The mood of the subordinate verb is governed by the semantics of the main verb and the construal of the situation denoted by the sentence. Generally speaking, indicative mood, as in the examples in (45) and (48), is related to factuality and objectivity, that is, the event expressed by the subordinate clause is presented as factual, with no interference of the speaker's personal opinions, considerations, feelings, etc.

(48) a. *So che **arrivano**/**arriveranno** domani sera.*
         'I know that they (will) arrive tomorrow evening.'
     b. *Riconoscono che **abbiamo fatto** un ottimo lavoro.*
         'They acknowledge that we did a great job.'

In contrast, subjunctive mood, as in (49) and (47a'–c') earlier, relates to non-factuality and subjectivity: the event denoted by the subordinate clause is linked to probability, uncertainty, negation, and/or speaker's personal involvement, while conditional mood is used to express hypotheses (50a) and future in the past (50b).

(49) a. *Penso che **vengano** anche loro.*
         'I think they are coming too.'
     b. *Non sapevo che Francesco **fosse** così permaloso.*
         'I didn't know that Francesco was so touchy.'

(50) a. *So che mi **aiuteresti** (se potessi).*
         'I know you would help me (if you could).'
     b. *Hanno promesso che ci **avrebbero aiutato**.*
         'They promised that they would help us.'

It should be noted, however, that although this generalization is still quite robust in Italian, there are verbs which may select either indicative or subjunctive in their subordinate clauses, leading to a different construal of the event denoted by the subordinate in terms of degrees of (un)certainty and speaker's subjectivity/objectivity. For instance, mood selection is semantically functional with the verb *sperare* 'hope' because indicative and subjunctive convey different, contrasting degrees of speaker's commitment to and/or attitude about the realizability (i.e., factuality) of the situation expressed by the embedded clause, but it is not with verbs like *credere* 'believe' or *pensare* 'think' (Squartini, 2010; Wandruszka, 2001; among others).

5.1.3.2.2 Adverbial clauses

Adverbial clauses resemble adjunct phrases from a semantic perspective in that they convey similar sorts of information. The array of adverbial clauses is fairly vast; in consideration of space, we will review only the main types, namely, causal, concessive, consecutive, final, temporal, and conditional.

    Causal sentences declare the cause of the event expressed by the main sentence. The most common causal subordinator in explicit clauses is *perché* 'because,' followed by *poiché/siccome* 'since,' *dato/visto che* 'given/seen that.' The position of the subordinate clause with respect to the matrix depends on the individual subordinators: clauses introduced by *perché* preferably follow the main clause, clauses introduced by *siccome* normally precede it, while some subordinators allow either order.

(51) a. *Vado a casa **perché** è tardi.*
  'I'm going home because it's late.'
 b. ***Siccome** piove, resto a casa.*
  'Since it's raining, I'm staying home.
 c. ***Dato che** non aveva l'ombrello, si è inzuppato./Si è inzuppato **dato che** . . .*
  'Given that he didn't have an umbrella, he got soaked.'

Implicit causal sentences, on the other hand, are introduced by *per* 'for' or, more marginally, *di* 'of' and *a* 'at; to.'

(52) a. *Ho preso una multa **per** aver parcheggiato vicino a un idrante.*
  'I got a ticket for parking by a fire hydrant.'
 b. *Ti ringrazio **di** avermi aiutato.*
  'Thank you for helping me.'
 c. *È fortunato **a** vivere in campagna.*
  'He's lucky to live in the country.'

Concessive clauses present a condition despite which the situation denoted by the main clause takes place (or doesn't), setting up a contrast between the matrix and the subordinate clause. The most frequent concessive subordinators in explicit constructions are *benché, nonostante/malgrado (che), sebbene* 'although,' which require the embedded verb in the subjunctive mood, and *anche/neanche se* 'even/not even though,' which impose no mood restrictions on the subordinate verb. Implicit concessive clauses are rendered by *pur* 'even though' and the verb in the gerund or past participle form; overall, they are restricted to formal (written) language.

(53) a. *È andato in vacanza alle Hawaii **benché** fosse pieno di debiti.*
  'He went to Hawaii on vacation although he was full of debts.'
 b. *Vado al cinema con Francesco **anche se** dovrei lavorare.*
  'I'm going to the movies with Francesco even though I should work.'
 c. *Ma c'è una cosa che mi tengo/Perdonami non puoi averla tu/ **Neanche se** piangi in cinese* (Vecchioni, 2007).
  'But there is one thing I will keep for myself/Forgive me; you cannot have it/Not even if you cry in Chinese.'
 d. ***Pur essendo** completamente diversi vanno d'accordo.*
  'Even though they are completely different, they get on well together.'
 e. ***Pur stremato** ha passato l'aspirapolvere in tutta la casa.*
  'Even though he was exhausted, he vacuum-cleaned the entire house.'

Consecutive clauses express a result or consequence of the state of affairs portrayed by the main clause. In the explicit format, they are commonly introduced by *che* 'that,' which is anchored to *così/tanto/talmente* 'so' in the main clause, or by *cosicché/sicchè, quindi, perciò* 'so (that).' In the implicit form, they are introduced by *da* 'from' or *per* 'for.'

(54) a. *Era **così** assorto nella lettura **che** non ha sentito il telefono.*
'He was so engrossed in reading that he didn't hear the phone.'

b. *C'era corrente **perciò** ho chiuso la finestra.*
'There was a draft, so I closed the window.'

c. *La puzza era talmente forte **da** togliere il respiro.*
'The smell was so strong that it took your breath away.'

d. *Sei abbastanza grande **per** restare a casa da solo.*
'You are old enough to stay home by yourself.

Final clauses convey the goal of the situation expressed by the main clause. Explicit ones are introduced by *affinché* 'in order/so that' and require the verb in the subjunctive, while implicit ones are introduced primarily by *per* 'for.'

(55) a. *Ti ho avvertito **affinché** tu non ti trovassi in una situazione imbarazzante.*
'I tipped you off so that you wouldn't find yourself in an awkward situation.'

b. *Ho fatto di tutto **per** convincerlo a venire con noi.*
'I did everything I could to convince him to come with us.'

Temporal clauses refer to the temporal relation between the events denoted by the main and the subordinate clause, which can be of contemporaneity (at the same time), anteriority (before), or posteriority (after). The most common temporal adverbs signaling **contemporaneity** are *quando* 'when' and *mentre* 'while,' and only the explicit format is available in this case, with the verb in indicative mood.

(56) a. *Ti telefono **quando** arrivo.*
'I'll call you when I arrive.'

b. *Francesco telefonato **mentre** stavamo cenando.*
'Francesco called while we were having dinner.'

Temporal clauses linked to the matrix by a relation of **anteriority** are introduced by *prima che* 'before that,' which calls for the subjunctive and *prima di* 'before of,' while *dopo che* with indicative and *dopo* followed by the verb in the past infinitive form mark posteriority.

(57) a. *Dovrei pulire la casa **prima che** arrivi mia suocera.*
'I should clean the house before my mother-in-law arrives.'

b. *Ho fatto il bucato **prima di** uscire.*
'I did the laundry before I went out.'

(58) a. *Non li ho più sentiti **dopo che** si sono trasferiti a Austin.*
'I never heard from them again after they moved to Austin.

b. ***Dopo che** ti avrò raccontato tutto capirai.*
'After I tell you everything, you'll understand.'

c. ***Dopo** aver fatto il bucato è andato a fare la spesa.*
'After doing the laundry, he went grocery shopping.

We conclude our review of subordinate clauses with **conditional** clauses, which express a prerequisite necessary for the realization of the situation denoted by the main clause and are most commonly introduced by *se* 'if' and less frequently by *talora/qualora* 'in case,' *a patto/*

condizione che, qualora 'on the condition that.' In Italian, constructions involving conditional clauses are also known as *periodo ipotetico* 'hypothetical sentence'; the conditional clause is called **protasis**, and the matrix **apodosis**. There are three types of hypothetical constructions which convey different degrees of factuality and are governed by a precise tense and mood correspondence between the verb of the main clause and the subordinate verb. The order of the two clauses is flexible, that is, the main clause can also precede the conditional clause.

(59) a. *Se nevica, andiamo a sciare.*
        'If it snows, we'll go skiing.'
     b. *Se nevicasse, andremmo a sciare.*
        'If it would snow, we would go skiing.'
     c. *Se avesse nevicato, saremmo andati a sciare.*
        'If it had snowed, we would have gone skiing.'

The sentence in (59a), where both the subordinate and the matrix verbs are in the indicative mood (and present tense), exemplifies the type of conditional construction which presents the situation as factual. The version in (59b), on the other hand, expresses a lower degree of factuality, presenting the situation as possible; in this case, the verb of the subordinate clause is in the imperfect subjunctive and the matrix verb is in the present conditional. Finally, (59c) presents the situation as impossible (i.e., counterfactual); the subordinate verb is in the pluperfect subjunctive, while the main verb is in the past conditional. Conditional constructions denoting possibility, with both the main and subordinate verb in the imperfect indicative (*se nevicava, andavamo a sciare*), which had been banished to low registers and uneducated speakers, have been gaining more and more acceptability.

5.1.3.2.3 Relative clauses

Relative clauses, like direct object clauses, are quite frequent in Italian. Their distinctive feature is that they are introduced by a relative pronoun which is anchored to a constituent of the main clause – called the **antecedent** (or **head**) and underlined in the examples in (60) – which expresses the relative pronoun's referent; the relative pronoun and its antecedent must be adjacent.

(60) a. <u>*La ragazza*</u> **che** *sta parlando con Francesco.*
        'The girl who is talking with Francesco.'
     b. <u>*La ragazza*</u> **che** *Francesco ha conosciuto a Austin.*
        'The girl whom Francesco met in Austin.'

Italian relative pronouns come in three forms and serve different syntactic functions. The first form is *che*, which is invariable (i.e., unmarked for gender/number) and functions as subject (60a) and direct object (60b). The second is a periphrastic form consisting of a preposition (which expresses the grammatical function of the pronoun) and invariable *cui* and serves for complements other than direct object.

(61) a. *La ragazza* **a cui** *Francesco ha mandato una dozzina di rose.*   (Indirect object)
        'The girl to whom I wrote.'
     b. *La ragazza* **con cui** *Francesco è andato in vacanza l'anno scorso.*   (Company)
        'The girl with whom Francesco went on vacation last year.'
     c. *Il coltello* **con cui** *Francesco ha affettato il pane.*   (Instrument)
        'The knife with which Francesco sliced the bread.'

The third form is also periphrastic and comprises the definite article (which agrees in gender and number with the referent of the relative pronoun) followed by the relative pronoun *quale* (which agrees with its antecedent in number only) and theoretically covers all functions, though in present-day standard Italian, it is rarely used as subject and direct object.

(62) a. *La ragazza **la quale** sta parlando con Francesco.*
b. *La ragazza **la quale** Francesco ha conosciuto a Austin.*
c. *La ragazza **alla quale** Francesco ha mandato una dozzina di rose.*
d. *La ragazza **con la quale** Francesco è andato in vacanza l'anno scorso.*
e. *Il coltello **con il quale** Francesco ha affettato il pane.*

Relative clauses come in two main types: **restrictive** relative clauses, which convey information that is necessary to determine the antecedent (63a), and **appositive** relative clauses, typically enclosed by commas in writing (63b), which provide supplementary information about the antecedent and therefore are optional.

(63) a. *La ragazza [per cui Francesco ha perso la testa] vive a Austin.*
'The girl for whom Francesco lost his head lives in Austin.
b. *Gaia, [per cui Francesco ha perso la testa], è arrivata ieri.*
'Gaia, for whom Francesco lost his head, arrived yesterday.'

Relative clauses can also carry specific semantic functions, thus resembling adverbial clauses.

(64) a. *Beata lei, **che** va in vacanza ai Caraibi.* (Causal)
'Lucky her, who (because he) is going on vacation to the Caribbean.'
b. *Francesco, **che** sapeva tutto, non ha detto niente.* (Concessive)
'Francesco, who (although he) knew everything, said nothing.'
c. *Hai bisogno di amici **che** ti aiutino in un momento così difficile.* (Final)
'You need friends who (so that they) help you at such a difficult time.'
d. *Ho visto Francesco **che** andava al supermercato.* (Temporal)
'I saw Francesco who (when he) was going to the supermarket.'
e. *Il 2019 è l'anno **in cui** è scoppiata la pandemia COVID-19.* (Temporal)
'2019 is the year in which the COVID pandemic broke out.'
f. *Il paese **in cui** è nato Francesco è sul mare.* (Locative)
'The town where she was born is by the sea.'

In locative and temporal relative clauses, the relative pronoun can be replaced, respectively, by *quando* 'when' and *dove* 'where,' particularly in contexts not characterized by a high degree of formality.

A phenomenon that is gaining ground in present-day Italian, though still associated by many with lower-class, semi-/illiterate speakers (i.e., *italiano popolare*), is the use of invariable *che* in contexts that would call for the either *cui* or *quale* (see preceding text), often accompanied by a clitic pronoun which expresses the syntactic function of the relative pronoun.[9]

(65) a. *È un ragazzo **che** [**a cui**] (**gli**) piacciono tutti gli sport.*
'He's a boy who likes all sports.'
b. *Il paesino **che** [**in cui/dove**] (**ci**) sono stato in ferie l'estate scorsa è una meraviglia.*
'The small town I went on vacation last summer is wonderful.'

c. *È una questione **che** [**di cui**] (**ne**) dobbiamo parlare.*
'It's an issue we have to talk about.'

d. '. . . *tu mi hai fatto convincere a me di una cosa **che** io prima non ero convinto*' (Fiorentino, 1999, p. 101)
'you convinced me of something I wasn't convinced about before'

Somewhat related to invariable relative *che* is the so-called *che polivalente* 'multifunctional *che*,' that is, *che* serving as a versatile, general-purpose subordinating conjunction used instead of a specific subordinator as the ones examined earlier, which express the semantic value/function of the subordinate clause. Pinpointing the precise semantic value of *che*, however, may not be straightforward, especially when it comes to distinguishing between consecutive and final value.

(66) a. *Apri la finestra **che** c'è aria viziata.*   (Causal)
'Open the window because the air is stale.'

b. *Sono mesi **che** non sento Francesco.*   (Temporal)
'It's been months since I have heard from Francesco.'

c. *Avvicinati **che** ti vedo meglio.*   (Final/Consecutive)
'Come closer so I can see you better.'

d. '*voi dovreste trovare un lavoro **che** la domenica restate libera*' (Fiorentino, 2007, p. 64)
'you should find a job so that you're free on Sundays'

Similar to invariable relative *che*, some uses of multifunctional *che* are still viewed as restricted to informal, colloquial speech and sub-standard Italian. There is general consensus, however, that this structure has been expanding increasingly, and multifunctional *che* is considered a phenomenon that pertains to the general process of restructuring of modern standard Italian into neo-standard Italian (Berruto, 1987, p. 69). Indeed, multifunctional *che* with temporal value is fully accepted and is now the only viable option to express the duration of an event in relation to a given unit of time, as in (66c) earlier (Serianni, 1988, p. 481). Conversely, the use of multifunctional *che* with final/consecutive function remains frowned upon.

Multifunctional *che* is by no means a recent phenomenon, nor is it restricted to the spoken language. Rather, it is attested fairly regularly throughout the history of the Italian language, starting from its very origins, even in major authors whose language played a key role in the development of modern standard Italian, such as Dante Alighieri, Giovanni Boccaccio, and Francesco Petrarca.[10]

(67) a. '*Quivi il lasciammo, **che** più non ne narro*'
'We left him there, that of him I will say no more'
(Alighieri, *Commedia*, *Inferno* VIII, 64)

b. '*o voi mi licenziate **che** io per li miei pensieri mi ritorni e steami nella città tribolata*'
'or you give me leave so that I go back for my cares and abide in the afflicted city'
(Boccaccio, *Decameron*, Day I, Introduction)

c. '*Era il giorno **ch**'al sol si scoloraro/per la pietà del suo Factore i rai*'
'It was the day when the sun's rays faded in pity of its Maker'
(Petrarca, *Canzoniere* III, 1–2)

Indeed, several forms frowned upon as 'incorrect' or sub-standard in modern Italian have actually been around for centuries. A renowned example is the use of the object pronouns *lui* '3.M.SG,' *lei* '3.F.SG,' and *loro* '3.PL' with subject function, which, though blacklisted by prescriptive grammars until not long ago, is attested as early as the thirteenth century (D'Achille, 1990, pp. 315–319).

5.2 Sentence form and communicative functions

This section touches on the interface between syntax and discourse pragmatics, or **information structure**. Briefly put, information structure examines how sentences are used in different communicative settings. Thus, rather than concerning lexical and sentence content, it addresses the different strategies whereby propositional content is transmitted and, consequently, addresses the relationship between linguistic forms and language users' (i.e., discourse participants') mental states. Knud Lambrecht, whose research on information structure is widely acknowledged as groundbreaking – many actually consider him one of this field's founders – defines *information structure* as:

> [The] component of sentence grammar in which propositions as conceptual representations of states of affairs are paired with lexico-grammatical structures in accordance with the mental states of interlocutors who use and interpret these structures as units of information in given discourse contexts.
>
> *(Lambrecht, 1994, p. 5)*

The order in which words, more properly constituents, occur within phrases and sentences, then, can correlate to communicative function. Though word order is governed by language-specific constraints, all languages allow for different word-order patterns, typically paired to certain prosodic features, each conveying a specific communicative function. A distinction is thus drawn between so-called **unmarked** (also basic, canonical, or neutral) and **marked** word-order patterns. The former basically instantiate declarative sentences, whereas the latter are variations of unmarked word-order configurations associated to differences in expressivity and specific communicative functions, most typically that of foregrounding and/or emphasizing a given constituent's appearances in some 'unexpected' position. Thus, unmarked and marked word-order patterns convey the same propositional content (i.e., evoke the same 'conceptual scene') but diverge in terms of contextual appropriateness since they fulfill different communicative functions, as illustrated in (68).

(68) a. *Francesco ha prestato dieci euro a Gaia.*
   'Francesco lent ten euro to Gaia.'

  b. | *Dieci* | *euro,* | *li* | | *ha* | *prestati* | *a* | *Gaia,* | *Francesco.* |
   |---|---|---|---|---|---|---|---|---|
   | ten | euro | them.M.PL | | has | lent.M.PL | to | G. | F. |

   'Ten euro, he lent them to Gaia, Francesco.'

  c. | *Francesco,* | *dieci* | *euro,* | *li* | | *ha* | *prestati* | *a* | *Gaia.* |
   |---|---|---|---|---|---|---|---|---|
   | F. | | ten | euro | them.M.PL | has | lent.M.PL | to | G. |

   'Francesco, ten euro, he lent them to Gaia.'

  d. | *A* | *Gaia,* | *Francesco le* | | *ha* | *prestato* | *dieci* | *euro.* |
   |---|---|---|---|---|---|---|---|
   | to | G. | F. | to.her | has | lent | ten | euro |

   'To Gaia, Francesco lent her ten euro.'

   e.   *Gaia,*   *le*   *ha*   *prestato* *dieci*   *euro,*   *Francesco.*

       G.   to.her has   lent   ten   euro   F.

       'Gaia, to her he lent ten euro, Francesco.'

   f.   *È Francesco che ha prestato dieci euro a Gaia.*

       'It's Francesco who lent ten euro to Gaia.'

   g.   *È a Gaia che Francesco ha prestato dieci euro.*

       'It's to Gaia that Francesco lent ten euro.'

We see in (68) that the same content – namely, 'Francesco lent ten euro to Gaia' – can be expressed in Italian in (at least) seven different structural configurations. The sentence in (68a) exemplifies the unmarked word-order pattern for Italian: subject-verb-complements, with DO preceding IO. Conversely, the other six configurations, which can be subsumed under two broad types of marked word-order constructions, dislocation (68b–e) and cleft sentences (68f, g), represent alternatives charged by specific communicative functions, so that the choice of one configuration over the others depends crucially on the speaker's ideas about, as well as on the discourse setting.

5.2.1 Dislocation and related constructions

The term **dislocation** refers to a type of (morpho)syntactic construction attested extensively across languages (Lambrecht, 2001). This term, which evokes the idea of 'movement,' stems from the generative (i.e., Chomskyan) linguistic framework that relies on the notion of movement from a basic position (so-called underlying structure/representation) to a derived position (so-called surface structure/representation), which might be misleading within different theoretical approaches to linguistic analysis. Nonetheless, we will adopt it since it has become the established term in the literature worldwide. It is generally agreed that the basic discourse function of dislocation is to mark a constituent's referent as **topic** (e.g., Dik, 1978; Gundel, 1988; Lambrecht, 1994, 2001), that is, to signal that it conveys given/old information, more precisely, information that the speaker presupposes to be known by the addressee, which typically constitutes the starting point of the communicative event. In Lambrecht's words:

> [A] referent is interpreted as the topic of a proposition if in a given situation the proposition is construed as being about this referent, i.e. as expressing information which is relevant to and which increases the addressee's knowledge of this referent. . . . [F]or a proposition to be construable as being about the referent of a topic expression this referent must be *pragmatically accessible in the discourse.*
>
> *(1994, p. 131; emphasis added)*

Topic referents, then, must either be under discussion in a given discourse context or retrievable from the context and stand in opposition with new information (also **focus, rheme**, or **comment**). Crucially, 'new' information is not to be interpreted as information that has not been previously mentioned, though this may well be (and often is) the case; rather, it is new in the sense that speakers present it as not being retrievable from previous discourse. That is, the focus of a proposition is 'that portion of a proposition which cannot be taken for granted at the time of speech. It is the UNPREDICTABLE or pragmatically NON-RECOVERABLE element in an utterance. The focus is what makes the utterance into an assertion' (Lambrecht, 1994, p. 207; original emphasis).

Summarizing, dislocation enables promoting the representation of a referent from non-active to active state in the addressee's mind, consequently allowing speakers to mark such referent as a preferred topic expression (Lambrecht, 1994, p. 181).

Two types of dislocation are distinguished, **left-** and **right-dislocation**, and they are addressed in the next subsections.

5.2.1.1 Left-dislocation

The sentence pair in (69) illustrates the contrast between the unmarked word-order configuration (69a) (i.e., the affirmative declarative construction) and left-dislocation (69b). In the former, the DO constituent *i carciofi* 'the artichokes' follows the verb, as expected, and instantiates the sentence focus. In (69b), on the other hand, *i carciofi* appears in sentence-initial position, which, as we know, is the position typically reserved to subject (topic) constituents in unmarked word-order constructions in Italian. Moreover, (69b) includes the unstressed DO pronoun *li* 'them.M.PL,' which is co-referential to the dislocated constituent *i carciofi* and links it to the sentence by signaling its syntactic function. In terms of intonation, left-dislocation may (though need not) involve a pause after the dislocated constituent, which in writing is traditionally rendered with a comma.

(69) a. *Francesco non mangia [i carciofi.]*_{NP/DO}
     'Francesco doesn't eat artichokes.'

    b. *[I carciofi]*_{NP/DO}, *Francesco non li*_{DO} *mangia.*
     'Artichokes, Francesco doesn't eat them.'

In Italian, left-dislocation most commonly involves NP constituents, though PPs and clauses can be left-dislocated as well, as seen in (70).

(70) a. *[A Francesco,]*_{PP/IO} *gli*_{IO} *ho regalato un romanzo di Camilleri.*
     'Francesco, I gave him a novel by Camilleri as a present.'

    b. *[A Baltimora,]*_{PP/LOC} *Francesco non ci*_{LOC} *è mai stato.*
     'Baltimore, Francesco has never been there.'

    c. *[Con Francesco,]*_{PP/COM} *non ci*_{COM} *parlo più.*
     'Francesco, I no longer speak to him.'

    d. *[Di questo argomento,]*_{PP/COM} *non ne*_{COM} *voglio parlare.*
     'This subject, I never want to talk about it.'

    e. *[Che Francesco non sarebbe venuto]*_S *lo*_S *avevo intuito.*
     'That Francesco wouldn't come, I had guessed that.'

According to some (e.g., Benincà, 2001; Zamora Muñoz, 2002), the co-referential pronoun is obligatory only if the dislocated constituent is a DO, as in (69b) or (70e), and also when it is a quantified NP (*due/alcune* mele 'three/some apples), in which case the pronoun involved is partitive *ne* (*mele* **ne** *mangio due ogni giorno* 'apples, I eat two of them every day'). For all the other types of constituents (i.e., PPs), either the pronoun or the preposition is required (e.g., *Francesco* **gli** *ho già telefonato* or **a** *Francesco ho già telefonato* 'Francesco, I already phoned him').

In sum, the key difference between non-dislocated and left-dislocated constructions lies in the discourse status speakers attribute to the dislocated constituent: in (69a) it is assumed to be new to the addressee, whereas in (69b) it is either assumed to be discourse old/presupposed by the speaker, and it is foregrounded to the addressee's consciousness, or it is considered discourse new, though known to the addressee or retrievable from the discourse context. Thus, left-dislocation most commonly signals that a constituent other than the subject is the discourse topic, that is, it promotes to topic status some previously non-topic constituent.

Left-dislocation involving subject constituents is somewhat less straightforward in Italian because the canonical position for subjects is sentence-initial and Italian lacks unstressed subject pronouns which would function as dislocation markers, as, for instance, in French (71b). However, Lambrecht (2001) proposes (71a) as an instance of Italian subject left-dislocation and identifies the verbal person/number inflectional suffix -*o* as a formal marker of dislocation equivalent to the unstressed object pronouns in (70).[11]

(71) a. [*I Romani*]$_i$ *son-o*$_i$ *pazzi.*
      b. [*Les Romains*]$_i$ *ils*$_i$ *sont fous.*
      c. [*The Romans*]$_i$ *they*$_i$ *are crazy.*
          (Adapted from Lambrecht, 2001, p. 1051, ex. (5))

Left-dislocation is to be distinguished from other superficially similar constructions which also involve 'displacement' of a constituent to the left. Two of them are worthy of a quick review. The first is known as **contrastive topicalization**, or, alternatively, **focus movement/pre-posing** (depending on the theoretical framework) and is illustrated in (72b).

(72) a. *I carciofi non li mangio.*
          'Artichokes, I don't eat them.'
      b. *I CARCIOFI non mangio (le rape sì).*
          'ARTICHOKES, I don't eat (turnips I do).'

Contrastive topicalization does not include an unstressed pronoun co-referential with the relevant constituent (*i carciofi*, in our case). It conveys new information (i.e., it is a focus referent) and is typically contrasted with another topic referent (*le rape* in (72b)). Moreover, it is phonetically marked as the only point of prosodic prominence in the sentence, indicated by the small caps.

Another construction resembling left-dislocation is **hanging topic**. Hanging topic differs from left-dislocation in two aspects: (a) if the relevant constituent is a PP, the preposition heading the PP is not present (73b–d), and (b) the 'displayed' constituent can be linked to the sentence by a stressed pronoun, a demonstrative, or a phrase (73a). Furthermore, in terms of intonation contour, hanging topic always involves a pause after the relevant constituent, again orthographically signaled by a comma.

(73) a. *Francesco, lui/quello/quel briccone lo conosco da dieci anni.*
      b. *Francesco, a lui/a quello/a quel briccone ho regalato un libro.*
          'Francesco, to him/to that rascal I gave a book as a present.'
      c. *Baltimora, Francesco lì/in quella città non è mai stato.*
          'Baltimore, Francesco has never been there.'
      d. *Francesco, con lui/con quello/con quel briccone non parlo più.*
          'Francesco, I no longer speak to him.'

Overall, hanging topic carries the same pragmatic function as left-dislocation.

Before moving to right-dislocation, a brief historical note about left-dislocation is in order. Left-dislocation is steadily attested throughout the entire history of the Italian language (e.g., Sabatini, 1985). In fact, we find it in one of the oldest attestations of Italo-Romance varieties, quoted in (74).

(74) *Sao ko [**kelle terre**], per kelle fini que ki contene, trenta anni [**le**] possette parte*
S(an)c(t)i Benedicti (Placito capuano, March 960)
'I know that those lands, within those boundaries which are described therein, the Monastery of Saint benedict owned them for thirty years'
(From Castellani, 1973, p. 59, my translation)

The text in (74) is the first of four very similar texts (the other three written in 963) collectively known as *Placiti campani* (or *Placiti cassinesi*), which were inserted on the margins of notarial records (written in Latin) documenting a lawsuit over a dispute on several lands among three Benedictine monasteries and a local landowner.

Despite being steadily attested since the origins of the Italian language, left-dislocation has endured widespread and vehement censure in (prescriptive) grammars and among language scholars in general and is considered to be a construction restricted to spoken (colloquial) and informal written language. This view has finally been cast off, and it is now agreed that left-dislocation is widespread in basically any variety and register of Italian (D'Achille, 2016, p. 182).

5.2.1.2 Right-dislocation

Right-dislocated constructions differ from unmarked word-order configurations only in (a) the presence of the unstressed pronoun co-referential to the relevant constituent, unless it is a subject (75g), and (b) it may involve a pause before the relevant 'dislocated' constituent, as usual noted in writing by a comma.

(75) a. *Francesco non **li**$_{DO}$ mangia, [**i carciofi**.]$_{NP/DO}$*
'Francesco doesn't eat them, artichokes.'
   b. ***Gli**$_{IO}$ ho regalato un romanzo di Camilleri, [**a Francesco**.]$_{PP/IO}$*
'I gave him a novel by Camilleri as a present, to Francesco.'
   c. *Francesco non **ci**$_{LOC}$ è mai stato, [**a Baltimora**.]$_{PP/LOC}$*
'Francesco has never been there, Baltimore.'
   d. *Non **ci**$_{COM}$ parlo più, [**con Francesco**.]$_{PP/COM}$*
'I no longer speak to him, Francesco.'
   e. *Non **ne**$_{COM}$ voglio parlare, [**di questo argomento**.]$_{PP/COM}$*
'I don't want to talk about it, this subject.'
   f. ***Lo**$_S$ avevo intuito, [**che Francesco non sarebbe venuto**.]$_S$*
'I guessed it/that, that Francesco wouldn't come.'
   g. *Sono pazzi, [**questi Romani**]$_{SUBJ}$*   (Adapted from Lambrecht, 2001, p. 1051)
'They are crazy, these Romans'

Right-dislocation is very widespread in the spoken language, particularly in the context of yes/no questions (*li mangi i carciofi* 'do you eat artichokes?'), and appears to have become the default in semi-fixed expressions as *lo sai che . . . ?* 'do you know that . . . ?'

The primary communicative function carried by right-dislocation is to foreground/highlight the verb phrase while backgrounding the referent of the dislocated constituent, which is the verb's complement. Another discourse function attributed to right-dislocation referred to as 'afterthought' (Berruto, 1987, p. 67) is to recall a current topic referent expressed by the dislocated constituent and identified by the unstressed pronoun, which the speaker may perceive as no longer active in the addressee's mind, a sort of clarification strategy, we could say, aimed at repairing potential ambiguity. In this case, the construction involves a break in the intonation contour before the relevant constituent.

Unlike left-dislocation, right-dislocation remains confined essentially to the spoken language (D'Achille, 2010, p. 227; Zamora Muñoz, 2002, p. 452).

Summarizing, there is common agreement in the literature in considering both left- and right-dislocation as topic marking constructions: they mark a constituent as the topic about which the sentence expresses a relevant comment which provides new information. The choice between the two relates to the relative pragmatic salience of the referent of the dislocated constituent in the discourse setting. Specifically, left-dislocation establishes a new topic relation between a referent and the predication (remember that establishing a new topic is not the same as introducing new information), while right-dislocation maintains an already-established topic relation.

5.2.2 Cleft and pseudo-cleft sentences

Cleft sentences comprise two syntactically separate components. The first consists of the verb *essere* 'be,' followed by a pronominal, phrasal, or clausal constituent carrying any kind of syntactic function, with which *essere* agrees in person and number if it is an NP. This constituent expresses new information (i.e., it has focus status); hence, it is prosodically marked (i.e., it is the peak on the intonation contour). The second component is a clause that conveys given or presupposed information (i.e., it is topical) and can be either explicit or implicit, though implicit clauses are only possible if the focalized constituent is a subject and typically human/animate. A generic schema of cleft sentences is sketched in (76), and some examples illustrating the range of specific configurations are given in (77), for explicit clauses, and (78), for implicit clauses. (Small caps symbolize marked intonation.)

(76) *essere* [phrase/clause]$_{FOCUS}$ + *che* [explicit clause]$_{TOPIC}$
      a [implicit clause]$_{TOPIC}$

(77) a. È [GAIA/LEI]$_{SUBJ}$ *che mangia i carciofi.*
          'It's Gaia/her that eats artichokes.'
     b. *Sono* [FRANCESCO E GAIA/LORO]$_{DO}$ *che ho incontrato in centro.*
          'It's Francesco and Gaia I met downtown.'
     c. È [*a* FRANCESCO E GAIA/LORO]$_{DO}$ *che ho mandato una cartolina.*
          'It's Francesco and Gaia I sent a postcard to.'
     d. È [STIRARE]$_{S/DO}$ *che odio.*
          'It's ironing that I hate.'

(78) a. *È stato* FRANCESCO/LUI *a mangiare tutti i cioccolatini.*
          'It was Francesco/him who ate all the chocolates.'
      b. *Sono stata* IO *a telefonarti.*
          'It was me to call you.'

Overall, cleft sentences instantiate a type of focalization/emphasizing strategy. Their primary communicative function is to mark the constituent following *essere* as focal, at the same time foregrounding/underscoring it (hence making it more easily identifiable) to the addressee. This is achieved by setting apart the constituent from old/presupposed information structurally and/or intonationally. Structurally, by linking it to *essere* and, in the case of complements, removing it from the position it would occupy in pragmatically unmarked constructions (e.g., *è **la torta** che ha bruciato* 'it's the cake s/he burned' vs. *ha bruciato **la torta***), and intonationally by stressing it. Furthermore, cleft sentences commonly bear an additional contrastive function in that the referent of the clefted constituent is contrasted (directly or indirectly) with another referent within a given set (*sei* TU *che non capisci (non io)* 'it's you who doesn't understand (not me)').

Cleft sentences are yet another construction which has been exposed to (prescriptive) grammar's severe censorship and condemned as a Gallicism but now appears to be fully accepted, both in the spoken and written language (Berruto, 1987, p. 68; D'Achille, 2010, p. 227).

Pseudo-cleft sentences exemplify yet another focalization strategy which divides a construction into two syntactically separate parts, as outlined in (79).

(79) [Introductory element + relative pronoun] + VP + *essere* + [phrase/clause]$_{FOCUS}$

The introductory element takes a variety of forms; most typically, it is the demonstrative pronoun *quello* 'that' (80a) or an NP with a generic noun (80b–c) that refers to the focal constituent. The syntactic function of the focal constituent is coded by the relative pronoun: *che* for subject and direct object (80a, b) and *cui* preceded by the appropriate preposition for all other complements (80c). The introductory element and relative pronoun can 'merge' in the form *chi* 'whoever' when the focal constituent is a subject NP (80d) with a human referent.

(80) a. ***Quello che** mi mancava di più durante la pandemia **era** [andare in palestra.]*$_{SUBJ}$
          'What I missed most during the pandemic was going to the gym.'
      b. ***La cosa che** odio **è** [stirar.e]*$_{DO}$
          'What I hate is ironing.'
      c. ***Il tizio con cui** ho parlato **era** [un impiegato che non sapeva niente.]*$_{COM}$
          'The guy I spoke with was an employee who didn't know anything.'
      d. ***Chi** cercavo **sei** [tu]*$_{DO}$.
          'The person I was looking for is you.'

Pseudo-cleft sentences carry the same communicative function as cleft sentences, but the focal constituent occupies the same position as in a pragmatically unmarked (declarative) sentence (e.g., *odio* [stirare]$_{DO}$, *ho parlato* [con un impiegato che non sapeva niente]$_{COM}$); its focal status is foregrounded by the introductory element and the relative pronoun and the verb *essere*.

Pseudo-cleft sentences remain somewhat restricted in the spoken language, appearing mostly in colloquial and informal registers.

5.3 Exercises

1. Give concise but complete answers to the following questions, illustrating with examples. Try to find original examples rather than relying on the textbook.

   a. What are the two main meanings of the term *grammar*?
   b. What is a *constituent*? What are some tests typically used to identify constituents?
   c. Briefly define the notions of *argument*, *adjunct*, and *oblique* (*argument*).
   d. What is the difference between *syntactic functions* and *semantic roles*? Explain why they are both important in syntactic analysis.
   e. The following sentence has two possible interpretations: *Francesco ha parlato all'uomo con il megafono*. After explaining what these are (by means of paraphrases), draw the corresponding syntactic structures using either a tree diagram or bracketing.
   f. Discuss the notions of valency and transitivity and how they relate to each other.
   g. What are unergative and unaccusative verbs? What are the main structural/semantic properties that differentiate them?
   h. What is a *clause*? How many core types of clauses are traditionally distinguished?
   i. What is meant by *coordination* and *subordination*?
   j. What is the domain of *information structure*? What are the main pragmatically marked constructions in Italian? What functions do they serve?

2. For each of the following sentences, identify the syntactic function and semantic role of the underlined constituents. Justify your answers.

   a. *Francesco vive a Austin*.
   b. *Il film è durato due ore*.
   c. *Non presto la macchina a nessuno*.
   d. *Ha aperto una scatola di fagioli con l'apriscatole*.
   e. *Il vento ha spalancato la finestra*.
   f. *A Gaia piace fare lunghe passeggiate sulla spiaggia*.
   g. *Il gelo ha ucciso i gerani*.
   h. *Adria ha tradotto un romanzo dall'italiano all'inglese*.
   i. *Aspirava a diventare il presidente della repubblica*.
   j. *Francesco ha paura degli scarafaggi*.
   k. *Ha sacrificato la carriera per la famiglia*.
   l. *Il fiume Po nasce a Pian del Re, sul Monviso*.
   m. *Il sicario ha assassinato il primo ministro*.

3. Determine whether the following statements are true or false, then explain why.

   a. The head of the phrase *sul davanzale della finestra* is *in*.
   b. *Spostare* is a bivalent verb.
   c. In the sentence *sono andata al cinema con Francesco*, the phrase *con Francesco* is an argument.
   d. In the sentence *mi fa male la testa*, the NP *la testa* bears the semantic role agent.
   e. *Nascere* is an unaccusative verb.
   f. In the sentence *spero che Francesco arrivi in orario*, the clause *che Francesco arrivi in orario* is implicit.
   g. *Quello che voglio è un gelato* is an example of right-dislocation.

h. In the sentence *è importante* [*bere almeno due litri d'acqua al giorno*], the bracketed constituent is the direct object.

4. Complete the following statement with the right element. Justify your answer.

a. The verb *grandinare* is:

   i.   avalent.
   ii. monovalent.
   iii. bivalent.
   iv. trivalent.

b. The verb *sognare* is:

   i.   transitive.
   ii. unergative.
   iii. unaccusative.
   iv. pronominal.

c. The syntactic function of the constituent *a Francesco* in the sentence *a Francesco fa male la testa* is:

   i.   subject.
   ii. direct object.
   iii. indirect object.
   iv. oblique argument.

d. The semantic role of the constituent *l'uragano* in the sentence *l'uragano ha distrutto il villaggio* is:

   i.   agent.
   ii. source.
   iii. instrument.
   iv. stimulus.

e. '*E gli errori li aveva pagati sulla sua pelle*' (Manzini, 2017, p. 107) is an example of:

   i.   hanging topic.
   ii. cleft sentence.
   iii. right–dislocation.
   iv. left–dislocation.

f. In the sentence *chiudi la finestra* **che** *fa freddo, che* is:

   i.   relative pronoun with temporal function.
   ii. relative pronoun with locative function.
   iii. relative pronoun with final function.
   iv. che polivalente.

Notes

1 Although in more recent generative (Chomskyan) approaches, NP has been replaced by DP (determiner phrase), we will stick to the older tradition here.

2 Null-subject languages are also known as 'pro-drop' languages, following the theoretical Chomskyan approach called 'principle and parameters' (or also 'government and binding theory'), which assumes the presence of a phonetically null element present whenever a finite verb has no overtly expressed subject. More specifically, a distinction is made between so-called 'little pro' (*pro*), which is posited for finite verb forms (*canta sempre sotto la doccia* 's/he always sings in the shower'), and 'big pro' (PRO), which is postulated for non-finite verb forms (*Francesco ama cantare* 'Francesco loves [PRO singing/to sing]).

3 Direct object complements agree with past participles only when they are instantiated by direct object atonic pronouns, for example, *Francesco ha mangiato*.M.SG [*i carciofi*]M.PL 'Francesco ate the artichokes' → *li*.M.PL *ha mangiati*.M.PL 'he ate them'.

4 The label 'indirect object complement' may be used also to refer to (a) a complement that is not adjacent to the verb; (b) a complement that corresponds to the Latin dative case; and (c) a complement whose thematic role is not that of patient.

5 The term *valency* comes from chemistry; it was applied to linguistics by the French linguist Lucien Tesnière (1893–1954), who used the term 'actant' for event participants.

6 I am indebted to Knud Lambrecht for this sentence.

7 In present-day Italian, *che cosa* is often rendered by either *che* or *cosa* only: *che/cosa vuoi?* 'what do you want?'

8 It should be noted that in some cases, both the implicit and explicit constructions may be available: *Penso di andare/che andrò a casa* 'I think I'll go home.' The two alternatives differ (slightly) in terms of the overall conceptualization of the event. This is a complex issue and cannot be addressed properly here in consideration of space.

9 *Italiano popolare* remains, at least to some extent, a controversial notion, and different definitions are found in the literature. De Mauro (1970, p. 49) defines it as the variety used by uneducated speakers when trying to communicate in standard Italian. According to Cortelazzo (1972, p. 11), it is the variety of standard Italian acquired by native speakers of a dialect.

10 The expression *le tre corone (fiorentine)* 'the three (Florentine) crowns' refers to the fourteenth-century Florentine authors Dante Alighieri (c. 1265–1321), Francesco Petrarca (1304–1374), and Giovanni Boccaccio (1313–1375). They authored three masterpieces (respectively, *Divine Comedy*, *Canzoniere*, and *Decameron*), which led fourteenth-century literary Florentine to become the foundation of modern standard Italian.

11 The subscript 'i' signals co-referentiality.

Bibliography

Benincà, P. (2001). L'ordine degli elementi della frase e le costruzioni marcate. In L. Renzi & G. Salvi (Eds.), *Grande grammatica italiana di consultazione* (Vol. 1, pp. 129–194). Il Mulino.

Berruto, G. (1987). *Sociolinguistica dell'italiano contemporaneo*. Carocci.

Burzio, L. (1986). *Italian syntax: A government-binding approach*. Reidel.

Castelfranchi, C., & Parisi, D. (1976). Towards one si. *Italian Linguistics*, 2, 83–121.

Castellani, A. (1973). *I più antichi testi italiani*. Pàtron.

Chomsky, N. (1957). *Syntactic structures*. Mouton & Co.

Cortelazzo, M. (1972). *Avviamento critico allo studio della dialettologia italiana. Vol. 3: Lineamenti di italiano popolare*. Pacini.

Cruschina, S. (2010). Syntactic extraposition and clitic resumption in Italian. *Lingua*, *120*(1), 50–73.

D'Achille, P. (1990). *Sintassi del parlato e tradizione scritta della lingua italiana: Analisi di testi dalle origini al secolo XVIII*. Bonacci.

D'Achille, P. (2010). *L'italiano contemporaneo* (3rd ed.). Il Mulino.

D'Achille, P. (2016). Architettura dell'italiano di oggi e linee di tendenza. In S. Lubello (Ed.), *Manuale di linguistica italiana* (pp. 165–189). Walter de Gruyter.

De Mauro, T. (1970). Per lo studio dell'italiano popolare unitario. In A. Rossi (Ed.), *Lettere da una taranta* (pp. 43–75). De Donato.

Dik, S. C. (1978). *Functional grammar*. North-Holland.

Ferrari, A. (2012). *Tipi di frase e ordine delle parole*. Carocci.

Fillmore, C. J. (1985). Frames and the semantics of understanding. *Quaderni di Semantica*, *6*(2), 222–254.

Fillmore, C. J. (1986). Pragmatically controlled zero anaphora. *Berkeley Linguistics Society*, *12*, 95–107.

Fillmore, C. J., & Kay, P. (1995). *Construction grammar coursebook*. University of California.

Fiorentino, G. (1999). *Relativa debole: Sintassi, uso, storia in italiano*. Franco Angeli.

Fiorentino, G. (2007). Relative "pragmatiche" in italiano. In F. Venier (Ed.), *Relative e pseudorelative tra grammatica e testo* (pp. 53–71). Edizioni dell'Orso.

Givón, T. (1984). *Syntax: A functional-typological introduction* (Vol. 1). John Benjamins.

Graffi, G. (2021). *Introduzione alla sintassi*. Carocci.

Gundel, J. K. (1988). Universals of topic-comment structure. In M. Hammond, E. Moravcsik, & J. Wirth (Eds.), *Studies in linguistic typology* (pp. 209–239). John Benjamins.

Hopper, P. J., & Thompson, S. A. (1980). Transitivity in grammar and discourse. *Language*, *56*(2), 251–299.

Kemmer, S. (1993). *Middle voice*. John Benjamins.

La Fauci, N. (2009). *Compendio di sintassi italiana*. Il Mulino.

Lambrecht, K. (1994). *Information structure and sentence form: Topic, focus and the mental representations of discourse referents*. Cambridge University Press.

Lambrecht, K. (2001). Dislocation. In M. Haspelmath, E. König, W. Oesterreich, & W. Raible (Eds.), *2. Halbband language typology and language universals 2. Teilband* (pp. 1050–1078). Mouton de Gruyter.

Langacker, R. W. (1987). *Foundations of cognitive grammar* (Vol. 1). Stanford University Press.

Langacker, R. W. (1990). *Concept, image, and symbol: The cognitive basis of grammar*. Mouton de Gruyter.

Langacker, R. W. (1991). *Foundations of cognitive grammar* (Vol. 2). Stanford University Press.

Levin, B., & Rappaport Hovav, M. (1995). *Unaccusativity: At the syntax-lexical semantics interface*. MIT Press.

Manzini, A. (2017). *Pulvis et umbra*. Sellerio.

Marazzini, C. (2006). *La storia della lingua italiana attraverso i testi*. Il Mulino.

Perlmutter, D. M. (1978). Impersonal passives and the unaccusative hypothesis. *Berkeley Linguistics Society*, *4*, 157–189.

Sabatini, F. (1985). L'"italiano dell'uso medio": Una realtà tra le varietà linguistiche italiane. In G. Holtus & E. Radtke (Eds.), *Gesprochenes Italienisch in gesichte und gegenwart* (pp. 154158). Narr.

Serianni, L. (1988). *Grammatica italiana: Italiano comune e lingua letteraria. Suoni forme costrutti*. UTET.

Squartini, M. (2010). Mood in Italian. In B. Rothstein & R. Thieroff (Eds.), *Mood in the languages of Europe* (pp. 237–250). John Benjamins.

Van Valin, R. D. Jr. (1987). The unaccusative hypothesis vs. lexical semantics: Syntactic vs. semantic approaches to verb classification. *North East Linguistics Society*, *17*, 641–661.

Van Valin, R. D. Jr. (1990). Semantic parameters of split intransitivity. *Language*, *66*, 221–260.

Vecchioni, R. (2007). *Neanche se piangi in cinese* [Song].

Voghera, M. (1992). *Sintassi e intonazione nell'italiano parlato*. Il Mulino.

Waltereit, R. (2000). What it means to deceive yourself: The semantic relation of French reflexive verbs and corresponding transitive verbs. In Z. Frajzyngier & T. S. Curl (Eds.), *Reflexive forms and functions* (pp. 257–278). John Benjamins.

Wandruszka, U. (2001). Frasi subordinate al congiuntivo. In L. Renzi & G. Salvi (Eds.), *Grande grammatica italiana di consultazione* (Vol. 2, pp. 415–481). Il Mulino.

Zamora Muñoz, P. (2002). Dislocazioni a destra e sinistra nell'italiano e nello spagnolo colloquiale parlato: Frequenza d'uso, funzioni e parametri linguistici. *Studi Italiani di Linguistica Teorica e Applicata*, *31*(3), 447–470.

6

FROM LATIN TO ITALIAN

Notes on historical grammar

This chapter sketches the earliest phases of the development of Italian, more precisely, Italo-Romance vernaculars, from Latin; in other words, it reviews the key phenomena that shaped the emerging grammar of early Italo-Romance. The focus will be on Old Florentine because it constitutes the foundations of the Italian language whose process of standardization (also known as the *questione della lingua* 'the language question') began in the sixteenth century. Hence, Old Florentine is used here as synonymous with Old Italian. After a brief discussion of the Latin origins of Italian (i.e., which variety of Latin should be considered as its 'source'), we address the most significant changes that occurred at the level of sounds (phonology), word (morphology), and phrase structure (morpho)syntax). The chapter ends with a review of a selection of the most representative (and best-known) earliest Italo-Romance attestations (dating from the end of the eighth to the beginning of the thirteenth century).

6.1 Latin roots

The adjective *Romance* designates all the languages and dialects/varieties that originated from Latin. Its source is Old French *romanz*, which comes from the Latin expression *ROMANĬCE (LOQUI) '(to speak) in the Roman way,' that is, to speak Latin as the people in Rome did. But what does it mean that Romance languages derive from Latin? This is a twofold question. First, we should clarify what 'derivation' means in relation to language; since natural languages do not emerge abruptly, the terms 'continuation' or 'evolution' are more appropriate. Second, we must determine which Latin was the source of Romance languages, because, as any natural language, Latin was characterized by wide variation along five (interrelated) dimensions: space, social class, register, communication channel (spoken vs. written), and of course, time. Let's briefly review these variables, starting with space.

At its greatest extent during the reign of the emperor Trajan (98–117 CE), the Roman Empire (hence, Latin) covered a sizable territory (traditionally referred to as Romània) stretching over Europe, Africa, and Asia. Although Latin was never imposed in the dominated territories, it was adopted by the conquered peoples due to its high prestige. Naturally, Latin was not uniform across these territories, as any language with such a wide

DOI: 10.4324/9781003057536-6

geographical distribution (think about English). Geographical variation is evinced by the fate of words with the same meaning in different Romance languages, such as the adjectives meaning 'beautiful': FORMOSUS (> Spanish *formoso*) vs. BELLUS (> Italian *bello*); or the verbs meaning 'to eat': COMEDERE (> Spanish *comer*) vs. MANDUCARE (> Italian *mangiare*). Concerning social class, register, and channel, variation is related to (degree of) literacy. Illiteracy or lower degree of education entails restricted linguistic proficiency, hence less variation; although any speaker, independent of their degree of education, employs a range of registers according to the communicative context, a higher degree of literacy enables wider differentiation both at the spoken and written level. In most of Europe, Latin remained the language of academic and administrative circles throughout the Middle Ages; it also was the liturgical language of the Roman Catholic Church until the Second Vatican Council (1962–1965), and it still is the official language of the Holy See. Furthermore, Latin continues to be taught and studied extensively in Europe and beyond. In a sense, then, Latin is still 'alive.' However, Latin is no longer a language spontaneously acquired during childhood and serving as primary, everyday channel of communication in any community, that is, it is no longer anyone's native language. Therefore, as a natural language, it is 'dead.'

The variety of Latin from which the Romance languages originated is traditionally referred to as Vulgar Latin, that is, the Latin used by the people (Lat. VULGUS), characterized by 'innovations and trends that turned up in the usage, *particularly but not exclusively spoken*, of the Latin speaking population who were little or not at all influenced by school education and by literary models' (Herman, 2000, p. 7, emphasis added). Although it was primarily a spoken variety, Vulgar Latin does not equate to spoken Latin *tout court*; rather, it was a specific variety of spoken Latin: 'a moving and unstable kind of Latin' (Herman, 2000, p. 8), a composite entity subject to variation along all the dimensions discussed previously. While an amazing, unique wealth of attestations of written Latin is available to us, we lack actual attestation of any variety of spoken Latin, including Vulgar Latin. Yet spoken/Vulgar Latin can be 'reconstructed' from different written sources, both direct, such as inscriptions, glossaries, and notes on grammar 'errors' (e.g., the *Appendix Probi*);[1] private documents (letters, commercial records); technical treatises; and manuals on various disciplines (medicine and veterinary science; architecture, for example, Vitruvius (first century BCE); agriculture; culinary arts), and indirect, such as literary works, including reproductions of spoken language (e.g., Plautus's (254–184BCE) and Terence's (ca. 185–159BCE) comedies, Petronius's (27–66CE) *Satyricon*), and Christian literature.

When did the Romance languages (or vernaculars) begin to emerge? There is general consensus that Romance vernaculars as separate linguistic systems detached from Vulgar Latin between the sixth and seventh century CE (Barbato, 2016). The Council of Tours (813) proclaimed that sermons be delivered in *rusticam romanam linguam aut theothiscam* 'rustic Roman (Romance) language or German' so to be accessible to anyone; this is the first clear, 'official' indication of a general awareness of Romance vernaculars being distinct from Latin, and some considered it their 'birth certificate.' Thus, by the early Middle Ages, Romance vernaculars were spoken by the people, though it would take some time before they started to replace Latin in formal writing and in the religious domain. Until the ninth century, original written attestations of Romance vernaculars are very scarce; their earliest attestation (specifically, of Gallo-Romance) is identified in the *Oaths of Strasbourg* (842).

6.2 Sound changes

This section outlines the major sound changes that occurred during the development of Italian from Latin – specifically, the changes pertaining to the Old Florentine vernacular, which, as noted previously, served as the foundation for standard Italian. Also, note that these changes are reflected only in the **hereditary** lexicon, that is, words that Italian inherited directly from Latin via uninterrupted transmission. **Latinisms** (i.e., Latin words which entered Italian indirectly through borrowing at different times in history starting from the thirteenth century), on the other hand, remained unaffected by the changes under examination since they were no longer operative. For example, the Latin noun CAUSA(M) 'cause, reason' survives in Italian in two forms: the directly inherited *cosa* 'thing,' which attests the change AU > *o*, and the Latinism *causa* 'cause, reason,' which doesn't. Similarly, the noun *neve* 'snow' < NĬVE(M) reflects the change Ĭ > *e* unattested in the adjective *niveo* 'snow-white, snowy' < NĬVEU(M).[2]

6.2.1 Vowels

The vowel system of Classical Latin, the literary standard language variety in use from about 75 BCE to the third century, included ten sounds (or phones) divided into two sets of long and short vowels, as listed in (1), with vowel length represented graphically by the diacritic marks macron (ˉ) for long vowels and breve (ˇ) for short ones. Thus, the distinguishing feature of the vocalic system of Classical Latin was **quantity,** which applied to both stressed and unstressed vowels.

(1) Ī Ĭ Ē Ĕ Ă Ā Ŏ Ō Ŭ Ū

Vowel length was distinctive both at the lexical and at the grammatical level, distinguishing different forms of the same word bearing different grammatical functions, as illustrated in Table 6.1.

At the spoken level, vowel length was accompanied by a phonetic difference (vowel **quality**) in the case of the high and mid vowels, since short vowels tend to be realized as more open than their long counterparts. This quality distinction, on the other hand, did not apply to the low vowels Ā and Ă, which were both pronounced [a].[3]

(2) a. Ī   Ĭ   Ē   Ĕ   Ā Ă   Ŏ   Ō   Ŭ   Ū
     b. [i] [ɪ] [e] [ɛ] [a] [ɔ] [o] [ʊ] [u]

TABLE 6.1 Contrastive vowel length in Latin

Lexical	
MĂLUM 'evil'	MĀLUM 'apple'
ĔSSE 'be'	ĒSSE 'eat'
LĬBERUM 'book'	LĪBERUM 'free'
PŎPULUS 'people'	PŌPULUS 'poplar'
Grammatical	
ROSĂ 'rose-NOM.SG'	ROSĀ 'rose-ACC.SG'
VĔNIT 'come-3SG.PRS.IND'	VĒNIT 'come-3SG.PRF.IND'
FŬGIT 'flee-3SG.PRS.IND'	FŪGIT 'flee-3SG.PRF.IND'

The quality distinction gradually strengthened in time, ultimately leading to the shift from a quantity-based to a quality-based vowel system in Late Latin, as in (2b). This shift represents a crucial transitional stage in the development of the Romance languages, all of which display vocalic systems characterized by a quality distinction, that is, systems based on the contrast between open and close vowels.[4]

A major pan-Romance change linked to the demise of the vocalic quality distinction is the merger of the front mid vowels Ē and Ĭ and the back mid vowels Ō and Ŭ. The vowel merger is sketched for Italian in (3) and illustrated by the examples in Table 6.2.

(3) The Proto-Romance vowel merger

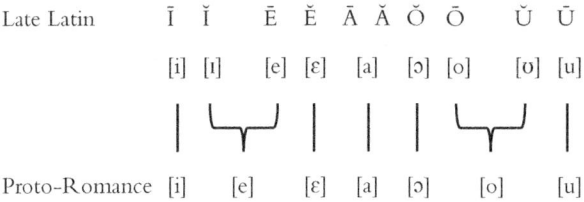

Late Latin   Ī Ĭ   Ē   Ĕ   Ā Ă   Ŏ   Ō   Ŭ Ū

                 [i] [ɪ] [e] [ɛ] [a] [ɔ] [o] [ʊ] [u]

Proto-Romance [i]   [e]   [ɛ] [a] [ɔ]   [o]   [u]

Thus, the vocalic merger gave rise to a seven-vowel system. However, the contrast between close-mid and open-mid vowels applies only to stressed vowels, while unstressed mid vowels are always realized as close – that is, the system of Italian stressed vowels comprises seven phones, but that of unstressed vowels includes only five.

The vocalic system of Classical Latin also included three diphthongs: AE, OE, and AU. Both OE and AE merged with Ē already in Latin, though the former was realized as [e] and the latter as [ɛ]. AU, on the other hand, resisted longer; after changing first to ō (but only in a few words, for example, CAUDAM > CŌDA 'tail,' FAUCEM > FŌCE 'mouth'), it became [ɔ] in eighth century (*còsa* 'thing' CAUSAM < 'cause,' *òro* 'gold' < AURUM). Two new diphthongs emerged in Old Italian through **diphthongization** of Latin stressed Ĕ [ɛ] and Ŏ [ɔ] in open syllables (i.e., syllables ending in a vowel); some examples are given in Table 6.3.[5]

Diphthongization was a very systematic change, yet exceptions can be found; some examples of common words which escaped it are *bene* 'well; good (noun)' < BĔNE, *pecora* 'sheep' < PĔCORA (NOM/ACC.N.PL), *nove* 'nine' < NŎVEM, *opera* 'work' < ŎPERA (NOM/ACC.N.PL).

TABLE 6.2 Vowel merger in Italian

Front vowels			
Latin Ē	Italian *e* [e]	Latin Ĭ	Italian *e* [e]
TĒLAM 'cloth'	*téla* [tela]	PĬRAM 'pear'	*péra* [pera]
VĒRUM 'truth'	*véro* [vero]	VĬTRUM 'glass'	*vétro* [vetro]
Back vowels			
Latin Ō	Italian *o* [o]	Latin Ŭ	Italian *o* [o]
VŌCEM 'voice'	*vóce* [votʃe]	NŬCEM 'nut'	*nóce* [notʃe]
SŌLEM 'sun'	*sóle* [sole]	CRŬCEM 'cross'	*cróce* [krotʃe]

TABLE 6.3 Diphthongization of ĕ and ŏ

Open syllable

Latin ĕ	Italian [jɛ]	Latin ŏ	Italian [wɔ]
HĔRI 'yesterday'	*ieri* [jɛri]	BŎNUM 'good'	*buono* [bwɔno]
FĔRUM 'wild'	*fiero* [fjɛro]	*CŎRE 'heart'	*cuore* [kwɔre]
PĔTRAM 'stone'	*pietra* [pjɛtra]	FŎCUM 'fire'	*fuoco* [fwɔko]
Closed syllable			
Latin ĕ	Italian [ɛ]	Latin ŏ	Italian [ɔ]
SĔPTEM 'seven'	*sette* [sɛtːe]	CŎRNUM 'horn'	*corno* [kɔrno]
VĔNTUM 'wind'	*vento* [vɛnto]	MŎRTEM 'death'	*morte* [mɔrte]

The diphthongs [jɛ] and [wɔ] eventually reversed to single vowels (i.e., they monophthongized) after consonant clusters of the type <Cr> (*brieve* > *breve* 'short,' *pruova* > *prova* 'test, trial'). Monophthongization first affected [jɛ] around the mid-fifteenth century, then [wɔ] in the sixteenth century, and was possibly due to the influence of western Tuscan varieties in which diphthongization never developed.

Another important change that affected stressed vowels is the raising of the close-mid vowels [e] and [o] (the outcomes of the vowel merger) to [i] and [u], respectively. This change – traditionally referred to as **anaphonesis** (< Greek *anà* 'on, above' e *phónēsis* 'sound'), a term introduced by Castellani (1952, 1980) – occurred in two specific contexts, illustrated in (4).

(4) a. [e] > [i] before the consonant clusters <nc> [ŋk] and <ng> [ŋg]: *tinca* 'tench' < TĬNCAM, *vinco* 'I win' < VĬNCO; *lingua* 'tongue' < LĬNGUAM, *cingere* < CĬNGERE 'to surround.'
b. [o] > [u] before <ng> [ŋg]: *lungo* 'long' < LŎNGUM, *fungo* 'mushroom' < FŬNGUM, *unghia* 'fingernail' < ŬNG(U)LAM.
c. [e] > [i] before the palatal consonants [ʎ] (< Latin [lj]) and [ɲ] (< Lat. [nj]): *famiglia* 'family' < FAMĬLIAM, > *gramigna* 'couch grass' < GRAMĬNEA 'grassy-SG.F.' (Anaphonesis did not occur before [ɲ] < Lat. [gn]: *légno* 'wood' < LĬGNUM).

Unstressed vowels are weaker than their stressed counterparts; therefore, they are more easily susceptible to undergo assimilation or dissimilation, or they may even be lost. The main changes that affected unstressed vowels are illustrated in (5) and (6).

(5) Raising of [e] and [o] before stressed syllables.
a. [e] > [i]: *finèstra* 'window' < FĔNESTRAM, *minóre* 'smaller' < MĬNOREM, *sicùro* 'safe; sure' < SĒCURUM.
b. [o] > [u]: *pulìre* 'to clean' < PŎLIRE, *uncìno* 'hook' < ŬNCINUM, *uccèllo* 'bird' < AUCELLUS. The change was less systematic for the back vowels, and several doublets are found (*olìvo/ulìvo* 'olive tree' < ŎLIVAM 'olive (fruit/tree),' *mulìno/molìno* 'mill' < MŎLINUM).

(6) Raising of [a] before [r] before or after stressed syllables: *gàmbero* 'shrimp' < CAMMĂRUM, *margherìta* 'daisy' < MARGĂRĪTAM 'pearl.'

Let's close this section with some brief notes on word stress. In Classical Latin, the position of word stress was determined by syllable structure; specifically, it relied on the distinction between heavy syllables (i.e., open syllables with a long vowel or a diphthong as their nucleus, or closed syllables) and light syllables (i.e., open syllables with a short vowel as its nucleus). Words comprising three or more syllables were stressed on the penultimate syllable if it was heavy; if the penultimate syllable was light, stress fell on the antepenultimate syllable, irrespective of its weight. Words consisting of two syllables were always stressed on the penultimate syllable. In Italian, on the other hand, the position of word stress is no longer governed by syllable structure and stress can fall on any syllable, as shown in (7). However, the most common pattern is (7b), and the pattern in (7d) is restricted to verb forms, precisely, some third-person plural forms and imperative forms with enclitic direct and indirect object pronouns.[6]

(7) a. Last – *metà* 'age,' *virtù* 'virtue,' *calamità* 'calamity.'
     b. Penultimate – *lùna* 'moon,' *ancóra* 'still; yet,' *calamìta* 'magnet.'
     c. Antepenultimate – *àncora* 'anchor,' *mùsica* 'music,' *tìtolo* 'title.'
     d. Fourth to last – *dùbitano* 'they doubt,' *cómpramelo* 'buy it for me.'

Another important change related to stress, which pertains to prosody, is that in Classical Latin, stressed syllables were pronounced with higher pitch, whereas in Italian, they are pronounced with greater articulatory strength (i.e., greater loudness). In other words, Classical Latin was a pitch-accent language and Italian is a stress-accented language. The fact that all Romance languages are stress-accent suggests that in Late Latin, pitch started to give way to loudness (Oniga, 2014, p. 28).

6.2.2 Consonants

The consonant system of Classical Latin comprised 15 phones, as illustrated in Table 6.4.

The voiceless velar stop [k] was spelled <c> (COLLUM 'neck'), and the labiovelar stops [kʷ] and [gʷ] were spelled <QU> (QUADRUM 'square') and <GU> (LINGUAM 'tongue'), respectively.

A major change that took place in the transition from Latin to Old Italian is loss of word-final consonants.[7] Although only a subset of the Latin consonants occurred regularly in word-final position, word-final consonants were highly frequent in Latin because they carried important morphological/morphosyntactic information (i.e., case, gender, and number for nouns, pronouns, and adjectives, and person, number, tense/aspect for verbs). The only word-final consonants which survived in Italian are [n], [l], [r], but they occur only in a handful of words (i.e., the negative adverb *non* 'not'; the prepositions *con* 'with,' *in* 'in,' *per* 'for'; and the articles *il* 'definite.M.SG' and *un* 'indefinite. M.SG').[8] On the other hand, in word-initial and intervocalic position, all Latin consonants except the glottal fricative [h] were retained,

TABLE 6.4 Classical Latin consonants

	Bilabial	Labiodental	Dental	Velar	Labiovelar	Glottal
Stop	p b		t d	k g	kʷ gʷ	
Nasal	m		n			
Fricative		f	s			h
Lateral		l				
Trill		r				

either in their original form or they underwent changes which resulted in the development of new phones.

A crucial change that systematically affected the consonant system of Latin in its transition to Italo-Romance (and Romance varieties in general), dated as early as the fifth century, is **palatalization**, an assimilation process whereby sounds become palatal due to adjacent palatal sounds, which led to the emergence of a set of consonants unknown to Latin.

As seen in Table 6.5, the main conditioning environment of palatalization was a following front vowel. Among the earliest targets were the velar stops [k] and [g], which changed respectively into the palatal affricates [tʃ] <c> and [dʒ] <g>, and the cluster [sk] <sc>, which changed into the palatal fricative [ʃ] <sc>.[9]

The sound inventory of Latin also included the semi-vowel <ĭ> [j], which only occurred before vowels.[10] <ĭ> systematically changed to [dʒ], even before [a] and back vowels, in which case it is spelled <gi> (ĬACERE 'to lounge' *giacere* >, 'to lie' > ĬOCUM 'joke' > *gioco* 'game,' ĬUDICEM 'judge' > *giudice*), lengthening in intervocalic position (MAĬUS (MENSIS) 'May' > *maggio*, PEĬOREM 'worse; worst' > *peggiore*).

In addition to undergoing palatalization itself, [j] triggered the palatalization of some preceding consonants, which led to the emergence of four more sounds unknown to Latin: the voiceless alveolar affricate [tz] and its voiced counterpart [dz] (both spelled <z>), and the palatal nasal [ɲ] <gn> and lateral [ʎ] <gli>.[11] These sounds are always long in intervocalic position. Some examples are given in Table 6.6.

One more change triggered by word-internal [j] was the lengthening of preceding bilabial stop (SEPĬAM 'cuttlefish' > *seppia*, RABĬAM 'force' > *rabbia*).

Another new sound that emerged in Italian is the voiced labiodental [v], which had two sources. It developed through spirantization (i.e., the change of an oral stop into a fricative)

TABLE 6.5 Palatalization of [k], [g], and [sk]

	[i]	[e]	[ɛ]
[k] > [tʃ]	CIBUM 'food' > *cibo*, VICINUM 'neighbor' > *vicino*	CERAM 'wax' > *cera*, SOCECRAM 'mother-in-lae' > *suocera*	CERVUM 'deer' > *cervo*, RECENTEM 'recent' > *recente*
[g] > [dʒ]	GENESTAM 'broom plant' > *ginestra*, MAGICUM 'magic' > *magico*	GENITOREM 'father; creator' > *genitore* 'parent,' ABIGEATUM 'rustling' > *abigeato*	GENERUM 'son-in law' > *genitore*, ARGENTU 'silver' > *argento*
[sk] > [ʃ]	SCINTILLAM 'spark' > *scintilla*, FASCINAM 'faggot' > *fascina*	PISCEM 'fish' > *pesce*,	SCAENAM 'scene' > *scena*

TABLE 6.6 Palatalization of [j]+C clusters

Latin	Italian	Examples
<TĬ>	[ts:]	PRETĬUM 'price' > *prezzo*, [ts], FORTĬAM 'force' > *forza*
<DĬ>	[dz:]	RADĬUM 'beam' > *razzo* 'rocket,' [dz], PRANDĬUM 'price' > *pranzo*
<SĬ>	[ʃ] > [tʃ] <ci>	BASĬUM 'kiss' > *bacio*
<NĬ>	[ɲ:]	CICONĬA 'stork' > *cicogna*
<LĬ>	[ʎ:]	ALĬU 'garlic' > *aglio*

TABLE 6.7 Regressive assimilation of Latin consonant clusters

Latin	Italian	Examples
–CT–	[t:]	LACTEM 'milk' > *latte*, NOCTEM 'night' > *notte*
–MN–	[n:]	SOMNUM 'sleep' > *sonno*, DOM(I)NAM 'lady' > *donna* 'woman'
–PT–	[t:]	SEPTEM 'seven' > *sette*, CAPTIVUM 'prisoner' > *cattivo* 'bad'
–PS–	[s:]	ECLIPSI 'eclipse' > *eclissi*, SCRIPSI 'I wrote' > *scrissi*
–X– [ks]	[s:]	SAXUM 'stone' > *sasso*, MAXIMUM 'big (superlative)' > *massimo*[12]

TABLE 6.8 Lenition

Latin	Italian	Intervocalic	Before [r]
–P–	[v]	(E)PISCOPUM 'bishop' > *vescovo*, RECIPERE 'receive' > *ricevere*	
–T–	[d]	BOTELLUM 'intestine' > *budello*, SCUTUM 'shield' > *scudo*	MATREM 'mother' > *madre*, PATRONUM 'patron' > *padrone* 'owner'
–K–	[g]	ACUM 'needle' > *ago*, LACUM 'lake' > *lago*	MACRUM 'thin' > *magro*, ACREM 'bitter, sour' > *agro*
–S–	[z] <s>	ROSAM 'rose' > *rosa*, VISUM 'sight' > *viso* 'face'	

of [b] in intervocalic position (HABERE 'to have' > *avere*, FABAM 'horse' > *fava*), and from the Latin labiovelar semi-vowel [w] < U>/<V > (VINO 'wine,' MALVA 'mallow').

The consonant system of Latin also included **geminate** (i.e., long) consonants (CUPPAM 'cup,' CATTUM 'cat,' VACCAM 'cow,' OSSUM 'bone,' FLAMMAM 'flame,' CAPILLUM 'hair,' CARRUM 'cart'). Geminate consonants generally disappeared in Romance languages but were preserved in Italian. In the development of Italian, several Latin consonant clusters underwent regressive assimilation (i.e., the first consonant assimilated to the following one), becoming geminate consonants. Table 6.7 provides some examples of non-inherited Italian geminate consonants.

The last change to be addressed is consonant **weakening** (or **lenition**). This change applied pervasively in western Romance varieties (where, in some cases, it also resulted in consonant loss), whereas it was marginally in eastern Romance varieties (hence, Italian); in fact, consonant weakening is one of the features that separates western from eastern varieties. As illustrated in Table 6.8, weakening in Italian amounted to voicing of voiceless consonants in intervocalic position. In the case of [t] and [g], the change occurred also before [r], and in the case of [p], it involved spirantization as well.

6.2.3 Other changes

This section reviews three unsystematic developments: addition and loss of sounds, and *rafforzamento fonosintattico* 'phonosyntactic strengthening,' a case of regressive assimilation occurring within phrases rather than word-internally.

Different technical terms are used to refer to addition and loss of sounds, depending on where they take place inside the word. Addition of a sound in word-final position is referred to as **epithesis**. In Old Italian, epithesis affected words ending in a consonant (mainly Latin names, *David > Davidde >Davide*) and words stressed on the last syllable, in which, however, it was eventually reversed (*più* > *piùe* > *più* 'more,' *sarò* > *saròe* > *sarò* 'I will be). **Prosthesis** denotes addition of a sound in word-initial position; it occurred primarily in words beginning in <s> + C clusters when preceded by words ending in a consonant (i.e., essentially, the prepositions *con* 'with,' *in* 'in, at,' and *per* 'for') and involved the vowel [i]: *con isdegno* 'with scorn/indignation, *in Ispagna* 'in Spain,' *per ischerzo* 'as a joke.' Prosthesis survives only marginally in contemporary Italian, mainly in written bureaucratic language (*per iscritto* 'in writing'). **Epenthesis** refers to insertion of a sound in word-internal position; it may involve either a vowel, most typically [i] (BAPTISMUM 'baptism' > *battesimo*, SPASMUM 'spasm' > *spasimo*), or a consonant, mainly [v] (MANUALEM 'easy to handle' > *manovale* 'manual worker,' VIDUAM 'widow' > *vedova*).

Loss of word-initial sounds is termed **aphaeresis**. Aphaeresis of the initial syllable affected very early the demonstrative pronoun ILLUM 'that,' which is the source of third-person pronouns (*lui* 'he' < *ILLUI, *lei* 'she' < *ILLAEI, *loro* 'the' < ILLORUM, *lo* 'him/it' < ILLUM, etc.) and the definite article (*lo* 'the.M.SG,' *la* 'the.F.SG,' etc.). In present-day spoken Italian, apheresis is quite productive in the forms of the demonstrative adjective *questo* 'this' (*sto libro* 'this book'). Temporal adverbs as *stamattina* 'this morning,' *stanotte* 'tonight,' *stavolta* 'this time' (< *questa mattina*, etc.), which are attested at very early stages of Italian, indicate that aphaeresis of the feminine form is an old phenomenon. **Syncope** refers to loss of sounds in word-internal position. Loss of word-internal unstressed vowels was rather frequent in Late (Spoken) Latin, leading to the development of several new consonant clusters, some of which underwent further changes (CEREBELLUM 'brain' > *cervello*, FRIGIDUM 'cold' > *freddo*, VIRIDEM 'green' > *verde*, MACULAM 'stain' > *macchia*, SPECULUM 'mirror' > *specchio*, UNGULAM 'hoof, talon' > *unghia* 'fingernail'). **Apocope** denotes loss of sounds in word-final position. A case of apocope that is particularly important from a diachronic perspective is that involving loss of an entire syllable because it gave rise to the class of nouns stressed on the last syllable (CARITATEM 'affection, love' > *carità* 'charity,' VANITATEM 'vanity' > *vanità*, VIRTUTEM 'vanity' *virtù*).

As noted earlier, *rafforzamento fonosintattico* denotes a phenomenon of regressive assimilation that targets a sound within phrases (hence the label 'phonosyntactic'). Specifically, it involves two-word phrases when uttered without a pause, causing lengthening of the initial consonant of the second word. It is considered a case of assimilation rather than lengthening, because historically it was triggered by a final consonant of the first word, which was eventually lost, leaving its trace in the pronunciation only. Thus, the phrase *a piedi* 'on foot' is pronounced [ap:jɛdi] (*a* < AD). The trace of the lost Latin consonant is still visible in some cases when what was originally a phrase became one word: *appunto* 'precisely' (*a* 'at' < AD *punto* 'point'), *ebbene* 'well' (*e* 'and' < ET *bene* 'well'), *ovvero* 'really' (*o* 'or' < AUT *vero* 'true'), *seppure* 'although' (*se* 'if' < SED *mai* 'ever'), *soprattutto* 'above all' (< SUPER 'above' *tutto* 'all').[13]

Synchronically, the triggers of *rafforzamento* can be divided into three main categories, as illustrated in (8), with examples of the most common words of each category.

(8) a. Stressed monosyllabic words. (Absence of orthographic stress is irrelevant here.)
   i. Prepositions: *a* 'at/to,' *da* 'from,' *fra/tra* 'between,' *su* 'on.'
   ii. Adverbs: *qui/qua* 'here,' *lì/là* 'there,' *già* 'already,' *più* 'more.'
   iii. Pronouns: *tu* 'you,' *che* 'what,' *chi* 'who,' *ciò* 'this/that.'
   iv. Conjunctions: *e* 'and,' *o* 'or,' *ma* 'but,' *se* 'if.'
   v. Verb forms: *è* 'is,' *ho* 'I have,' *ha* 'has,' *do* 'I give,' *dà* 'gives,' *fa* 'does'
   vi. Others: *sì* 'yes,' *no* 'no,' *tre* 'three.'

b. All words stressed on the last syllable (*città* 'city,' *dirò* 'I will say').
c. Some disyllabic words stressed on the first syllable: *come* 'as,' *dove* 'where,' *qualche* 'some,' *sopra* 'on, above.'

The fact that in modern Italian *rafforzamento* is also triggered by words that originally didn't end in a consonant is explained by analogical extension. Finally, it should be noted that *rafforzamento* is present only in central and southern Italian varieties.

6.3 Morphological and morphosyntactic changes

Morphology designates the subfield of linguistics that examines how words can be partitioned into subparts, addressing the systematic associations between forms and meanings that hold among words. **Morphosyntax**, on the other hand, deals with language features and structures which can be analyzed by criteria of morphology and syntax (which studies the structure of sentences), thus capturing the close interaction between the two. This section reviews the most important morphological and morphosyntactic changes pertaining to nouns, adjectives, pronouns, and verbs. We will see that, overall, these changes reveal a transition from a predominantly synthetic system (i.e., a system where the syntactic relations within sentences are expressed by inflectional suffixes) to a system where analytic (or periphrastic) structures acquire more prominence.

6.3.1 Nouns and adjectives

Latin marked nouns and adjectives for the grammatical categories of number, gender, and case (which expressed the grammatical functions words served in sentences), distinguishing two numbers (singular and plural), three genders (masculine, feminine, and neuter), and six cases (nominative, genitive, dative, accusative, ablative, and vocative). These three categories were expressed together by means of single inflectional endings (or suffixes). Grammatical gender was essentially arbitrary, although it usually matched biological sex in nouns with animate referents, especially nouns denoting humans (feminine PŬELLĂ 'girl.NOM,' masculine PŬĔR 'boy.NOM'), while nouns with inanimate referents were often neuter. Although each case governed several grammatical functions, their core functions were the following: nominative marked subjects; genitive signaled possession; dative and accusative marked indirect and direct object, respectively; ablative expressed a variety of relations (e.g., locative, temporal, manner, comitative), often accompanied by a preposition; and vocative marked entities addressed or invoked. Thanks to case marking, word order in Latin was very flexible.

Based on their inflectional suffixes, Latin nouns were grouped into five **declensions** (or classes), illustrated in Table 6.9.

Concerning gender, the first declension comprised primarily feminine nouns, though it also featured some masculine ones (ĂGRĬCŎLĂ 'farmer,' PŎĒTĂ 'poet'), the second included mainly masculine and neuter nouns and some feminine ones, the third contained nouns of all three genders, the fourth consisted of feminine and neuter nouns, and the nouns of the fifth declensions were all feminine.

A crucial change that affected the nominal morphology of Latin in its transition to Romance was the demise of case marking. As seen in Table 6.9, the same suffix could express multiple cases, indicating that the Latin case system was not very strong. The loss of word-final

TABLE 6.9 Latin declensions

	1	2		3		4		5
	PŬELL-Ā 'girl.F'	LŬP-US 'wolf.M,' DŌN-UM 'gift.N		VOLP-ĒS 'fox.F,' MĂR-Ĕ 'sea.N'		MĂN-ŬS 'hand.F,'CŎRN-Ŭ 'horn.N'		R-ĒS 'thing.F'
SINGULAR								
NOM	-Ă	-US	UM	-ĒS	-Ĕ	-ŬS	-Ŭ	ĒS
GEN	-AE	-I		-IS		-ŪS		-EĪ
DAT	-AE	-O		-I		-UI	-U	-EĪ
ACC	-AM	-UM		-EM		-UM	-U	-EM
VOC	-Ă	-E		-ES	-Ĕ		-U	-ES
ABL	-Ā	-O		-E	-I	- ŬS		-Ē
PLURAL								
NOM	-AE	-I		-ĒS		- U		-ES
GEN	-ĀRUM	-ŌRUM		-ĬUM	-ĬA	-ŪS	-ŬA	-ĒRUM
DAT	-IS	-IS		-ĬBUS		-ĬBUS		-ĒBUS
ACC	-AS	-OS		-ES	-ĬA	-ŪS	-ŬA	-ES
VOC	-AE	-I		-ES	-ĬA	-ŪS	-ŬA	-ES
ABL	-IS	-IS		-ĬBUS		-ĬBUS		-ĒBUS

consonants and of the contrast between long and short vowels further weakened it, and cases were eventually lost in all Romance varieties. Consequently, grammatical functions came to be signaled by prepositions and word order, which became essentially fixed (i.e., subject-verb-direct object-indirect object/other complements).

(9) a. MARIUS   JULIAM   AMAT
           Marius.NOM.M.SG Julia.ACC.F.SG loves
           'Marius loves Julia'
     a'. *Mario ama Giulia*
     b. MARIUS   ROSAM   JULIAE   DEDIT
           Marius.NOM.M.SG rose.ACC.F.SG Julia.DAT.F.SG gave
           'Marius gave a/the rose to Giulia'
     b'. *Mario diede la/una rosa a Giulia*
     c. MARIUS   GLADIO   FILIUM   BRUTI   NECAVIT
           Marius.NOM.M.SG sword.ABL.M.SG son.ACC.M.SG Brutus.GEN.M.SG killed
           'Marius killed Brutus' son with a sword'
           Mario uccise il figlio di Bruto con la spada

The Italian examples in (9a', b', c'), moreover, reveal another important Romance innovation: the emergence of the definite and indefinite article, both absent in Latin. The source of the indefinite article was the numeral UNU(M) 'one,' while (as already mentioned) the definite article derived from the demonstrative pronoun ILLU(M) 'that' via apocope.

(10) a. UNU(M) > masculine *un, uno*; UNA(M) > feminine *una*.
      b. ILLU(M) > masculine singular *lo*; ILLA(M) > feminine singular *la*; ILLI > masculine plural *li* (> *gli*); ILLAS (or ILLAE) > feminine plural *le*.[14]

Another major change that impacted the development of the Italian nominal system (as well as that of all Romance languages except Romanian) was the loss of the neuter gender. Latin neuter nouns of the second (FILU(M) 'thread'), third (LATU(M) 'side'), and fourth declension (CORNU 'horn, CORPU(s) 'body') became masculine since they were practically undistinguishable from masculine nouns of the second declension (MURU(M) 'wall'). Neuter nouns with other endings became masculine as well (MARE 'sea,' SANGUE(N) 'blood').

The number distinction singular vs. plural, on the other hand, continued in Italian. Both number and gender are expressed inflectionally. (Old) Italian, then, developed a nominal system comprising three main inflectional classes, as illustrated in Table 6.10.

A small noun class which, however, includes many common nouns deserves mention because it evinces a trace of the neuter. This class comprises nouns which were neuter in Latin but became masculine in the singular and feminine, ending in -*a* rather than -*e*, in the plural. Among the most common are *braccio* 'arm'/*braccia*, *dito* 'finger'/*dita*, *ginocchio* 'knee'/*ginocchia*, *labbro* 'lip'/*labbra*, *lenzuolo* 'bed sheet'/*lenzuola*, *osso* 'bone'/*ossa*, *uovo* 'egg'/*uova*. The plural forms are a continuation of the Latin neuter forms, which were reinterpreted as feminine since -*a* is the canonical feminine singular nominal suffix. Many of these nouns developed also the 'regular' plural form (*bracci*, *ossi*), which may have a different meaning. Typically, the 'new' plural bears singulative rather than collective meaning (*lo scheletro umano è formato da 206* **ossa** 'the human skeleton is composed of 206 bones' vs. *un mucchio di* **ossi** 'a heap of bones'), or a non-literal/metaphorical meaning (*ha* **le braccia** *muscolose* 's/he have muscular arms' vs. *un candelabro a tre* **bracci** 'a candelabra with three arms,' **i fondamenti** *della matematica* 'the principles of mathematics' vs. **le fondamenta** *di un edificio* 'the foundations of a building').

Qualifying adjectives denote gradable notions, usually distinguishing three degrees: positive (*beautiful*), comparative (*more/less beautiful, as beautiful as*), and superlative (*most/least beautiful, very beautiful*). Latin qualitative adjectives were divided into two classes, depending on how they distinguished gender. Adjectives of the first class followed the same inflectional pattern as nouns of the first and second declension nouns (FORMŎS-US, -A, -UM 'beautiful'), while adjectives of the second class had either two forms, one for masculine and feminine vs. one for neuter (DULCIS, -E 'sweet'), or only one form for all genders (VETŬS 'old'). Both classes continue in Italian, that is, Italian developed one class of adjectives that distinguishes gender, following the inflectional pattern of nominal class 1 (*bello/-a* 'beautiful,' *freddo/-a* 'cold'), and one that doesn't and follows the inflectional pattern of nominal class 3 (*acre* 'acrid,' *debole* 'weak').

Latin comparative forms denoting 'more' were synthetic forms, that is, they were formed by adding the suffixes -IOR (masculine and feminine) and -IUS (neuter) to the adjective stem (11a). Comparative forms denoting 'less' and 'same,' on the other hand, were analytic, that is, they were expressed by periphrasis involving adverbs meaning 'less' or 'same' (11b, c).

TABLE 6.10 Italian main nominal classes

Class	Inflectional suffix	Gender	Examples
1	SG -*o*, PL -*i*	masculine	*cielo* 'sky,' *fuoco* 'fire,' *gatto* 'cat,' *medico* 'doctor'
2	SG -*a*, PL -*e*	feminine	*alba* 'dawn,' *capra* 'goat,' *luna* 'moon,' *sorella* 'sister'
3	SG -*e*, PL -*i*	masculine	*cane* 'dog,' *fiore* 'flower,' *padre* 'father,' *sale* 'salt'
		feminine	*ape* 'bee,' *cenere* 'ash,' *notte* 'night,' *madre* 'mother'

Superlative forms were derived either inflectionally by the suffix -ISSIMUS, -ISSIMA, ISSIMUM or analytically by adverbs meaning 'very' (MULTUM, MAXIME, VALDE) (10d).

(11) a. CLAUDIA FORMOS**IOR** QUAM JULIA EST.
'Claudia is more beautiful than Julia.'
b. CLAUDIA **MINUS** FORMOSA **QUAM** JULIA EST.
'Claudia is less beautiful than Julia.'
c. CLAUDIA **TAM/TANTUM** FORMOSA **QUAM** JULIA EST.
'Claudia is as beautiful as Julia.'
d. CLAUDIA FORMOS**ISSIMA/MULTUM** FORMOSA EST.
'Claudia is very beautiful.'

As shown in (12), all the forms in (11) are inherited by Italian except the synthetic comparative in (11a), which was replaced by an analytic form involving the adverb *più* 'more' (< PLUS).

(12) a. *Claudia è **più** bella **di** Giulia.*
b. *Claudia è **meno** bella **di** Giulia.*
c. *Claudia è **tanto** bella **quanto** Giulia.*
d. *Claudia è **bellissima**/**molto** bella.*

Finally, note that four (high-frequency) adjectives have also kept their synthetic comparative forms: *buono* 'good'/ *migliore* 'better' (< MELIORE(M)), *cattivo* 'bad'/ *peggiore* 'worse' (< PEIORE(M)), *grande* 'big'/ *maggiore* 'greater, bigger' (< MAIORE(M)), and *piccolo* 'small,' *minore* 'smaller' (< MINORE(M)).

6.3.2 Pronouns

This section provides a diachronic sketch of four series of pronouns: personal, relative, possessive, and demonstrative.

The forms of first and second **personal pronouns** continue their Latin counterparts, as shown in Table 6.11. The Latin nominative forms give the Italian subject forms, and the complement forms derive from the accusative forms; more precisely, the bare forms serve as direct object pronouns, while the other grammatical functions are marked by prepositions (*a* 'to' indirect object, *di* 'of' possessive, *con* 'with' company).

Latin lacked third-person pronouns, using instead the demonstratives IS and ĬLLE, both meaning 'that,' and IPSE 'self.' We already know that the Italian third-person pronouns derive from ĬLLE; a few forms, however, developed from ĬPSE. As illustrated in Table 6.12, Old Italian has a rather-large set of third-person subject pronouns, most of which were lost.

TABLE 6.11 First- and second-person pronouns

	Latin NOM > *Italian* SUBJ	*Latin* ACC > *Italian* COM
1SG	ĔGŌ > *ĔŌ > *io*	MĒ > *me*
2SG	TŪ > *tu*	TĒ > *te*
1PL	NŌS > *noi*	NŌS > *noi*
2PL	VŌS > *voi*	VŌS > *voi*

TABLE 6.12 Old Italian third-person pronouns

		Italian SUBJ	Italian COM
SG	M	⋆ĬLLĪ > *elli, egli, gli, ei, e'* ĬPSŬ(M) > *esso*	⋆ĬLLŪI > *lui*
	F	ĬLLA(M) > *ella, la* ĬPSA(M) > *essa*	⋆ĬLLAEI > *lei*
PL	M	⋆ĬLLĪ > *elli, egli, eglino*[15] ĬPSĪ > *essi*	ĬLLORŬ(M) > *loro*
	F	ĬLLA(S) > *elle, elleno* ĬPSA(S) > *esse*	

TABLE 6.13 Old Italian clitic pronouns

	DO	IO
1SG	*mi*	
2SG	*ti*	
3SG.M	*lo, il, el, 'l*	*li, gli, igli, lgli, i*
3SG.F	*la*	*le, li*
1PL	*ci, no*	
2PL	*vi, vo*	
3PL.M	*li, i, gli*	*i, li*
3PL.F	*le*	*le, li*

Indeed, we could say that none of the subject pronouns in Table 6.12 survives in present-day (spoken) Italian, because they have been replaced by the complement forms. The use of *lui*, *lei*, and *loro* with subject function actually dates back to Old Italian but was subject to severe censorship by prescriptive grammars until very recently. The forms derived from ĬPSE first became restricted to inanimate referents, then eventually fell out of use.

The pronouns reviewed so far are all stressed. A parallel series of unstressed pronouns developed for the object forms in all Romance varieties. These are known in the literature as clitic (< Gr. *klínein* 'to lean on') pronouns because since they are unstressed they have to 'lean on' the adjacent verb for pronunciation. Clitic pronouns are a major pan-Romance innovation and have been one of the most investigated topics in (Romance) linguistics. Table 6.13 gives the forms of Old Italian clitic pronouns.

Like their subject counterparts, the third-person object pronouns come from ĬLLE and, particularly the masculine pronoun, have several variants. Moreover, they differ notably from the first and second pronouns by being marked for gender and having separate forms for direct and indirect object. The first and second singular forms *mi* and *ti* derive from the same source as their tonic counterparts, MĒ and TĒ. The plural forms *ci* and *vi*, which replaced the etymological forms *no* and *vo* (< NŌS and VŌS) very early, are actually locative pronouns: *ci* 'here' (< ⋆(ĔC)CE HĪ(C) 'here') and *vi* 'there' (< (Ĭ)BĬ 'there'). *Ci* and *vi* continued in their locative function as well, although *vi* increasingly weakened and is extremely marginal in contemporary Italian, where *ci* has acquired both meanings. The set of third-person pronouns reduced considerably, possibly also due to the fact that *gli*, *i*, *li*, and *le* fulfilled multiple functions. Contemporary Italian has four direct object forms (*lo, la, li, le*) and three indirect object forms: masculine singular *gli*, feminine singular *le*, and plural *loro* unmarked for gender, which in fact is not a clitic pronoun. It must be noted, though, that the use of *gli* for plural and feminine singular referents has expanded sizably and is considered a feature of *neo-standard* Italian (Berruto, 1987).

Depending on the position they occupy with respect to the verb, we distinguish proclitic pronouns, which precede the verb (13a), and enclitic pronouns, which follow it (13b). In modern Italian, clitic pronouns are proclitic with finite (i.e., conjugated) verb forms, while non-finite verb forms and imperatives require enclitic pronouns which attach to the verb also orthographically.

(13) a. **lo** mangio,   **lo** mangiavo,   **lo** mangerò,   **lo**   mangerei
         it eat.1SG.PRS.IND it eat.1SG.PRS.IPF it eat.1SG.FUT it   eat.1sg.PRS.COND
    b. *per mangiar**lo**,   mangiando**lo**, mangia**lo**!,   mangiamo**lo**!, mangia**te**lo!*
         for eat.INF–it   eating–it   eat.2SG.IMP–it eat.1PL.IMP–it eat.2PL.IMP–it

The distribution of proclitic and enclitic pronouns was different in Old Italian. In essence, enclitic pronouns were obligatory in clause-initial position irrespective of whether the verb was finite or non-finite, as shown in (14).

(14) a. 'il signore Cristo sì **li** disse: "Che vuo' tu comperare, giovane?"'
         'the Lord Christ so said to him: "What do you want to buy, boy?"'
         (Anonymous, *Leggenda aurea*, fourteenth century, p. a68)[16]
    b. 'Disse**li** santo Vito: "Vegnano gli dei tuoi e guariscanti, se possono!"'
         'St. Vito said to him: "May your gods come and heal you if they can!'
         (Anonymous, *Leggenda aurea*, fourteenth century, p. b679)

When direct and indirect object clitics co-occur, the indirect pronoun precedes the indirect one. First and second pronouns undergo a phonological change: the final *-i* becomes *-e* (*te lo darò* 'I'll give it to you'); also, *gli* is the only third-person indirect object form allowed, and the pronoun cluster is written as one word (**glielo** *darò* 'I'll give it to him'). The original order, however, was DO-IO; starting around the beginning of the fourteenth century, both orders were possible (seemingly in free variation), until the DO-IO order eventually disappeared.

(15) a. 'E io **lo ti** mosterrò'
         'And I will show it to you'
         (Anonymous, *Leggenda aurea*, fourteenth century, p. b520)
    b. 'domandali, e ellino **te lo** diranno'
         'ask them, and they will tell you'
         (Anonymous, *Leggenda aurea*, fourteenth century, p. c1354)

Italian **relative pronouns** developed from their Latin counterparts rather straightforwardly and underwent only minor changes. *Che* 'that' (< neuter interrogative/indefinite pronoun QUĬD) still functions both as subject (16a) and direct object (16b) but has been replaced by *cui* when expressing other complements (16c–f).

(16) a. '*diremo d'altri signori e donne* **che** *in questi dì passarono per Firenze*'
'we will tell of other gentlemen and women who passed through Florence in these
days'
(Giovanni Villani, *Cronica*, 1348, p. c555)
b. '*il più pessimo e feroce animale* **che** *Idio crease*'
'the vilest and wildest animal that God created'
(Giordano da Pisa, *Quaresimale fiorentino (1305–1306)*, p. 19)
c. '*tirando la fune* **con che** *la falce era legata*'
'pulling the rope with which the scythe was tied'
(Giamboni, *Delle Storie contra i Pagani di Paolo Orosio libri VII*, 1292, p. 368)
d. '*questa è la ragione* **per che** *li Santi non hanno tra loro invidia*'
'this is the reason for which Saints are not envious of each other'
(Dante Alighieri, *Il Convivio*, 1304, p. 247)
e. '*Vanità sono le cose* **di che** *gli uomini vanamente si gloriano*'
'Vanity are those things of which men'
(Passavanti, *Trattato della vanagloria*, 1355, p. 263)
f. '*L'altro modo* **a che** *si possono conoscere i pensieri*'
'The other manner in which thoughts can be known'
(Passavanti, *Trattato della scienza*, 1355, p. 298)

Cui (< CUI the dative form of QUI 'who/that') served as interrogative and indefinite
pronoun (16b) and could bear any grammatical function except subject; when expressing possessive function, *cui* was often preceded by the definite article agreeing in gender and number to its referent (17e). It eventually lost interrogative and direct object
function.

(17) a. '*Dunque* **a cui** *sono necessarj i comandamenti?*'
'Thus, to whom are the commandments necessary?'
(Anonymous, *Pistole di Seneca volgarizzate*, 1325, p. 4)
b. '*Questi sono i nomi degli arcivescovi e vescovi principali* **cui** *fece suoi esecutori*'
'These are the names of the chief archbishops and bishops whom he appointed as his
executors'
(Villani, *Cronica*, 1348, a134)
c. '*voi,* **cui** *io amo più che niuna altra cosa*'
'you, whom I love more than anything else'
(Boccaccio, *Filocolo*, 1336, p. 137)
d. '*Jacob figliuolo d'Isaac,* **a cui** *Idio puose nome poi Isdrael*'
'Jacob, son of Isaac, to whom God later gave the name Isdrael'
(Anonymous, *Ottimo commento della Commedia. Inferno*, 1334, p. 39)
e. '*intorniato d'alberi d'oro,* **le cui** *frondi non temevano l'autunno*'
'surrounded by golden trees, whose leaves did not fear the autumn'
(Boccaccio, *Filocolo*, 1336, p. 171)

The form *quale* (< interrogative QUALE(M) 'what/which') expresses the same functions as
che and *cui*. Unlike *che* and *cui*, though, *quale* agrees with its antecedent in number and in
gender by means of the definite article.

(18) a. *'fuvvi morto uno <u>Rinuccio di Pepo</u>, lo quale era prod'uomo et molto nomato'*
'a Rinuccio of Pepo died there, who was a valiant man and very renowned'
(Pieri, *Cronica*, 1305, p. 50)

    b. *'<u>Meleagro amoe una giovane</u>, . . ., a la quale elli presentoe la testa del cinghiaro'*
'Meleagro loved a girl, . . ., to whom he presented the wild boar's head'
(Anonymous, *Commento ai Rimedi d'amore di Ovidio (Volgarizzamento B)*, 1313, p. 874)

    c. *'<u>le tue lagrime</u> con le quali non solamente il tuo viso bagnasti, ma ancora il mio'*
'your tears, with whom you wet not only your face but also mine'
(Boccaccio, *L'elegia di Madonna Fiammetta*, 1343, p. 108)

    d. *'la Luna ha più <u>nomi</u>, delli quali l'uno è Diana'*
'the Moon has many names, one of which is Diana'
(Anonymous, *L'Ottimo Commento della Commedia III*, 1334, p. 63)

Finally, interrogative indefinite *chi* 'who' (< interrogative/indefinite QUIS '(one)who') functions as subject and any type of complement.

(19) a. *'**Chi** l'abandonò?'*
'Who abandoned him?'
(Sacchetti, *Sposizioni di Vangeli*, 1378, p. 274)

    b. *'**chi** la vedea diventava di pietra'*
'whoever saw her turned into stone'
(Anonymous, *Chiose all' 'Inferno,'* 1321, p. 121)

    c. *'stavano al bordello e davansi a chi le volea'*
'they were at the brothel and gave themselves to whomever wanted them'
(*Novellino*, early thirteenth century, p. 307)

    d. *'lo smeraldo chiarifica il viso di chi 'l porta'*
'the emerald illuminates the face of whom wears it'
(Pucci, *Libro di varie storie*, 1362, p. 95)

As seen in Table 6.14, the paradigm/system of Italian **possessive** pronouns (which function as adjectives as well) developed straightforwardly from Latin.

The 1SG/PL and 2PL masculine forms derive from the Latin nominative rather than accusative forms. The expected outcomes of nominative TŬI and SŬI would be *tòi* and *sòi* since, as we

TABLE 6.14 Possessive pronouns/adjectives

	MASCULINE		*FEMININE*	
	SG	PL	SG	PL
1SG	MĔŬ(M) > *mio*	MĔI 'NOM' > *miei*	MĔA(M) > *mia*	MĔA(S) > *mie*
2SG	TŬŬ(M) > *tuo*	*tuoi*	TŬA(M) > *tua*	TŬA(S) > *tue*
3SG	SŬŬ(M) > *suo*	*suoi*	SŬA(M) > *sua*	SŬA(S) > *sue*
1PL	NŎSTRŬ(M) > *nostro*	NŎSTRI > *nostri*	NŎSTRA(M) > *nostra*	NŎSTRA(S) > *nostre*
2PL	VŎSTRŬ(M) > *vostro*	VŎSTRI > *vostri*	VŎSTRA(M) > *vostra*	VŎSTRŬ(S) > *vostre*
3PL	ĬLLORŬ(M) > *loro*			

recall, the diphtnong <uo> comes from <ŏ>. Therefore, the forms *tuoi* and *suoi* were possibly modeled by analogy with *miei*. The invariable 3PL form *loro* comes from the masculine/ neuter genitive plural of the demonstrative ILLE 'that.'

Let's close this brief overview of possessives with pointing out a distinctive feature of Italian possessives, namely, that they agree in gender and number with the possessed entity rather than with the possessor, as shown in (20).

(20) '*Fitone fu un grandissimo serpente, il quale <u>Apollo</u> con **le sue saette** uccise.'*
'Python was a huge snake, which Apollo killed with his arrows.'
(Boccaccio, *Teseida delle nozze d'Emilia. Chiose*, 1339, p. 625)

The Latin system of **demonstrative** pronouns made a three-way distinction as for spatial, temporal, or discourse position of a referent with respect to the discourse participants.

(21) a. HIC, HAEC, HOC 'this': near the speaker.
b. ISTE, –A, –UD 'that': near the addressee.
c. ILLE, –A, –UD 'that': away from speaker and addressee.

This three-way distinction continues in Italian, but with different forms, due to shifts in the Latin system brought about by the loss of HIC and other pronouns. The development of the Italian forms is sketched in (22), where we see that all three demonstratives developed from periphrastic expressions involving the adverb ĔCCU(M) 'here,' which carried reinforcing emphatic value.

(22) a. ĔCCU(M) ĬSTŬ(M) 'here this' > *coesto* > **questo** 'this (by the speaker).'
b. ĔCCU(M) TĬBĬ ĬSTŬ(M) 'here to you this' > *cote(v)esto* > **codesto** 'that (by the addressee).'
c. ĔCCU(M) ĬLLŬ(M) 'here that' > *coello* > **quello** 'that (away from the speaker and addressee).'

Codesto, however, is no longer used in present-day Italian (it survives marginally only in written bureaucratic register), so the demonstrative system is actually based on a two-way opposition.

6.3.3 Adverbs

Adverbs (< Lat. ADVERBIUM, AD '' + VERBUM 'word, verb') are invariable words that modify verb phrases (*I slept badly/soundly*), adjectives (*she's very pretty*), and other adverbs (*you talk too loudly*), typically providing information pertaining to space (*here, outside*), time (*now, always*), manner (*slowly, well*), quantity (*less, a lot*). They can be primitive forms (*soon*); alternatively, they can be derivative forms, either resulting from phrases (*upside down, upstairs*) or obtained by adding a suffix to adjectives (*-ly*, in English). Latin had two productive adverbial suffixes: -E for adjectives of the first class, and -ITER for adjectives of the second class (23a, b). Neither suffix survived in Italian, but a new adverbial suffix emerged, *-mente* (23c) (and in many other Romance varieties).

(23) a. AVDIUS, -A, -UM 'avid' → AVIDE 'avidly,' LAETUS, -A, -UM 'usual' → LAETE 'usually'
    b. BREVIS, -E 'brief' → BREVITER 'briefly,' SUAVIS, -E 'gentle' → SUAVITER 'gently'
    c. *avida**mente**, breve**mente**, lieta**mente**, soave**mente***

The suffix -*mente* is the outcome of a process of grammaticalization, a type of language change pervasively attested across languages 'whereby lexical items and constructions come in certain linguistic contexts to serve grammatical functions, and, once grammaticalized, continue to develop new grammatical functions' (Hopper & Traugott, 2003, p. xv). The suffix -*mente* originated from the ablative form of the Latin noun MENTE(M) 'mind' in the context exemplified in (24), where it could be used to indicate the way an action is performed.

(24) a. ADJ.ABL.SG.F + MENTE.ABL.SG.F
    b. CLARA/IRATA MENTE 'with a clear/furious mind.'

The origins of -*mente*, thus, account for the fact that it attaches to the feminine form of adjectives. While the suffix was originally restricted to adjectives semantically compatible with MENTE(M), it can now be used with nearly any qualifying adjective (*ultimamente* 'lately' < *ultimo* 'last').

6.3.4 Verbs

The verb system of Latin marked the grammatical categories given in (25):

(25) a. **Tense** establishes temporal relations between the event/situation denoted by the verb and some other temporal point (typically, the time of the utterance). Latin had three tenses: past, present, and future tense.
    b. **Aspect** provides a temporal view of the event/situation denoted by the verb; although closely correlated to tense, aspect is a separate category. Latin distinguished between perfective aspect, which views the event/situation in its entirety, as a single unit, and imperfective aspect, which points to the internal temporal structure of the event/situation (e.g., progressive, habitual, iterative).
    c. **Mood** conveys the degree of reality/factuality speakers assign to the content of utterances. Latin distinguished between indicative mood, which relates to reality/factuality, and subjunctive mood, which expresses possibility, uncertainty; it also had imperative mood to express commands and exhortations.
    d. **Voice** links participant roles (e.g., agent, patient, recipient) to grammatical relations (e.g., subject, direct/indirect object). Latin distinguished **active** voice, where the subject denotes the agent performing the action expressed by the verb, whereas the direct object undergoes it (*John kissed Mary*), and **passive** voice, where the subject denotes the undergoer and the agent, if expressed overtly, appears in the form of a PP (*Mary was kissed by John*).
    e. **Person** (1, 2, and 3) and **number** (SG and PL).

Latin verbs were divided in four verb classes (or **conjugations**) on the basis of their inflectional endings for the infinitive forms, as shown in (26).

(26) a. 1 -ĀRE: AMĀRE 'to love,' CANTĀRE 'to sing,' LAUDĀRE 'to praise,' PUGNĀRE 'to fight.'

    b. 2 -ĒRE: DEBĒRE 'to own,' HABĒRE 'to have,' TIMĒRE 'to fear,' VIDĒRE 'to see.'

    c. 3 -ĔRE: DUCĔRE 'to lead,' LEGĔRE 'to read,' MITTĔRE 'to send,' REGĔRE 'to guide.'

    d. 4 -ĪRE: AUDĪRE 'to hear,' DORMĪRE 'to sleep,' SENTĪRE 'to feel,' VĔNĪRE 'to come.'

Table 6.15 illustrates the paradigm of the primary forms of LAUDARE in the first-person singular.

We see that passive forms were either synthetic (inflectional) or analytic (periphrastic); precisely, imperfective forms were obtained inflectionally adding the suffix -R, while perfective forms were periphrases comprising the past participle followed by ESSE 'to be.'

In addition to the active infinitive LAUDĀRE and the forms in Table 6.15, the Latin verb system included other partially inflected or non-inflected forms, given in (27).

(27) a. Imperative. Active present LAUDĀ 'praise.2SG,' LAUDĀTE 'praise.2PL'; future LAUDĀTO 'praise.2SG,' LAUDĀTŌTE 'prais.2PL.' Passive LAUDĀRE 'be praised.2SG,' LAUDĀMINI 'be praised.2PL.'

    b. Participles. Present LAUDĀNS 'praising' (inflected as class 2 adjectives), perfect LAUDĀTUS 'praised,' and future LAUDĀTŪRUS 'going to praise' (inflected as class 1 adjectives).

    c. Infinitive. Passive LAUDĀRI 'to be praised,' perfect active LAUDĀVISSE 'to have praised,' perfect passive LAUDĀTUM ESSE 'to have been praised.'

    d. Gerund. Genitive LAUDANDĪ 'of praising,' dative/ablative LAUDANDŌ 'by/for praising,' accusative AD LAUDANDUM 'in order to praise.'

    e. Gerundive. A verbal adjective (inflected as class 1 adjectives) which conveyed necessity or fitness: LAUDANDUS 'needing to be praised.'

    f. Supine. It mainly expressed purpose or the beginning of an action: accusative LAUDATUM and ablative LAUDATU.

TABLE 6.15 LAUDARE 'primary' forms

		Indicative			*Subjunctive*	
		Present	*Imperfect*	*Future*	*Present*	*Imperfect*
Imperfective	Active	LAUDO 'I praise'	LAUDABAM 'I was praising'	LAUDABO 'I will praise'	LAUDEM 'I may praise'	LAUDAREM 'I might praise'
	Passive	LAUDOR 'I am praised'	LAUDABAR 'I was being praised'	LAUDABOR 'I will be praised'	LAUDER 'I may be praised'	LAUDARER 'I might be praised'
		Perfect	Pluperfect	Future perfect	Perfect	Pluperfect
Perfective	Active	LAUDAVI 'I praised'	LAUDAVERAM 'I had praised'	LAUDAVERO 'I will have praised'	LAUDAVERIM 'I praised'	LAUDAVISSEM 'I had praised'
	Passive	LAUDATUS, -A, UM SUM 'I was praised'	LAUDATUS, -A, UM ERAM 'I had been praised'	LAUDATUS, -A, UM ERO 'I will have been praised'	LAUDATUS, -A, UM SIM 'I was praised'	LAUDATUS, -A, UM ESSEM 'I had been praised'

It's apparent, then, that the verb system of Latin was quite complex. Italian (and Romance languages as well) inherits much of its complexity but also experiences some important innovations, the most notable of which will be addressed shortly.

First, while the first (-ĀRE) and fourth (ĪRE) Latin conjugation continued in Italian, second (-ĒRE) and third (-ĔRE) conjugations merged (due to loss of distinctive vocalic quantity). Italian has three conjugations: -are, -ere, and -ire. Moreover, several verb forms disappeared altogether, namely, the synthetic future (LAUDABO) and passive (LAUDABOR, etc.), the imperfect subjunctive (LAUDAREM), the future participle (LAUDĀTŪRUS), and all the infinitive forms except the active present. The class of deponent verbs, which are verbs with passive form but active meaning (LOQUI 'to speak') was also lost, and the verbs that continued in Italian were 'regularized' (MŎRI 'to die' > *MORIRE > morire, NASCI 'to be born; to originate' > *NASCERE > nascere). Some forms, conversely, continued essentially with their original function, such as the present, imperfect and perfect indicative, the present subjunctive, and the imperative.

Most importantly, new verb forms emerged via grammaticalization, a type of language change widely attested across languages introduced previously when addressing the development of adverbs in -mente. One of them is a new synthetic future, which originates from a periphrastic construction involving HABERE 'to have' in the present indicative, followed by a verb in the infinitive: LAUDARE HABEO 'to praise I have' > *LAUDAR(E) AO > lodarò > loderò 'I will praise.' The same periphrasis but with HABERE in the perfect was the source of the conditional, a verb form unknown to Latin: LAUDARE HABUI 'to praise I had' > *LAUDAR(E) (H)E(BU)I > lodarei > loderei 'I would praise.'

Another novel verb form that emerged through grammaticalization is the analytic past perfect, *passato prossimo* 'near past,' which also involves the present indicative of HABERE and a past participle: HABEO LAUDATUM > ho lodato 'I have praised.' In this case, HABERE maintains its full phonological shape, though it functions as an auxiliary verb. As seen in (28a), HABERE was a lexical verb meaning 'to own,' which continued in Italian as *avere*. The source of *passato prossimo* is exemplified in (28b), where the direct object of HABERE is a noun modified by a past participle.

(28) a. PECUNIAS MAGNAS HABENT money.ACC.F.PL much.ACC.F.PL have.3PL.PRS.IND 'They have a lot of money.'

   b. IN EA PROVINCIA **PECUNIAS MAGNAS** in that.ABL.F.SG province ABL.F.SG money.ACC.F.PL much.ACC.F.PL **COLLOCATAS HABENT** (Cicero, *De imperio Cn. Pompei*, 7, p. 18) invested.ACC.F.PL have. 3PL.PRS.IND 'They have a lot of money invested in that province.'

In (28b), HABERE is still a lexical verb, and the past participle expresses the state of the noun's referent, a state that results from the performance of the event the participle denotes. In this type of context, HABERE does not really entail possession/ownership, and its subject may be different from the agent that causes the state conveyed by participle. Weakening of HABERE's lexical meaning promotes the interpretation of HABERE's subject as the one who caused the direct object referent's state, that is, HABERE becomes an auxiliary verb, and the past participle loses its 'adjectival' value, becoming the only lexical verb so that even intransitive verbs can occur in this construction. In short, the change is from a construction conveying the result of an event ('I have money which is invested') to a construction denoting a past event ('I have invested money'). Auxiliary *avere* eventually became restricted to transitive verbs and a subclass of intransitive verbs known as **unergative**, while it was replaced by *essere* for the subclass of intransitive verbs known as **unaccusatives**.[17]

As noted previously, Latin had only one form of the past indicative, the perfect LAUDAVI, which functioned both as present perfective ('I have praised') and past punctual ('I praised'). In Italian (and Romance languages in general), the Latin perfect indicative continued as a past tense with punctual value (i.e., *passato remoto* 'remote past'), while *passato prossimo* took on the present perfective value. This new form brought about an array of analytic verb forms featuring *avere/essere* in different tenses/moods (see Table 6.16).

Regarding the passive voice, loss of the synthetic forms resulted in some shifts in the paradigm; specifically, Latin periphrastic past form LAUDATUS EST 'it was praised' was reinterpreted as the present form, *è lodato* 'it is praised,' leading to the past form *fu lodato* (< LAUDATUS FUIT).

Table 6.16 illustrates all the tenses and moods of the Italian verb system for the active voice through the first-person singular forms of *lodare*.

In closing this section, I would like to draw attention to an important issue. According to a widespread view that received much consensus not too long ago, the (morpho)syntactic changes which characterized the shift from Latin to the Romance languages evidence a transition from a synthetic to an analytic system. Although this view is overall correct, it is important to note that it is too broad since Latin did display several analytic constructions. Consequently, the shift from synthesis to analysis should be addressed and evaluated, taking into consideration individual (sets of) constructions rather than languages in their entirety (see Schwegler, 1990 for a thorough discussion on this issue; cf. also Vincent, 2016, among others).

6.4 Earliest Italo-Romance attestations

The earliest Italo-Romance attestations date between the end of the eighth century and the first decade of thirteenth century; they are almost exclusively practical texts (i.e., non-literary

TABLE 6.16 The Italian verb system

Indicative			
Present	*lodo* 'I praise'	*Passato prossimo*	*ho lodato* 'I (have) praised'
Imperfect	*lodavo* 'I used to praise'	Pluperfect 1	*avevo lodato* 'I had praised'
Passato remoto	*lodai* 'I praised'	Pluperfect 2	*ebbi lodato* 'I had praised'
Future	*loderò* 'I will praise'	Future perfect	*avrò lodato* 'I will have praised'
Subjunctive			
Present	*lodi* 'I praise'	Past	*abbia lodato* 'I have praised'
Imperfect	*lodassi* 'I praised'	Pluperfect	*avessi lodato* 'I had praised'
Conditional			
Present	*loderei* 'I would praise'	Past	*avrei lodato* 'I would have praised'
Infinitive			
Present	*lodare* 'to praise'	Past	*avere lodato* 'to have praised'
Gerund			
Present	*lodando* 'praising'	Past	*avendo lodato* 'having praised'
Imperative			
Present	*loda* 'you.SG praise'		
	lodiamo 'let's praise'		
	lodate 'you.PL praise'		

texts, such as legal documents; town, religious, and guilds statutes; and official or private correspondence) and come primarily from central and southern Italy. Traditionally, they are chronologically subdivided into three main groups. The oldest of them (until the beginning of ninth century) comprise a handful of very short notes penned down inside texts written in Latin. These are 'casual' texts in that they ensued from unique erratic situations where the 'writer' deemed the choice of the vernacular more appropriate than Latin, which was still the regular written language.

Dated between the end of the eighth and the beginning of the ninth century (i.e., about 50 years earlier than the *Oaths of Strasbourg* (842)), the *Indovinello Veronese* 'The Verona Riddle' amounts to three lines of text written in Italian minuscule cursive on a liturgical codex which originated from early eighth-century Spain and was later brought to Verona, Italy. The text is given in (29a), accompanied by translations in modern Italian (29b) and English (29c).

(29) a. *Se pareba boves alba pratalia araba & albo versorio teneba & negro semen | seminaba gratias tibi agimus omnip(oten)s sempiterne d(eu)s*
   b. *Spingeva davanti a sé i buoi, arava bianchi prati, e un bianco aratro teneva e un nero seme seminava Rendiamo grazia a te Dio onnipotente e sempiterno*
   c. 'He pushed the oxen in front of himself, plowed the white fields, and held a white steering rope and sowed black seed' (From Castellani, 1973, p. 13; my translations)

As seen in (29a), a prominent feature of the text is the sharp contrast between the riddle itself, written in vernacular, and the last line (*gratias tibi . . .*) in flawless Latin. This sharp contrast and some graphical discrepancies between the two parts raise the question of whether different hands were involved in writing the riddle. Moreover, the vernacular part does not display some expected Romance features, and those it does display apply inconsistently, as summarized in (30).

(30) a. Third-person reflexive pronoun *se* vs. SIBI.
   b. Imperfect indicative ending *-eba* (vs. -ABAT) in *pareba*, but not in *araba* and *seminaba*.
   c. Word-final consonant loss: *-t* in third-person imperfect indicative forms, but final, the consonant is still present in *semen*.
   d. Vowel merger: *negro* (vs. NIGRU(M)) but *seminaba* not *semenaba*.
   e. Enclitic pronoun in sentence-initial position, *se pareba*, violating the Tobler-Mussafia Law.
   f. Lack of consonant voicing in intervocalic position: *pratalia* not *pradalia*.

Thus, ascertaining whether *Indovinello* evidences an (Italo-)Romance vernacular or Medieval Latin is hard, and there is no general consensus on considering it the earliest Italo-Romance attestation. As for the solution, I trust that you found it by now.

The *Graffito della Catacomba di Commodilla*, discovered in 1903, is a four-line inscription of 11 × 6.5 cm in size located in the decorative border of a fresco in the crypt of Saint Felice and Saint Adàutto in the Roman catacomb of Commodilla.

(31) a. NON/DICE/RE IL/LE SE/CRITA/A B^BOCE
   Non dicere ille secrita a b^boce
   b. 'Don't recite/utter the secret orations aloud'
   (From Marazzini, 2006, p. 35; my translation)

While the fresco was presumably painted in the sixth or seventh century, archeological, historical-liturgical, and paleographical evidence allows us to date the inscription to the mid-ninth century. Precisely, the crypt was used as a place of worship until the ninth century, when Pope Leo IV (847–855) had the saints' remains removed from the chapel, fearing further Saracen attacks after the sack of the nearby Saint Paul's Basilica in 844, and the silent (or in a low voice) reading of liturgical rites spread during the first Carolingian period (ninth century). Also, the inscription displays both Roman capital and uncial characters (the latter in use until the eighth to ninth century), but ornamental traits in the 'L' in the fourth line point to the ninth century. The Romance features found in the inscription are given in (32).

(32) a. *Ille* functioning as definite article rather than demonstrative.
   b. *Secrita* (Lat. SECRETA): <i> for <e> ([e] < Lat. ē), following the pre-Carolingian writing usage; lack of sonorization of <c> [k] and feminine collective plural in *-a* (*secrita* vs. It. *segreti*), both distinctive features of texts in old *romanesco* vernacular.
   c. *Non dicere*: 'not' + infinitive is the typical negative imperative form of Italian and Italian dialects vs. Latin 'NE + perfect subjunctive.'
   d. *A bʰoce* reflects betacism (Latin <v>/<u> [w] > [b]); the smaller size of the second indicates that it was added later to represent *rafforzamento fonosintattico*, a distinctive feature of central and southern Italian dialects as well as Italian.

This document is truly unique since besides being one of the earliest Italo-Romance attestations not to appear in legal documents, it only displays Romance features (Castellani, 1976, p. 34) and attests to a deliberate use of the vernacular (i.e., a reminder on how to properly officiate the liturgy).

The next attestation we will address comprises four documents known as the *Placiti Campani* (or *Cassinesi*), referring to the region(s) from which they originate (i.e., Campania and nearby Cassino, Lazio). Their dating is uncontroversial since the date of composition is recorded and ranges from 960 to 963. The *Placiti* are official judicial records concerning an ownership dispute on some lands between three Benedictine monasteries and a local landowner. The documents themselves are written in Latin, while the witnesses' testimony is recorded verbatim in the local Italo-Romance vernacular. This evinces a clear awareness of Latin and Romance vernaculars being two distinct linguistic entities and a deliberate use of a language that represented the direct speech of witnesses. It is also why *Placiti* have been considered the 'birth certificate' of the Italian language, although they are less old than *Indovinello* and the *Graffito of Commodilla*. As seen in (32), the testimonies are very similar in both content and language due to the highly formulaic nature of the documents.

(32) a. *Sao ko kelle terre, per kelle fini que ki contene, trenta anni le possette parte Sancti Benedicti.* (Capua, March 960)
   'I know that those lands, within those boundaries which are described therein, the Monastery of Saint Benedict has owned them for thirty years.'
   b. *Sao cco kelle terre, per kelle fini que tebe monstrai, Pergoaldi foro, que ki contene, et trenta anni le possette.* (Sessa Arunca, March 963)
   'I know that those lands, within those boundaries which I showed you were of Pergoaldi, which are described therein, and he has owned them for thirty years.'

   c.   *Kella terra, per kelle fini que bobe mostrai, Sancte Marie è, et trenta anni la posset parte Sancte Marie.* (Teano, July 963)

        'That land, within those boundaries that I showed you, is of Saint Mary, and the Monastery of Saint Mary has owned it for thirty years.'

   d.   *Sao cco kelle terre, per kelle fini que tebe mostrai, trenta anni le possette parte Sancte Marie.* (Teano, October 963)

        'I know that those lands, within those boundaries that I showed you, the Monastery of Saint Mary has owned them for thirty years.' (Adapted from Castellani, 1973, pp. 59–62, my translation)

Patent (central-southern) Italo-Romance phonological and morphological features found in the *Placiti* are given in (33).

(33) a.   Loss of Latin labiovelar [kʷ] <qu> (*ko, cco* 'that' (< Lat. QUOD), *kelle* 'those' (< Lat. ECCU(M) ILLAE), and *ki* 'here' (< Lat. ECCU(M) HIC)).

     b.   The archaic verb form *sao* 'I know' (< Lat. sapio), later ousted by *saccio* [sat:o] displaying palatalization of [p].

     c.   Direct object clitic pronouns: *la* 'it.F' and *le* 'them.F.'

     d.   Rafforzamento fonosintattico: sao **cc**o.

Particularly notable is the presence of left-dislocation (*kelle terre . . . le possette* (33a, b, d), *Kella terra . . . la posset* (33c)), a feature destined to become increasingly frequent yet frowned upon by prescriptive grammar until recently. The texts also display some Latinisms, such as *que* 'which,' lack of simplification of the clusters <ct> (*Sancti, Sancte* 'Saint'), the synthetic genitive forms *Sancti Benedicti, Sancte Marie,* and *Pergoaldi,* and the indirect object pronouns *tebe* 'to you.SG' (< Lat. TIBI) and *bobe* 'to you.pl' (< Lat. VOBIS), which, however, evidence the merger of the front mid vowels Ē and Ĭ.

    Among the texts of the second group (second half of ninth to first half of twelfth century), we single out the *Postilla amiatina* (1087), the *Iscrizione di San Clemente* (end of eleventh to beginning of twelfth century), and the *Formula di confessione umbra* (ca. between 1037 and 1080).

    The *Postilla amiatina* (34) is a brief note added to a legal document from Mount Amiata (Tuscany) that records the donation of all their possessions to Saint Salvatore's Abbey by a certain Miciasello and his wife, Gualdrada. It is written by the notary who drew up the document and reveals an attempt at maintaining a 'Latin' style.

(34) *Ista cartula est de caput coctu ille adiuvet de ill rebottu qui mal consiliu li mise in corpu* (adapted from Castellani, 1973, p. 103, my translation)

     'This scrap of paper is Capocotto's: may it help him from that rascal who put that bad advice in his body'

Notable linguistic features include the Latinisms *ille* and *ill,* the demonstrative *ista,* and [u] instead of [o] (*Capu**cottu*** 'hard head' *rebott**u*** 'rascal' < Old Fr. *ribaut*), a distinctive feature of the region of Mount Amiata.

    The *Iscrizione di San Clemente* appears in a fresco located in the underground basilica named after the saint (Rome), and it basically consists of captions which identify the characters and illustrate their role in the story depicted in the fresco. It is characterized by the intentional contrastive use of Latin and vernacular: Latin (lines B and C) is reserved for the lofty parts of the text (the person who commissioned the work and the expression of moral judgment on the scene), whereas the vernacular is used for narrating the story. Furthermore, this text stands out for its manifest vulgarity.

(35) A: 'FALITE DERETO/COLO PALO/CARVONCELLE'
         'Put yourself behind him with the pole, Carvoncello!'
      B: 'D/U/R/I/TIAM COR/DIS/V(EST)/RIS'
         'Because of your hearts' hardness'
      C: 'S/A/X/A/TRAERE/MERUI/S/TIS'
         'you deserved to drag stones'
      D: 'ALBERTEL/TRAI(TE)'
         'Albertel, drag (him)!'
      E: 'GOS/MARI'
      F: 'SISIN/IUM'
      G: 'FILI/DELE/P/U/T/E/TRA/I/TE'
         'Figli di puttane, tirate(lo)!'
         'Sons of whores, drag (him)!'
         (Adapted from Castellani, 1973, pp. 112–114)

The inscription tells the miraculous story of the Roman patrician Sisinnius, who ordered three servants (Albertello, Carboncello, and Gosmari) to capture Saint Clemente, whom he believed to be a sorcerer, though the fresco portrays the servants laboriously dragging a column. The interpretation of the text, however, remains uncertain because some parts are not clearly visible due to the very poor conditions of the fresco. Its notable linguistic features include the order of the pronouns that are enclitic to the imperative *fa* with the indirect object pronoun *li* preceding the direct object pronoun *te*, following the same order as modern Italian rather than the expected direct-indirect object, and the forms *dele* 'of the' and *colo* 'with the' displaying coalescence of preposition and definite article.

Formula di confessione umbra is a confessional formula included into a compilation of liturgical and para-liturgical texts structured into three parts: an introductory paragraph consisting of a general inventory of sins; a list of more specific sins, each introduced by the Latin verb form *miserere* 'have mercy' and *accusome* 'I accuse myself,' as illustrated in (36); and a closing section where the confessor pronounces the penitence for the confessed sins. The text is characterized by a conspicuous presence of Latin, as shown by (36c), which is basically entirely in Latin.

(36) a. *Miserere. Accusome delu corpus Domini, k'io indignamente lu accepi.*
         'Have mercy. I accuse myself regarding the body of Christ, because I undeservingly received it.'
      b. *Miserere. Accusome deli mei appatrini sanctuli et delu sanctu baptismu ke promiseru pro me et noll'observai.*
         'Have mercy. I accuse myself regarding my godfathers and the holy baptism that they promised for me, and I did not observe it.'
      c. *Miserere. Accusome de V sensus corpori mei, visus, auditus, gustus, odoratus et tactus.*
         'Have mercy. I accuse myself regarding my five bodily senses, sight, hearing, taste, smell, and touch'
         (Adapted from Castellani, 1973, pp. 88, 90, 95, my translation)

A distinctive phonological feature displayed by this text is **metaphony**, an instance of distant regressive assimilation found extensively across Italian dialects/varieties but absent in Tuscan ones (therefore, in standard Italian). In this case, metaphony systematically targets stressed [e] and [o], which raise to [i] and [u], respectively, and is triggered by following [i]/[e] and [u] (e.g., *baptismu* vs. *battesimo* 'baptism' (XYb), *illi* vs. *elli* 'they,' *pusero* vs. *posero* 'they imposed'). Another noteworthy phonological feature is word-final [u] vs. [o], which also applies consistently (*lu* vs. *lo* 'the/it.M.SG,' *sanctu* vs. *santo* 'saint,' *promiseru* vs. *promisero* they promised'). Some notable morphological/morphosyntactic traits are summarized in (37).

(37) a. Definite articles (*lu*, *li* 'the.M.PL'), which combine to prepositions (*delu*, *deli*).
 b. Possessive adjective (*mei* 'my.M.PL').
 c. Direct object clitic pronouns (*me* 'me,' *lu* and *l'* 'it.M.SG').
 d. Enclisis in sentence-initial position (*accusome* vs. *mi accuso* 'I accuse myself'), conforming to the Tobler-Mussafia Law.
 e. *Rafforzamento morfosintattico* (*noll'* vs. *non l'* also showing assimilation of [n] to [ll]).
 f. Adverbs in *-mente* (*indignamente* 'undeservingly').

The establishment of medieval communes and the expansion of an urban culture promoted the consolidation of vernaculars as written languages. This new status of the vernaculars is evinced by the texts from the end of the twelfth to the beginning of the thirteenth century, which, along with practical texts linked to the authors' professional sphere (administrative and juridical texts and records of accounts, taxes, debts, goods, etc.), also include the first literary texts. One of the most prominent practical texts is the *Frammenti d'un libro di conti di banchieri fiorentini* (1211), which is the oldest Florentine document currently available to us. Some noteworthy features of this text are the co-occurrence of three forms of the first-person plural indirect object clitic pronoun, the archaic forms *no* (38a) and *ne* (38b), and the modern form *ci* (38c); the clitic pronoun *li* functioning as both third-person plural direct object and third-person singular indirect object (38a); the periphrastic past (*passato prossimo*) *à dato* (36c); and palatalization of [ʎ] not reflected in the orthography (*lulio* vs. *luglio* (36b)).

(38) a. '***no*** *die dare s. x, ke* **li li** *prestammo*'
 'he must give us ten *soldi*, which we lent him'
 (*Frammenti*, p. 31)
 b. '***dene*** *pagare otto dì anzi kl. lulio*'
 'he must pay us eight days before July kalends'
 (*Frammenti*, p. 36)
 c. '***ci*** *à dato di sua mano s. xl*'
 'he has given us of his own hand forty *soldi*'
 (*Frammenti*, p. 25)

 The first decade of the thirteenth century, then, is taken to delimit the end of the archaic stage of Italo-Romance, with *Frammenti d'un libro di conti di banchieri fiorentini* showing that the language of practical texts had reached its formalization. Around the same time (end of the twelfth, beginning of the thirteenth century at the latest), the language of poetry had also achieved its formalization. Among the best-known examples, we remember the works of Cecco Angiolieri (1260–ca. 1312), Folgóre da San Gimignano (ca. 1270–ca. 1332), and the *Dolce stil novo* 'sweet new style' poets Guido Guinizzelli (ca. 1225–1276) and Guido Cavalcanti (between 1250 and 1259–1300)). Regarding prose, the oldest Florentine texts include several *volgarizzamenti* 'vulgarizations,' that is, translations (or, more properly, adaptations) of works written in Latin or Greek, or other Italian *volgari* (e.g., Brunetto Latin's *Rettorica* (1260), the vulgarization of the first 17 chapters of Cicero's *De inventione*), treatises (e.g., Bono Giamboni's *Il libro de' vizî e delle virtudi* (1292)), as well as chronicles (e.g., by Dino Compagni, Giovanni Villani's *Nuova cronica* (started ca. 1322), and Donato Velluti's *Cronica domestica* (between 1367 and 1370)). The oldest narrative text is *Novellino* (late thirteenth century), an anonymous collection of short stories, a brief excerpt of which is given in (39a), accompanied by its modern Italian rendering (39b).

(39) a. '*Questi figliuoli, ciascuno pregava il padre ch'alla sua fine **li** lasciasse questo anello; e il padre, vedendo che **catuno il volea**, **mandò per** un **fino** orafo e disse: Maestro, fammi due **anella così a punto** come questo, e metti in ciascuno una pietra che **asomigli** a questa. **Lo** maestro fece **l'anella così a punto**, che **niuno conoscea** il fine, **altro che** 'l padre.*' (Novellino, p. 296)

   b. '*Questi figli, ciascuno pregava il padre che alla sua fine **gli** lasciasse questo anello; e il padre, vedendo che **ciascuno lo voleva**, **chiamò** un orafo **esperto** e disse: Maestro, fammi due **anelli proprio come** questo, e metti in ciascuno una pietra che **assomigli** a questa. **Il** maestro fece gli anelli **così**, senza che nessuno conoscesse il fine, **eccetto il** padre.*'

   'These children, each of them begged the father to leave them this ring when he'd die. And the father, seeing that each of them wanted it, sent for a skilled goldsmith and said: Master, make me two rings exactly like this one, and inside each put a stone that resembles this one. The goldsmith made the rings as requested, without anybody knowing why but the father.'

The parallel with modern Italian is striking, and the differences (in bold) overall do not hamper comprehension.

6.5 Exercises

1. Provide concise but complete answers to the following questions, illustrating with examples.

   a. Which variety of Latin is the 'source' of Italian? Why?

   b. Outline the main phonological, morphological, and (morpho)syntactic changes that characterize the development of Italo-Romance from Latin.

   i.   Phonological changes.
   ii. Morphological changes.
   iii. (Morpho)syntactic changes.

   c. What are the most distinctive features of the early Italo-Romance attestations?

2. Provide the Italian outcomes, both in orthographic and phonetic transcription, for the following Latin items.

   a. DISCĬPŬLU(M) >
   b. FŎCU(M) >
   c. FABŬLA >
   d. VĪNEA(M) >
   e. TĔPĬDU(M) >

    f.   CŬRTU(M) >

    g.   *PLAN(Ŭ)LA(M) >

    h.   SAGĪNA(M) >

    i.   CONSĬLIUM >

    j.   PŬTEU(M) >

3.   Identify the phenomena illustrated by the following items.

    a.   COLŬMNA(M) > *colónna* 'pillar.'

    b.   PĚTRA(M) > *piètra* 'rock.'

    c.   BASIU(M) > *bacio* 'kiss.'

    d.   TABŬLA(M) > *tavola* 'plank.'

    e.   SŎNU(M) > *suono* 'sound.'

    f.   VĬRĬDE(M) > *vérde* 'green.'

    g.   NURUS non NURA 'daugther-in-law' (*Appendix Probi*)

    h.   *PŪTIU(M) > *puzzo* 'stink.'

    i.   AMAR(E) HABEO > *AMAR(E) AO > *amerò* 'I will love.'

    j.   CLARA MENTE > *chiaramente* 'clearly.'

4.   Complete with the appropriate option.

    a.   The consonant inventory of Latin lacked the

        i.   voiceless labiodental fricative [f].

        ii.   voiced labiodental fricative [v].

        iii. voiceless dental fricative [s].

        iv. voiced bilabial stop [b].

    b.   Due to the vowel merger,

        i.   ī and ĭ > [i], ŭ and ū > [u].

        ii.   ĭ and ē > [ɛ], ō and ŭ > [ɔ].

        iii. ē and ě > [e], ŏ and ō > [o].

        iv. ĭ and ē > [e], ō and ŭ > [o].

    c.   The [o] in *fòrte* 'strong' < FŎRTEM does not diphthongize because

        i.   diphthongization affected only ō.

        ii.   it occurs in a closed syllable.

        iii. this adjective is a Latinism.

        iv. diphthongization affected only the front vowels ē and ě.

    d.   The development SŎLEAM > *sòglia* 'doorstep; threshold' illustrates

        i.   regressive assimilation.

        ii.   vowel merger.

        iii. palatalization.

        iv. anaphonesis.

e. A small group of Italian masculine nouns has two forms for the plural (e.g., *braccio* 'arm,' *bracci*/*braccia* 'arms'). This phenomenon is,

    i. purely accidental.

    ii. the plural in *-a* is a relic of the neuter gender, while the plural in *–i* is an innovation.

    iii. the two forms derive from different Latin words.

    iv. the plural in *–i* continues from Latin, while the plural in *-a* is an innovation.

f. Rafforzamento morfosintattico

    i. is triggered by all monosyllabic words.

    ii. is a distinctive trait of northern Italian varieties.

    iii. is triggered by any word stressed on the last syllable.

    iv. applies uniformly across central and southern Italian varieties.

5. True or false? Justify your choices.

a. The development LACU(M) > *lago* 'lake' illustrates consonant lenition.

b. The development PĪNEA(M) > *pigna* 'pinecone' illustrates anaphonesis.

c. Diphthongization of [ɛ] (< ĕ) and [ɔ] (< ŏ) occurred in both open and closed syllable.

d. In Italian, word stress is governed by syllable weight.

e. In the development of Italian from Latin, the grammatical category of number underwent radical changes.

f. Atonic/Clitic pronouns constitute a Romance innovation.

g. Italian definite and indefinite articles are directly inherited from Latin.

h. Word order in Latin was free.

Notes

1 The *Appendix Probi*, perhaps the most enlightening source of Vulgar Latin from a grammarian, is an unnumbered list of 227 word/phrase pairs, the first one corresponding to the correct Latin form, and the second representing the 'incorrect' form, that is, the form actually used by the people. The list follows the schema 'A not B' (e.g., COLUMNA NON COLOMNA) and evinces several key pan-Romance phonological and morphosyntactic features. It appears after a copy made in Bobbio (Piedmont) around 700 CE of a grammatical treatise presumably composed in Rome between the third and fourth century CE and attributed to a certain Probus (hence its name).

2 Following traditional conventions, Latin is written in small caps, and nouns and adjectives are given in the ACC SG form, with the final -M in parentheses to indicate that it was lost early. Graphemes (i.e., letters or combination of letters that represent sounds in orthography) are enclosed in angled brackets <>, and sounds are transcribed using the *International Phonetic Alphabet* (IPA), enclosed in // if they have phonemic status and in [] if they don't.

3 In technical works, open and close vowels are represented graphically by distinct IPA symbols. Orthographically, the distinction is traditionally marked by the grave accent (`) for open vowels and the acute accent (´) for close vowels. For example, the front open-mid vowel is written è, and the IPA symbol for it is [ɛ].

4 The following correlation exists in Italian between word stress and vowel length: stressed vowels in word-initial open syllable are long (*pala* /ˈpaːla/ 'shovel' vs. *palla* /palˈla/ 'ball' and *parola* /paˈrola/

'word'), whereas stressed vowels in word-final position are always short (*caffè* /kaf fɛ/ 'coffee'). Unstressed vowels are always short, and the only unstressed vowel that cannot occur in word-final position is /u/.

5 In Italian, diphthongization of Ĕ [ɛ] and Ŏ [ɔ] is traditionally referred to as *dittongamento spontaneo* 'spontaneous diphthongization' or also *toscano* 'Tuscan' because it is considered a distinctive feature of Tuscan varieties (Castellani, 1962, 1970; Wartburg, 1967). Although with different dynamics, this chance also occurred in other Romance varieties.

6 In Italian, marking stress in orthography is obligatory only for pluri-syllabic words stressed on the last syllable, as in (5a), and for a small group of monosyllabic words (*già* 'already,' *giù* 'down'). In pluri-syllabic words that are not stressed on the last syllable, stress may be marked orthographically if it is contrastive (*prìncipi* 'princes' ~ *princìpi* 'principles'). In general, however, orthographic marking of stress is not common and is basically restricted to dictionaries and texts dealing with language/linguistics. As mentioned in note 2, the acute and grave accents may be used to differentiate between close-mid and open-mid vowels, respectively; for the other vowels, the more widespread tendency is to mark stress always with the grave accent (<à>, <ì>, <ù>). Using the acute accent for high vowels (<í>, <ú>) and the grave for the low vowel (<à>) is also possible, but this practice is much less common.

7 Loss of word-final consonants is a pan-Romance phenomenon. This type of change is not unusual, since word-final position is considered a weak position. However, word-final [s] is retained in western Romance varieties and is one of the classic diagnostics for the distinction between western and eastern varieties, especially because it carries important morphological/morphosyntactic values (e.g., plural marker).

8 All the other words ending in a consonant found in Italian (e.g., *bar, computer, stop*) are borrowings.

9 [ʃ] lengthened systematically in intervocalic position, though consonant length (represented by [:] in IPA) is not reflected in the orthography. Intervocalic [dʒ] also underwent lengthening in some cases; in this case, consonant length is expressed by <gg> in spelling (LEGEM 'law' > *legge*).

10 Semi-vowels are also referred to as semi-consonants, approximants, or glides. Latin also had the labiovelar semi-vowel [w] <ŭ> (ŬENIRE 'to come').

11 Note that [ɲ] and [ʎ] are very rare in word-initial position; the former occurs in *gnomo* 'gnome' and *gnocchi* 'potato dumplings,' and the latter in *gli*, which is both one of the forms of the masculine plural definite article and the form of the 3PL indirect object pronoun. Another source of [ɲ] is the cluster -GN- (LIGNUM 'wood' > *legno*, PUGNUM 'fist' > *pugno*).

12 In some cases, -x- [ks] palatalized into [ʃ:] (MAXILLAM 'jaw' > *mascella*, LAXARE 'to leave' > *lasciare*).

13 *Rafforzamento fonosintattico* is systematically reflected in spelling in the case of monosyllabic 2SG imperatives, followed by an unstressed pronoun (*dimmi* 'tell me', *fallo* 'do it').

14 The forms *un, il, i* modify nouns/adjectives beginning with any consonant, but <sc-i/e> [ʃ] and /<gn> [ɲ]; *uno, lo, gli* occur with nouns/adjectives beginning with <s> plus consonant (*studente* 'student'), <z> [ts]/[dz] (*zaino* 'backpack'), [j] (*iodio* 'iodine'), [ʃ] (*sciroppo* 'syrup'), and [ɲ] (*gnomo* 'gnome'); *un, l', gli* modify nouns/adjectives beginning with a vowel.

15 The pronoun *eglino* was derived adding the 3PL verbal suffix *-no* (*parlano* 'they speak,' *parlavano* 'they sopke') to *egli*, serving then as a model for the feminine counterpart, *elleno*.

16 Unless otherwise noted, all Old Italian examples come from the database *Opera del vocabolario italiano* (OVI, https://artfl-project-uchicago-edu.ezproxy.lib.utexas.edu/content/ovi).

17 Unaccusative verbs are characterized by a non-agentive subject (i.e., a subject that is not the initiator of the event denoted by the verb; *cadere* 'fall,' *morire* 'die'), whereas unergative verbs have agentive subjects instead (*lavorare* 'work,' *parlare* 'speak').

Bibliography

Banniard, M. (2013). The transition from Latin to the Romance languages. In M. Maiden, J. C. Smith, & A. Ledgeway (Eds.), *The Cambridge history of the Romance languages* (Vol. 2, pp. 57–106). Cambridge University Press.

Barbato, M. (2016). Dal latino alle *scriptae* italoromanze. In S. Lubello (Ed.), *Manuale di linguistica italiana* (pp. 9–30). Walter de Gruyter.

Berruto, G. (1987). *Sociolinguistica dell'italiano contemporaneo*. Carocci.

Castellani, A. (1952). *Nuovi testi fiorentini del dugento* (Vol. 1). Sansoni.

Castellani, A. (1962). Quelques remarques à propos de la diphtongaison romane. *Zeitschrift für romanische Philologie, 78,* 494–502.

Castellani, A. (1970). Ancora sui dittongamento italiano e romanzo: Seconda risposta a Friedrich Schürr. *Cultura Neolatina, 30,* 117–130.

Castellani, A. (1973). *I più antichi testi italiani: Edizione e commento.* Patron.

Castellani, A. (1980). Sulla formazione del tipo fonetico italiano. In A. Castellani (Ed.), *Saggi di linguistica e filologia romanza (1946–1976)* (Vol. I, pp. 73–122). Salerno.

Castellani, A. (2000). *Grammatica storica italiana.* Il Mulino.

D'Achille, P. (1990). *Sintassi del parlato e tradizione scritta della lingua italiana: Analisi di testi dalle origini al secolo XVIII.* Bonacci.

D'Achille, P. (2007). *Breve grammatica storica dell'italiano.* Carocci.

Dardano, M. (Ed.). (2012). *Sintassi dell'italiano antico: La prosa del Duecento e del Trecento.* Carocci.

Formentin, V. (2007). *Poesia italiana delle origini.* Carocci.

Herman, J. (2000). *Vulgar Latin* (R. Wright, Trans.). Pennsylvania State University Press.

Hilty, G. (2001). I primi testi romanzi. In P. Boitani, M. Mancini, & A. Varvaro (Eds.), *Lo spazio letterario del Medioevo. Vol. 2: Il Medioevo volgare, tomo 1/2: La produzione del testo* (pp. 57–89). Salerno.

Hopper, P., & Traugott, E. C. (2003). *Grammaticalization* (2nd ed.). Cambridge University Press.

Larson, P. (2003). Il volgare del Mille: Fonti per la conoscenza dell'italiano preletterario. In N. Maraschio & T. Poggi Salani (Eds.), *Italia linguistica anno Mille, Italia linguistica anno Duemila. Atti del XXXIV Congresso della SLI (Firenze, 19–21 ottobre 2000)* (pp. 129–137). Bulzoni.

Maiden, M. (1995). *A linguistic history of Italian.* Routledge.

Mancini, M. (2000). Tra latino dialettale e latino preromanzo: Fratture e continuità. In J. Herman & L. Mondin (Eds.), *La transizione dal latino alle lingue romanze: Atti della Tavola Rotonda di linguistica storica (Università Ca' Foscari di Venezia, 14–15 giugno 1996)* (pp. 41–59). Niemeyer.

Marazzini, C. (2006). *La storia della lingua italiana attraverso i testi.* Il Mulino.

Oniga, R. (2014). *Latin: A linguistic introduction* (N. Schifano, Ed. & Trans.). Oxford University Press.

Patota, G. (2007). *Nuovi lineamenti di grammatica storica dell'italiano.* Il Mulino.

Petrucci, L. (1994). Il problema delle Origini e i più antichi testi italiani. In L. Serianni & P. Trifone (Eds.), *Storia della lingua italiana. Vol. 3: Le altre lingue* (pp. 5–73). Einaudi.

Petrucci, L. (2010). *Alle origini dell'epigrafia volgare. Iscrizioni italiane e romanze fino al 1275.* Edizioni Plus/Pisa University Press.

Poletto, C. (2014). *Word order in old Italian.* Oxford University Press.

Renzi, L. (1994). Egli-lui-il-lo. In T. De Mauro (Ed.), *Come parlano gli italiani* (pp. 247–250). La Nuova Italia.

Renzi, L. (2012). *Come cambia la lingua: L'italiano in movimento.* Il Mulino.

Rohlfs, G. (1966–1969). *Grammatica storica della lingua italiana e dei suoi dialetti.* Einaudi.

Sabatini, F. (1966). Un'iscrizione volgare romana della prima metà del IX secolo. *Studi Linguistici Italiani, 6,* 49–80.

Salvi, G. (2004). *La formazione della struttura di frase romanza: Ordine delle parole e clitici dal latino alle lingue romanze antiche.* Niemeyer.

Salvi, G. (2016). Sintassi dell'italiano antico. In In S. Lubello (Ed.), *Manuale di linguistica italiana* (pp. 62–89). Walter de Gruyter.

Salvi, G., & Renzi, L. (Eds.). (2010). *Grammatica dell'italiano antico.* Il Mulino.

Schwegler, A. (1990). *Analycity and syntheticity: A diachronic perspective with special reference to Romance languages.* Mouton de Gruyter.

Tekavčić, P. (1972). *Grammatica storica dell'italiano.* Il Mulino.

Varvaro, A. (2003). L'italiano dell'anno Mille: Le origini dell'italiano. In N. Maraschio & T. Poggi Salani (Eds.), *Italia linguistica anno Mille, Italia linguistica anno Duemila: Atti del XXXIV Congresso della SLI (Firenze, 19–21 ottobre 2000)* (pp. 19–35). Bulzoni.

Varvaro, A. (2013). Latin and the making of the Romance languages. In M. Maiden, J. C. Smith, & A. Ledgeway (Eds.), *The Cambridge history of the Romance languages* (Vol. 2, pp. 6–56). Cambridge University Press.

Vincent, N. (2016). A structural comparison of Latin and Romance. In A. Ledgeway & M. Maiden (Eds.), *The Oxford guide to the Romance languages* (pp. 37–49). Oxford University Press.

von Wartburg, W. (1967). *La fragmentation linguistique de la Romania.* Klincksiek.

Zamboni, A. (2000). *Alle origini dell'italiano: Dinamiche e tipologie della transizione dal latino.* Carocci.

Zamora Muñoz, P. (2002). Dislocazioni a destra e a sinistra nell'italiano e nello spagnolo colloquial parlato: frequenza d'uso, funzioni e parametri linguistici. *Studi Italiani di Linguistica Teorica e Applicata, 31*(3), 447–470.

INDEX

Note: numbers in **bold** indicate a table. Numbers in *italics* indicate a figure. Unless otherwise specified, terms refer to Italian language.

Printed in Great Britain
by Amazon

36380950R00117